Successful Marketing Communications

The Chartered Institute of Marketing/Butterworth-Heinemann Marketing Series is the most comprehensive, widely used and important collection of books in marketing and sales currently available worldwide.

As the CIM's official publisher, Butterworth-Heinemann develops, produces and publishes the complete series in association with the CIM. We aim to provide definitive marketing books for students and practitioners that promote excellence in marketing education and practice.

The series titles are written by CIM senior examiners and leading marketing educators for professionals, students and those studying the CIMs Certificate, Advanced Certificate and Postgraduate Diploma courses. Now firmly established, these titles provide practical study support to CIM and other marketing students and to practitioners at all levels.

The Chartered
Institute of Marketing

Formed in 1911, the Chartered Institute of Marketing is now the largest professional marketing management body in the world with over 60 000 members located worldwide. Its primary objectives are focused on the development of awareness and understanding of marketing throughout UK industry and commerce and in the raising of standards of professionalism in the education, training and practice of this key business discipline.

Books in the series

Creating Powerful Brands (second edition), Leslie de Chernatony and Malcolm McDonald
Cybermarketing (second edition), Pauline Bickerton, Matthew Bickerton and Upkar Pardesi
Cyberstrategy, Pauline Bickerton, Matthew Bickerton and Kate Simpson-Holley
Excellence in Advertising (second edition), Leslie Butterfield
Fashion Marketing, Margaret Bruce and Tony Hines
From Brand Vision to Brand Evaluation, Leslie de Chernatony
Innovation in Marketing, Peter Doyle and Susan Bridgewater
International Marketing (third edition), Stanley J. Paliwoda and Michael J. Thomas
Integrated Marketing Communications, Tony Yeshin
Key Customers, Malcolm McDonald, Beth Rogers, Diana Woodburn
Marketing Briefs, Sally Dibb and Lyndon Simkin
Marketing Logistics, Martin Christopher
Marketing Plans (fourth edition), Malcolm McDonald
Marketing Planning for Services, Malcolm McDonald and Adrian Payne
Marketing Professional Services, Michael Roe
Marketing Research for Managers (second edition), Sunny Crouch and Matthew Housden
Marketing Strategy (second edition), Paul Fifield
Relationship Marketing for Competitive Advantage, Adrian Payne, Martin Christopher, Moira Clark and Helen Peck
Relationship Marketing: Strategy and Implementation, Helen Peck, Adrian Payne, Martin Christopher and Moira Clark
Strategic Marketing Management (second edition), Richard M. S. Wilson and Colin Gilligan
Strategic Marketing: Planning and Control (second edition), Graeme Drummond and John Ensor
Successful Marketing Communications, Cathy Ace
Tales from the Market Place, Nigel Piercy
The CIM Handbook of Export Marketing, Chris Noonan
The CIM Handbook of Strategic Marketing, Colin Egan and Michael J. Thomas
The Customer Service Planner, Martin Christopher
The Fundamentals of Corporate Communications, Richard Dolphin
The Marketing Book (fourth edition), Michael J. Baker
The Marketing Manual, Michael J. Baker
Total Relationship Marketing, Evert Gummesson

Forthcoming

Direct Marketing, Brian Thomas and Matthew Housden
Effective Promotional Practice for eBusiness, Cathy Ace
eMarketing Excellence, Paul Smith and Dave Chaffey
Market-Led Strategic Change (third edition), Nigel Piercy
Political Marketing, Phil Harris and Dominic Wring
Relationship Marketing (second edition), Martin Christopher, Adrian Payne and David Ballantyne

Successful Marketing Communications

A practical guide to planning and implementation

Cathy Ace

Published in association with The Chartered Institute of Marketing

BUTTERWORTH
HEINEMANN

OXFORD AUCKLAND BOSTON JOHANNESBURG MELBOURNE NEW DELHI

Butterworth-Heinemann
Linacre House, Jordan Hill, Oxford OX2 8DP
225 Wildwood Avenue, Woburn, MA 01801-2041
A division of Reed Educational and Professional Publishing Ltd

 A member of the Reed Elsevier plc group

First published 2001

© Catherine Ace 2001

British Library Cataloguing in Publication Data
A catalogue record for this book is available from the British Library

Library of Congress Cataloguing in Publication Data
A catalogue record for this book is available from the Library of Congress

For information on all Butterworth-Heinemann publications visit our
website at www.bh.com

ISBN 0 7506 5027 3

Composition by Genesis Typesetting, Laser Quay, Rochester, Kent
Printed and bound in Great Britain

FOR EVERY TITLE THAT WE PUBLISH, BUTTERWORTH-HEINEMANN
WILL PAY FOR BTCV TO PLANT AND CARE FOR A TREE.

Contents

Introduction

Are you one of our target readers?

Getting ready for CIM exams?

Then this book is for you! From 2000 onwards the CIM syallabi for Certificate and Advanced Certificate address the broad field of marketing communications across several subjects. So this book has the advantage of bringing the whole subject together between these covers. Equally, if you are about to get ready for the CIM Diploma paper, Integrated Marketing Communications, you will find that this one text 'brings you up to speed' on the topic, prior to beginning your Diploma studies.

Getting ready for CAM exams?

Then this book is for you! Whilst the CAM syllabi ask you to look at separate parts of marketing communications in depth, this book will give you an excellent overview and will allow you to build your understanding across the topic of marketing communications planning. Equally, if you are about to enter the CAM qualification route at the higher level, this text will bring you 'up to speed' before you begin your studies.

Tackling marketing communications as part of your degree course?

Then this book is for you! Whilst you will always need to get advice from tutors about the specific emphasis of your syllabus, this text is a good 'catch all' introductory text to kick off with!

Managing marketing communications in real life?

Then this book is for you! When learning 'on the job' it is sometimes difficult to find the time to fill in the gaps in your knowledge and make sure you understand the bigger picture. This book should give you a good grounding of what each marketing communications tool can do, and how it fits into successful marketing communications planning overall.

Will you like the style?

I hope so! I have spent hundreds of hours addressing thousands of people who want to learn about marketing communications, and I have tried to bring that conversational style to the page. Writing this book has given me the chance to pull together real hints and tips on how to do things, rather than just address the academic content required by various syllabi. The case studies from real life are here to give you an insight into how theory is put into practice and the links with the suggested websites will allow you to keep up to date with this living, ever-changing topic.

Don't forget that you can access these websites to beef up your understanding of the topic under discussion and, by using this device, I have been able to avoid including data in the book that could well be out of date by the time you read it! Indeed, one of the most problematic issues with writing a book these days is that, purely because of the printing processes involved, books can seem to lose immediacy when compared with the Internet. I am pleased that the publisher has come up with an ideal way of overcoming this potential problem and has, at the same time, built in added value for you, the reader, by offering access to a website that will be updated as time passes.

If you are studying for exams you will find that the 'Self-test questions and opinion development' sections at the end of each chapter should challenge your understanding and thoughts on topics related to the chapter in question. Equally, the 'Extending knowledge and understanding' sections will encourage you to undertake activities that will enhance your knowledge.

I hope you find that the writing and layout styles keep you wanting to read, and learn – I can't claim that it will prove to be as riveting a read as your favourite novel, but I do hope that you find the style easy to read and engaging.

Why aren't there any pictures?

To be honest, as a writer, it is very tempting to want to put lots of photographs into a book – it makes it look sexy and it means you have to write fewer words to fill up the same number of pages! But, seriously, I haven't asked for lots of photographs or web screen grabs to be included because they date so very quickly and I really want to encourage you to visit the websites I highlight, where you can see up-to-the-minute visuals in glorious colour! That means, of course, that if you don't use the website you'll be denying yourself access to a whole dimension of this book – so go there and use it!

A final hint to get you started . . .

To use the book and websites to best advantage, know *why* you are reading it before you start: if you have a syllabus you are using to help you prepare for an exam or project, use that as your template against the pages that tell you what is covered in each chapter and the index. Hopefully each chapter is either short enough in its own right, or sufficiently well sub-divided, to allow you to find and focus on what you need but, if it's an overview you are after, then hopefully the progression of topics will prove to be logical for you.

If you are studying – good luck, and if you're reading this from professional interest – good for you . . . I hope it helps!

The marketing context

1

By the end of this chapter you should:

▶ have a better understanding of the context of marketing communications within the overall marketing planning process;
▶ understand clearly the relationship between the marketer's focus on the marketing mix and the customers' focus on the marketing mix;
▶ have an insight into some theories of how the communication process might work;
▶ have a better idea of how the mass communications industry developed to reach its current position;
▶ have a better understanding of how the communications business works as a whole;
▶ be aware of many of the bodies within the communications industry within the UK, and understand what they do.

Overview

Understanding marketing planning

This book is not about marketing planning, but about marketing communications. But without understanding the role of marketing communications within the marketing mix, you will never be able to do the best you can in terms of marketing communications itself. This is because the job of marketing communications is, essentially, to communicate what is attractive within the other elements of the marketing mix to those whose interest needs to be gained (buyers, specifiers, influencers, etc). Marketing communications can itself be used to differentiate a product, service or brand, building a unique personality for the offering in question that crystallizes the reason to purchase within the mind of the customer. But before we look at the detail of marketing communications planning, let's take a moment to look at the issues that surround marketing planning in the round.

Marketing planning rests on the same pillars as all planning: six key questions that have to be addressed and answered to allow an organization to move ahead effectively and efficiently. Those questions are:

1

Where are we now?
This means that you have to carry out an audit of all the internal and external aspects of your current position.

How did we get here?
You have to ask this question to be able to determine all the factors that might have influenced your current position over time (e.g., are you market leaders because for three years you were the only players in the market?).

Where do we want to be?
This gives the organization the chance to decide what its aims and goals are.

How might we get there?
This is the process of assessing the alternative routes by which you might arrive at your goals, in other words it is the stage when you assess alternative strategies that would deliver your agreed objectives.

How is it best to get there?
This is where the organization decides on its strategic path and details that set of activities.

How will we monitor and manage our progress?
As with any journey, it is never wise to wait until the journey *should* be over to discover that you didn't make it to your destination: constant monitoring of progress against agreed milestones allows effective management along the way.

With this fairly standard planning outline, the marketer will be carrying out a marketing audit, assessing possible objectives and strategies and deciding the direction in which to travel. Marketing communications will be the element of the marketing mix that we will concentrate upon in this book. But what about the others, and it's relationship to them all?

Getting back to basics – minding your Ps and Cs

The Chartered Institute of Marketing defines marketing as '. . .the management process which identifies, anticipates and supplies customer requirements efficiently and profitably'. This is our focus and our starting point. We must consider marketing communications within this context. Thus, it is worth reiterating the basics of the marketing mix to remind ourselves just where promotion fits into the overall picture. So let us go back to basics by looking at the Marketing Mix – not just the four Ps of the Marketing Mix, but the full seven Ps of the mix:

Product
Price
Place
Promotion
People
Processes
Physical evidence.

These seven key elements form what is often referred to as the Marketing Mix (the first four Ps) and the Service Mix (the last three Ps). My argument would be that all seven Ps need to be considered for all marketing decision making – all seven P's contribute to the success of a marketing and a marketing communications plan.

However, even all seven P's have one major drawback – they look at marketing from the point of view of the producer of the goods (or the provider of the service). With this perspective then, yes, it is fair to think of successful marketing as offering the right product/service at the right price and the right place to the right people through the right form of promotion, with the right people producing the products or providing the service, using effective management processes and delivering the right type of physical evidence of either service or product performance.

The problem with this approach is highlighted by the fact that as marketers we are supposed to believe that we are customer-orientated, so we really should look at marketing from the customer's perspective too. This is where the seven Cs come in – where each P is replaced by a customer-orientated 'C' alternative, which deals with the same issues as its corresponding 'P', but from the customer's point of view, thus:

Product: customers do not see products, they do not see product portfolio management techniques, matrices and product life cycles – they see that they have to make a *choice*. This choice might be direct ('Which cinema shall I go to?') or it could be indirect ('Shall I go to the theatre or the cinema or the pub?') or it could even be very indirect ('I will stay at home tonight because I am saving up for a new car'). Marketers have to carry out research that will show them how customers make choices, what they choose between and try to understand why they choose what they do – only then will true customer understanding begin to be at the heart of marketing planning.

Price: customers do not see price, but perceive a *cost* they have to bear, a part of which might well be something other than purely a financial consideration. It might be that a contract can be fulfilled more cheaply, in purely financial terms, by one contractor than another, but only if the customer is happy to wait three extra weeks for delivery: sometimes the customer will see the wait as a cost worth bearing to be able to pay the lower price, sometimes the cost of waiting will be unacceptable – so they will go with the more expensive supplier who can deliver next week. Equally, if the government wants to encourage us to stop drinking and driving, we have to bear the cost of not doing one or the other in order to comply and to benefit from our continued ability to legally drive on the roads because we haven't lost our licence, or our continued clear conscience because we haven't hurt anyone on the road, or our continued good health because we haven't hurt ourselves.

Place: customers don't see channel management decisions, or outlet selection or distribution strategy – they see *convenience*, and they see convenience on their terms, not those of the producer or provider. Marketers must gain a real insight into what their customers, and potential customers, see as convenience. A case in point is the recent rush to make almost everything available on the Internet (e.g., UK high street banks moving to more Internet banking and closing bricks-and-mortar branches), when, in fact, many customers do not have access to the Internet and feel disaffected by the move.

Promotion: the producer or provider might be seeking to promote their goods or services to an audience, but what the customer actually wants is *communication* – in other words, they want the chance to listen to what the marketer has to say but, increasingly, also want the chance to talk back! The word 'communication' implies this two-way process, whereas 'promotion' smacks of just highlighting the good bits! Marketers stick to simplistic promotion at their peril.

People: in face-to-face service delivery it is easy to see how people provide *care* – airlines emphasize the caring, smiling nature of their in-flight service, supermarkets make sure we all know how much the stackers, and checkers and packers care about our shopping experience, but what about when it comes to product manufacturing or non-frontline service staff in the service sector? Does the role of 'People' as providing 'Care' from the customer perspective still hold true? Well, yes, in that every worker on a production line can, and does, affect the delivery of the brand promise by how much they Care about what they are doing and how much Care they take in doing it: quality control systems are not infallible and every organization wants to produce as little waste, or below-average product, as possible, so the amount of care with which people pack, wrap, check, fit or finish a part of a whole job, whether it is a television set or a packet of crisps, makes a big difference to the overall effectiveness of the organization, which has a direct knock-on effect to the customer.

Processes: it is true to say that without business management processes in place, which allow best business practice to be connected and replicated throughout the organization, all organizations would offer a constantly varying level of quality or service to their customers across the range they offer, across the departments they house and over time. Thus it is *corporate competence* that is being sought by the customer – they expect the whole organization to be able to deliver what is promised – from the sales person, to the service engineer, to the delivery driver, to the quality control manager. Many organizations suffer because the customers' perception of them is that they are corporately incompetent, with expectations of service or reliability running at a very low level – this, in turn, affects the morale of the staff, who turn in lower levels of business performance, which serves to fulfil the low expectations of the customers – it is a vicious, downward spiral. Organizations need to understand the levels of competence expected of them, not just by industry standards or even by legal requirements, but by those they serve – their customers and potential customers.

Physical evidence: this is probably the most difficult part of the mix to pin down in terms of specific meaning, as it can mean different things depending upon specific circumstances, but if you think of it as meaning anything to do with the customers' expectations of *consistency* being met, this might help. We all expect to be able to pick out a particular bank on the high street, because we know what logo to look out for, and this goes for, say, McDonalds on a global scale as well. But it's about more than just the logo above the door. To take the McDonalds example further, wherever you visit a McDonalds around the world you will find not only the same logo, but the same food (with some regional variations), the same quality and service, the same standards of cleanliness and facilities: in other words, McDonalds makes a real virtue of the fact that it is essentially the same all over the world, and attracts a lot of customers on this basis – because people like to know what they are going to get, and then, of course, like to get it, so consistency isn't just about consistency of the promise, but also means consistency of delivery too.

Thus, as summarized in Fig. 1.1 we can view the seven Ps as having a Producer's focus, whilst the seven Cs have a Customer focus.

It is only once the marketer utilizes true customer orientation that the customer, long hailed as king, will finally be crowned. It is the synergistic effect of the full marketing mix, with both its P and C elements, which makes a successful product or service.

And what about the applicability of the marketing mix? It is quite easy to see from the examples above that the mix is applicable to fast-moving consumer goods (fmcg) marketing. But what about the more subtle, complex types of marketing, such as social marketing or health service marketing, for example? Well, if the mix didn't have an acceptable level of applicability across the board then it would have been replaced by something else by now – theories such as the marketing mix only continue to be used because they are relevant and useful.

With every pound spent on marketing communications needing to produce a real effect in terms of an impact on profitable sales, it is important for both practitioners and students to weigh carefully the balance of the promotional mix. It is also important to approach marketing communications planning with both an understanding of marketing planning and the actual business environment of the world of marketing communications itself, so this is where we will look now.

How communication might work – some theories

If it weren't for all the work put in on building theories of how communication works we would all flounder with each new programme that needed to be organized. If the basic truths at the heart of what is now recognized as standard promotional theory are, after all, myths, then they have been working their magic for a very long time and continue to do so today. Thus, it is by research, observation and practice that these concepts of how promotion works have become an accepted part of promotional planning and evaluation, and it is because campaigns that are running today are still bearing out the theories put forward many years ago that these theories still have credence.

Figure 1.1	*Producer–customer focus*

Producer/Provider Focus

Customer/Consumer Focus

Product

or service provided by supplier. Seen by producer/provider as planned product/service mix

Choice

Customer/consumer sees range of goods or services from which one needs to be selected

Price

When establishing the price to charge, marketers must consider all elements of the price mix

Cost

Customers see aspects of cost other than price – their own perspective may differ from that of the marketer

Place

Distribution channels and distributive outlets must be researched and planned, even for services

Convenience

Products and services that are not easily available will be seen as less desirable by customers who can choose from alternatives

Promotion

When planning a promotional campaign, marketers will research audience expectations and will aim to persuade customers that their product/service most closely meets their needs

Communication

Customers know that promotional tools are being used to persuade them; as consumer sophistication increases, communication rather than persuasion is sought by customers

People

People are what make marketing happen, and not just service staff. Usually the marketer will have training programmes in place for those members of staff who come into direct contact with the customer, delivering customer service either face to face or on the telephone

Care

Customers feel the care that the organization shows when doing ALL parts of its business, including the efforts of 'back room' staff such as accounting departments and cleaners, etc. All people within an organization should understand how the care that they put into their role will play a part in delivering the brand promise

Processes

Every organization needs to control its operations and activities, this is why there are management processes in place to make sure that things take place in a specified way, e.g. customer queries going through a certain checking procedure

Corporate Competence

Customers are only really concerned that an organization does what it promises it will do, rather than how it achieves this. Thus, it is important for marketers to never fall into the trap of telling customers about the process, but to concentrate on how this will deliver the required and expected level of product/service performance and satisfaction

Physical Evidence

This is the area where all the physical factors of the product or service are considered – it might relate to the livery of a delivery truck, flags outside headquarters or even the cleanliness of the loos at the office

Consistency

Customers will expect one product or service experience to be like another, so all your physical cues have to be consistent so that they know what to look out for, as well as your delivery being consistent too. A bad experience will lead a customer to expect a bad experience NEXT time, so always aim for positive delivery

During the middle and latter parts of the last century, there were numerous theories proposed of how promotion works. Most are based upon the common psychological concepts of perception, attitude formation and behavioural patterns. That sounds fairly straightforward, until you dig deeper into each of those areas and begin to realize that each topic is inextricably linked to so many other areas within psychology, sociology and behavioural studies that, in order to follow the most simplistic arguments you need to be a pretty well-versed student of the human mind and society in general!

Why address all these issues? Well, if promotion is to work at all it must:

- *be seen* – it must be physically placed where we will stand some chance of perceiving it;
- *be noticed* – seeing and noticing are different, noticing it means we actually give it our selective attention, selecting it from all the other stimuli around us at the time;
- *be interesting and relevant* – we must believe the message is for us, it must mean something to us at the time;
- *be appealing* – we must like the message in some way in order for us to feel positive about the object of the message;
- make us *want to do something about it* – we need to know what we can do and how to do it, or what is the point of having sent the message in the first place.

When you receive a stimulus, a promotional message, you may not feel yourself passing noticeably through each of these stages, but we all do, all the time, with promotional work that is successful. Successful promotional work takes us through three stages of response: the cognitive, affective and conative stages, each of which needs to precede the others in order for promotion to work.

The *cognitive* stage refers to the knowledge stage – awareness, comprehension, attention to the message. If you don't even know about something, how can you formulate an opinion or attitude?

The *affective* stage refers to the liking stage – you are convinced it will do what the message says, you desire it because it is relevant and interesting, you prefer it because it is most relevant.

The *conative* stage is that stage where the knowledge and the positive feelings now are likely to affect behaviour, so action will be taken, a purchase made, adoption of the product or service will result.

All the major theories of how promotion works are based upon these three key stages, and all are, thereafter, variations on a theme, whether it is a useful mnemonic like AIDA (Attention, Interest, Desire, Action) or a more complex proposition such as the Hierarchy of Effects (where we study the interrelationship between the stages rather than the stages themselves).

When it comes to the crunch, what marketers and promoters are really interested in, of course, is how behaviour is affected by promotion. If it is not affected at all, why bother? If we therefore agree that behaviour is affected by promotion, to what extent does promotion work? How can we tell ahead of time so that we can plan to spend exactly the right amount of money on just the right sort of promotional mix at just the right time? Well,

| **Figure 1.2** | *The psychological theory underlying how advertising might work* |

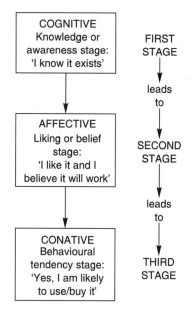

| **Figure 1.3** | *The AIDA principle* |

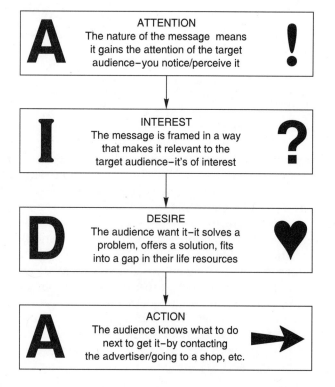

How attitudes and experience affect behaviour **Figure 1.4**

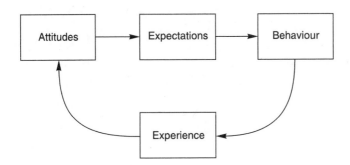

it seems like a truism, but if anyone knew the answers to those questions for certain, all promotional campaigns would be perfect and achieve all their objectives on time and within budget. Unfortunately, or fortunately, human beings are not 100 per cent predictable: even the most engrained habits can be broken once the reason for the habit is understood, so why shouldn't it be possible for a person to suddenly fancy trying out a new brand of washing powder?

Indeed, an understanding of why we do what we do is at the bottom of what the marketer wants to acquire about all consumers. Fig. 1.5 shows

Maslow's hierarchy of needs **Figure 1.5**

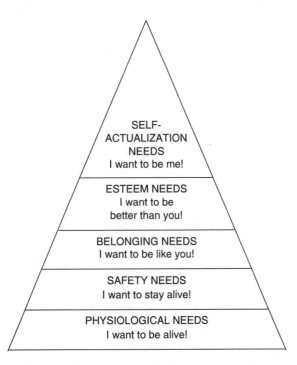

Maslow's hierarchy of needs, one of the most popular theories today that tries to address this terribly complex question.

Following from the idea that we all have needs (necessities – water), wants (preferences – lager) and desires (ideals – champagne), Maslow put forward the proposition that we have, in fact, a multi-layered approach to our requirements:

- *physiological needs* must be met first – unless we are alive all else is pointless;
- *safety needs* are next – once we are alive we want to be sure we will stay that way;
- next *we want to belong* – we are social animals and want to belong to some reference group;
- once we belong *we want esteem within our chosen group* – we all need to know our place, even if it isn't on top of the pile we like to know who to look up to and who to look down on;
- finally, and sometimes not even achievable by all, is *the desire to be what we truly believe we can be* – we seek to achieve self-actualization, a state where we are expressing as true a representation of the real 'us' as we can.

Many products are marketed using these concepts as a basis for not only their promotional messages, but their entire positioning strategy.

One way in which we can try to get a better understanding of why people choose what they do is by beginning to come to terms with the black box concept.

We can measure inputs, such as advertisements seen, and we can measure outputs, such as whether the product was bought, but everything that makes one stimulus turn into the other response is hidden from us within the human mind – as though it were a black box, all the decision making processes are hidden away (Fig. 1.6).

Imagine that the black box contains not one process but many dozen, some happen because they are basic and physiological, others are psychological. We would get a much better idea of what was going on inside the black box if we could break down the inputs into small pieces, measure the smaller outputs and develop a series of black box inputs and outputs that make the size of what is going on in the box smaller and smaller.

Figure 1.6   │   *The black-box model*

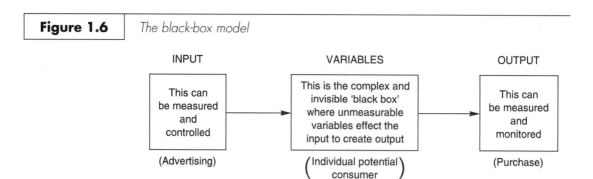

A good example of how to consider the range of variables within the black box (a comprehensive model, as it is called) is the model first put forward by Howard, and refined with the assistance of Sheth. The Howard–Sheth model of buyer behaviour (Fig. 1.7) shows how inputs are transmuted by perceptual constructs and learning constructs to produce outputs, including purchase.

This model was a major move forward in its time, and remains a standard today. When you first look at it it seems rather complex, but just reading through it once will show you that it is not that complicated, indeed, when you boil it down it really seems like common sense – as most of the best theories do!

Bear in mind, however, that even though individual purchasing behaviour is complex, it still is not as complex as organizational behaviour, where extra influences on behaviour are also evident. Sheth, who worked on the Howard–Sheth model, came up with one key mode, on his own this time, depicting organizational behaviour that certainly has implications for the business-to-business marketer.

The business of communicating

The development of communication methods

The Industrial Revolution was the real catalyst for the emergence of mass markets, as we understand them today: the move to towns meant people could no longer subsist or rely upon simple barter, they had paid jobs so began to deal in cash rather than in kind. Various providers of goods and services found themselves in competition with each other for the money in their potential customers' pockets, and so had to begin to differentiate their goods and services within the growing marketplace.

By the twentieth century the gradual rise in literacy amongst the working classes, together with the emergence of a merchant, or middle class, meant that producers could begin to develop brand identities and brand images that set them apart from their competitors and would remain at the front of the mind of the potential purchaser when they selected their goods or services.

With the development of mass-appeal brands such as Persil, Pear's Soap, Sunlight Soapflakes, and so on, the use of the new mass media to communicate brand messages soon followed. Newspapers and magazines carried more advertisements, now with illustrations added; the cinema, the most popular mass medium of the early twentieth century, allowed brand identities to be shown to the majority of the population on a regular basis. Posters, one of the earliest and most effective forms of simple mass communication, continue to reach millions today, as they have done since the nineteenth century.

Commercial radio, Radio Luxembourg only until the 1960s, brought aural messages into the home, and eventually into the car, whilst the advent of commercial television in the latter part of the twentieth century means

Figure 1.7 The Howard–Sheth model of buyer behaviour

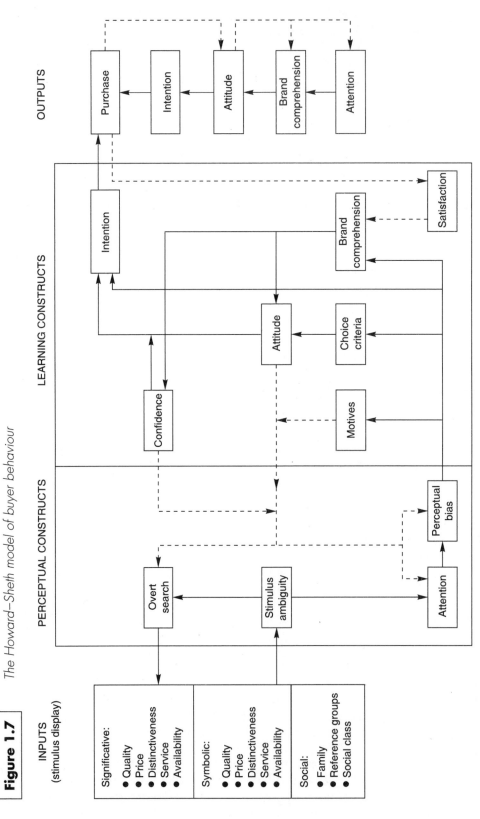

INPUTS
(stimulus display)

PERCEPTUAL CONSTRUCTS

LEARNING CONSTRUCTS

OUTPUTS

Significative:
● Quality
● Price
● Distinctiveness
● Service
● Availability

Symbolic:
● Quality
● Price
● Distinctiveness
● Service
● Availability

Social:
● Family
● Reference groups
● Social class

Overt search

Stimulus ambiguity

Attention

Perceptual bias

Confidence

Intention

Attitude

Brand comprehension

Choice criteria

Motives

Satisfaction

Purchase

Intention

Attitude

Brand comprehension

Attention

(Source: Howard, J.A. and Sheth, J.N. (1969) The Theory Of Buyer Behaviour (New York, John Wiley & Sons. By permission of John Wiley & Sons)

that it is now possible to send a very detailed visual and aural message into almost every home in the country.

Perhaps the biggest change in mass communication has taken place, however, within the last five years: faster and cheaper computing facilities mean that mass communication can now also be personalized communication at one and the same time. Huge amounts of information can be stored, manipulated and cross-referenced at a fraction of the cost of, say, ten years ago. The growth in both sales promotions that generate customer information and the methods of direct marketing that have been developed to capitalize upon this new information technology has been phenomenal. The Internet and all the possibilities it offers in terms of internal and external communication is another obvious addition to the communications toolbox.

The wheel has now turned full circle: in the early days it was often personal selling that captured customers. Then came the day when cost per thousand ruled, followed by the growth of non-contact personal communication with the customer. Today it is not unusual to see a television advertising campaign where the sole purpose is to generate telephone enquiries from the target audience. Who would have thought, even ten years ago, that systems would be available to allow the generation of hundreds of thousands of sales leads to be followed up almost immediately on an individual basis. Although many fight against the wealth of information about individuals held on databases, it is only through the proliferation of such systems that the marketer can truly move ahead to the, for some, ideal world of building a one-to-one relationship with each and every customer.

However, we should be aware that the rush towards personalized everything and Internet interactivity must be tempered with the need to communicate with groups of people who already have something in common – they form the segment of the market for whom the product or service in question is most relevant. As promoters we lose sight of this simple point at our peril. Even personal communication needs to be planned within an overall framework of promotion.

The business of communication today

As described earlier, the twentieth century saw a rapid growth in the use of mass communication and, latterly, in personal or direct communication. This has not happened in a vacuum: service industries have provided the resources demanded by the manufacturers and providers of services.

With the main demand for promotional capabilities coming from the fast-moving consumer goods (fmcg) sector, most of these mass manufacturers initially had their own internal experts in communication – a type of in-house advertising and promotional function. However, as time passed, those working in the industry saw a business opportunity for setting up centres of excellence, staffed by those best at, say, coming up with creative ideas, copy for advertisements etc., and for offering these services for sale to companies who might rather not carry the overhead of an in-house advertising department. Thus, the advertising agency was born.

| **Figure 1.8** | *Traditional full-service agency* |

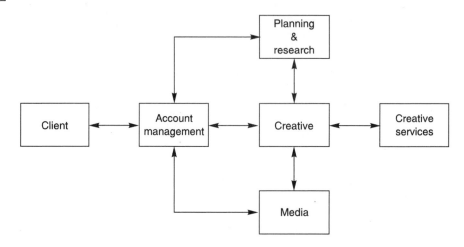

The full service advertising agency, as it is known, offers the client company a range of services. Initially these services mirrored those found in the client company, but over time they became more specialized, with the classic full service agency functions becoming well defined by the 1960s.

Over time the special functions within the agency were seen by those who delivered the services in question as prime opportunities for setting up even more specialized centres of excellence. Thus, from about 1970 to 2000 we saw the emergence of creative hot-shops, media independents, sales promotion houses, direct marketing agencies, sponsorship agencies, web design agencies, as well as increased specialization from PR agencies, design houses and the emergence of e-communication agencies.

Now, in the twenty-first century it is possible for the client to select a full service agency from the hundreds that exist, or to act as their own account handler and buy any and all promotional services *à la carte*. The client must decide whether it is better to use a full service agency, and bear the costs that would be incurred, or whether to spend more time, and thus incur internal costs, co-ordinating their own promotional effort. The client's requirements might mean it makes good commercial sense to employ one main full service agency and split out only their media buying, for example.

If a marketer chooses to buy *à la carte* then the range of services, and the number of people supplying them, is endless. Creative, production, packaging design, sponsorship, public relations, web design, sales promotion, media planning, media buying, point of sale display material construction – all these services, and many more, are available through specialist providers. Should the marketer choose to do so then each can be planned, bought and controlled separately and directly. However, it is clear that the planning of such communications services purchasing must be a priority if synergy and integration are the desired outcomes.

Whether the marketer chooses to use a full service agency, with its affiliated specialized sister companies, or to buy such services *à la carte*, the marketer and the agency are only two points in the triangle of reliance (see

The promotional triangle of reliance　　　　　　　　　　**Figure 1.9**

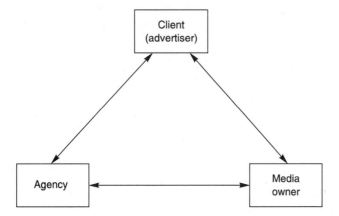

Figure 1.9). The third point is the media. Marketers need the mass media to allow them to reach their target audiences more effectively. Media might mean television or press, or even the postal system.

It is quite clear that the marketer needs the media to reach their customers, and that the marketer needs the services provided by the range of agencies available. It is also clear that the agency needs the marketer to provide them with business and needs the media to allow them to communicate with their client's customers. It is also clear that the media need the clients to provide them with advertising revenue. But why do the media need agencies? Why could they not just deal direct with the clients? Well, in reality, many media owners' sales forces do actually communicate a great deal with client companies direct, but usually only those who spend a great deal of money on the particular medium. It makes sense for the media to deal with agencies, or media houses, because these act as bulk purchasing centres and allow the media to concentrate their sales effort, keeping sales forces to a manageable size, rather than having to deal direct with all potential advertisers.

The balance within the triangle of reliance is key to its continued success. With the current pressures upon all parties to ensure value for money it is in the interests of all parties that the balance is maintained.

Business relationships today

In 1992 the Incorporated Society of British Advertisers (ISBA) published its Best Practice guidelines on managing the advertiser/agency relationship (see next section for an explanation of ISBA's role in the communication business). This document addresses the key issues of how the marketer should set about dealing with their agency and what they should expect from it. Whilst some controversy arose at the time of its publication it is true to say that the document is based upon the concepts of fair dealing and on clarity of purpose on the part of all parties concerned. The guidelines make it clear that in the advertiser/agency relationship, as in all business relationships, there should be trust on both sides, and suggests that that trust is best based upon discussion and written agreements.

It contains sections on selecting and appointing an agency, the agreement that should be drawn up and signed between a client and its agency, agency remuneration procedures, the day-to-day relationship between agency and client, briefing procedures, creative and media issues. It has been written to help both advertisers and agencies to be clearer and more informed about some of the key areas in which problems and disagreements can arise. The user-friendly approach of a question-and-answer format has proved popular. (N.B. at the time of writing the ISBA is planning to publish an updated version of this document.)

The relationship between agencies and media owners is also under scrutiny at all times. Media owners need to be certain that those who buy advertising space from them can actually afford to pay the bills, whilst the agency needs to be sure that the media selected achieves the audience coverage they believe they are buying for their clients.

In all dealings within the business, and the triangle of reliance, there must be both understanding of the other parties' interests and a clarity of purpose. The industry has recognized this for many years, and the bodies it has set up for itself play a leading role in ensuring that all parties benefit as they should.

As mentioned earlier in this unit, all the functions offered by a full service agency, namely account handling, account planning, media planning and buying, creative conceptual work and production facilities can all be bought direct by the client from independent companies or even freelance individuals. From the client's perspective, the advantage of using a full service agency is that there is immediate access to a whole range of experts who are able to bring a fresh and un-jaundiced point of view to bear on your problems. However, it is a very expensive way of operating if you do not intend using all the services on offer: your fees are having to service the overhead, so you might as well use the facilities!

This has to be balanced with the huge amount of extra time that the client who chooses to buy each element of service individually must dedicate to the task. Sometimes it is easy to lose sight of the fact that the internal costs of staff who co-ordinate matters in-house is as real a cost to your company as the fees paid to an agency. The client should weigh up the objective pros and cons of using a full service agency as opposed to buying *à la carte* as circumstances change with time.

The business that looks after itself

Let us take a look at the various industry bodies that are greatly involved in providing the business framework for the industry itself. All these bodies work together – they need to in order for the client, the person who finally pays the bill, to get what they need. Also, of course, all these bodies have at the back of their organizational 'mind' the fact that, unless the business as a whole runs smoothly the process of communication with the potential customer will break down, an end they will all seek to avoid at all costs.

Trade associations and bodies

Trade associations exist in all business fields with a common purpose – to represent the interest of their members as appropriate to the prevailing circumstances. This is certainly the case in the field of communication and promotion. There are literally dozens of trade associations and voluntary bodies; what follows is not an exhaustive list but a résumé of the ones you are most likely to encounter, read about and need to know about for the examinations.

Statutory bodies

These bodies are given their powers by Parliament. They have responsibilities laid down in law, or statute, and are funded by public monies. Both bodies were created as a result of the 1990 Broadcasting Act. 2001 will see a re-vamping of the Authorities, although at the time of writing the Government's White Paper, which proposes a new body OFCOM, has still to be enacted.

Independent Television Commission – ITC

This body licenses and regulates the independent television industry in the UK. It is responsible for drawing up and enforcing a code governing standards and practice in television advertising and the sponsoring of programmes, as well as ensuring all statutes affecting television advertising are adhered to. Under its powers, derived from the Broadcasting Acts of 1990 and 1996, the ITC:

- issues licences that allow commercial television companies to broadcast in and from the UK – whether the services are received by conventional aerials, cable or satellite; and whether delivered by analogue or digital means. These licences vary according to the type of service, but they all set out conditions on matters such as standards of programmes and advertising;
- regulates these services by monitoring broadcasters' performance against the requirements of the ITC's published licences and codes, and guidelines on programme content, advertising and sponsorship and technical performance. There is a range of penalties for failure to comply with them;
- has a duty to ensure that a wide range of television services is available throughout the UK and that, taken as a whole, these are of a high quality and appeal to a range of tastes and interests;
- has a duty to ensure fair and effective competition in the provision of these services;
- investigates complaints and regularly publishes its findings.

Radio Authority – RA

The Authority licenses and regulates all commercial radio services. These comprise national, local, cable, national FM subcarrier, satellite and restricted services. The latter includes all short-term, freely radiating services (for example, 'special event' radio) and highly localized permanent services such as hospital and student radio. The Authority will also be licensing digital radio services, both national and local, over the next few years. The Authority is responsible for monitoring the obligations on its licensees required by the Broadcasting Acts 1990 and 1996. The Authority has three main tasks: to plan frequencies; to appoint licensees with a view to broadening listener choice; and to regulate programming and advertising. It is required, after consultation, to publish Codes to which licensees must adhere. These cover programmes, advertising and sponsorship, and engineering. There are also rules on ownership. The Authority can apply sanctions to licensees who break the rules. Sanctions include broadcast apologies and/or corrections, fines and the shortening or revocation of licences. Licensees pay annual fees to the Authority and application fees are charged to applicants applying for licences. These fees are the Authority's only source of income and cover all its operating costs.

Some media-owner trade associations

Cinema Advertising Association – CAA

The CAA is a trade association of cinema advertising contractors operating in the UK and Eire. Its primary functions are to promote, monitor and maintain standards of cinema advertising, including pre-vetting all cinema commercials to ensure conformity with the British Codes of Advertising and Sales Promotion and the Advertising Standards Authority for Ireland, and to commission and conduct research into the cinema as an advertising medium. This includes the UK cinema admissions monitor, publishing master lists of cinemas taking advertising and providing an industry umbrella for the annual CAVIAR (Cinema and Video Industry Audience Research) studies. The CAA has also commissioned a series of cinema advertising recall studies, for further details please contact the CAA.

Commercial Radio Companies Association – CRCA

The Commercial Radio Companies Association is the trade body for commercial radio companies in the UK. It is a voluntary, non-profit-making body, incorporated as a company limited by guarantee, and was formed by the first radio companies when independent radio began in 1973. It has always enjoyed the overwhelming support of the radio industry – all but a handful of stations are in membership – and has been an influential force in British broadcasting throughout its existence. It is funded by the subscriptions of its member radio companies, who share the cost of CRCA in proportion to their shares of the industry's broadcasting revenue. CRCA affairs are managed by a board of nine non-executive directors, who are elected annually, and one executive director, the Chief Executive of CRCA, who manages the seven-person directorate.

http://www.crca.org.uk

The ITV Network – ITV

The ITV Network commissions and schedules the network programmes transmitted to all 15 ITV regions. It also carries out other functions, including network programming promotions and marketing. The Network provides a platform on which policies common to all the ITV companies can be discussed and determined and an organization through which this can be communicated. Although the companies preserve their independence and formulate their own policies, the Network acts on common cause issues including public affairs (domestic and European), the maintenance of TV advertising standards, engineering and the formulation of digital policy.

http://www.itv.co.uk

Newspaper Publishers' Association – NPA

The NPA is the trade association for Britain's national daily and Sunday newspapers and the Evening Standard. Founded in 1906, its aims are to promote and protect national press interests. Activities include:

- promotion of the national press;
- monitoring and lobbying activities on UK and European legislation affecting the newspaper industry, especially on advertising, copyright, environment and social areas;
- promotion of good practice in advertising, including vetting and monitoring of agencies and advertisers for credit-worthiness;
- provision of accreditation and other services including issuing press cards and administering press rotas for major royal, political and sporting events.

Outdoor Advertising Association – OAA

The OAA is the trade association representing the UK Poster Contractors (both Outdoor and Transport). It is the central reference point for the Outdoor or Poster industry with the objective of advancing and protecting the general trade interests of its members. It is also charged with maintaining the OAA Code of Practice. The primary function is to contribute to the provision of an environment that encourages growth of business.

http://www.oaa.org.uk

Periodical Publishers' Association – PPA

The PPA, established in 1913, has member-publishers covering the full spectrum of magazine publishing, from mass-circulation consumer magazines to highly technical business and professional journals. Approximately 80 per cent of the revenue from magazine publishing is represented by the association.

The main aims of the PPA are to promote and protect the interests and freedom of the periodical press. It maintains a system of agency recognition, oversees the mail order protection schemes operated by members and plays a crucial part in determining the policy and monitoring the daily application of advertising standards. PPA maintains close contacts with magazine distribution organizations, print and paper associations, the Post Office and government departments. Current activity includes the promotion of magazines as an effective advertising medium, the enhancement of editorial standards, the protection of publisher copyright and the provision of accurate data on the magazine industry.

http://www.ppa.co.uk

All these bodies have as their members the companies that are involved as media owners in the relevant field. For example, the OAA has as its members the contractors that erect poster hoardings and who have the right to sell the advertising space, whilst the NPA has as its members the companies that publish national daily newspapers, with the PPA being the body that deals with magazine publishers. Other bodies also exist, and will continue to be developed, within this field, as interest groups consider it desirable to have a trade association that can speak on their behalf, whether to the general public, to government or to the European legislature.

Most media owner trade associations have a small secretariat financed by the subscription of their members, but carry out a great deal of work by committee, with committee members being drawn from member companies. Committees might deal with anything from research to setting the standards against which agency recognition is granted.

Other trade associations

Most of the names of the following associations describe exactly the nature of their membership. Where there might be some ambiguity a brief explanation has been given.

Direct Marketing Association – DMA (formerly BDMA)

The DMA is the only industry association dedicated to promoting and protecting the direct marketing industry as a whole, in all its forms, including both advertisers and suppliers of services. The mission of the DMA is to represent the best interests of its members by raising the stature of the Direct Marketing Industry and gaining consumer trust and confidence in direct marketing. The DMA fulfils many roles including presenting a unified voice for the industry in discussions with the British Government and the institutions of the EU, and with statutory and other bodies. It promotes the use and understanding of direct marketing to members and consumers alike through seminars, conferences, public relations and market development activity.

The members of the Association adhere to a Code of Practice, derived from the codes of the four founding associations, which is administered by the Direct Marketing Authority – chaired by Lord Borrie QC. The Code includes a requirement that all members abide by the British Codes of Advertising and Sales Promotion.

http://www.dma.org.uk

Institute of Practitioners in Advertising – IPA

The IPA is the industry body and professional institute for UK advertising agencies. It has been servicing the needs of advertising agencies since 1917. The IPA serves two purposes:

- it acts as spokesman for agencies, representing them on issues of common concern and speaking on their behalf in negotiations with media bodies, government departments, trade unions and industry and consumer organizations;
- it makes an important contribution to the effective operation of advertising agencies through its advisory, training and information services.

Its objective is to represent all those companies concerned primarily with providing strategic advice on marketing communications, creating and/or placing advertising. There are 210 member companies who collectively handle over 80 per cent of all advertising placed by UK agencies.

http://www.ipa.co.uk

Incorporated Society of British Advertisers – ISBA

ISBA is the only body representing the interests of British advertisers in all areas of commercial communications, including TV advertising, radio, press, outdoor, new media, direct marketing, sponsorship, sales promotion, PR and exhibitions. Founded in 1900, ISBA has around 300 member-companies, whose total communications spend is over £8 billion.

ISBA's membership includes most of the UK's largest advertisers. These include companies operating in all areas of business, including financial services, technology, packaged food and goods, telecoms, automotive, entertainment and leisure. The single factor that binds ISBA members is that they each rely on advertising to promote their goods and services to the public.

ISBA works together with government, media owners and advertising agencies to promote the importance of advertising in driving competition in our economy, to promote the argument for self-regulation of commercial communications, especially in light of the changing media environment, and – always – to defend the freedom of businesses to advertise responsibly. ISBA exists to voice the interests and opinions of its members both to the public at large and to the key decision makers. It is through expression and discussion of members' concerns, interests and ambitions within ISBA's Council, Executive Committees and Action Groups, that the organization's direction is set and the policies of British advertisers are formalized.

ISBA's key strategic aims are to:

1 Achieve recognition of government and business of the fundamental importance of marketing communications to the nation's economy and consumer choice, and the key role of advertisers in funding the media.
2 Resist unwarranted media cost inflation and strive for a more competitive TV airtime marketplace.
3 Encourage a constructive and workable legislative and regulatory framework within which to advertise legally marketable products.

4 Build member involvement and ISBA profile especially at senior management level and create a sense of ownership in ISBA through a more effective internal marketing programme.
5 Encourage excellence of marketing communications practice among members.
6 Stimulate maximum effectiveness and commercial transparency from communication agencies/consultancies.
7 Assist in the effective utilization of new media channels to the benefit of advertisers.

Institute of Sales Promotion – ISP

The ISP is the pre-eminent professional association for everyone in the UK promotional marketing industry. From its inception in 1979, the ISP has aimed to ensure the highest professional standards in all issues relating to promotional marketing and is firmly committed to providing all members with the essential services and professional advice they need.

The ISP has a vital function to fulfil as the 'neutral ground' on which promoters, consultancies and marketing service companies can meet to the mutual advantage of all industry practitioners. The Institute provides the following services and activities for members: Legal Advice and Guidance, Education, European Lobbying, Industry Task Forces, Research and Marketing Intelligence, Publications Service, Social Events.

http://www.isp.org.uk

Public Relations Consultants' Association – PRCA

The PRCA Mission Statement states that the organization exists to encourage and promote the advancement of companies and firms engaged in public relations consultancy. Its stated objectives are:

1 To raise and maintain professional and ethical standards in consultancy practice including the encouragement of Quality ISO 9000, Investors in People, Best Practice and the use of Evaluation.
2 To provide facilities for government, public bodies, associations representing industry, trade and others to confer with public relations consultants as a body and to ascertain their collective views.
3 To promote confidence in public relations consultancy and, consequently, in public relations as a whole, and to act as spokesman for consultancy practice.
4 To educate potential clients, establishing the reputation of professionalism of members who conform to the Professional Charter.
5 To promote that members are registered and that there is a Professional Practices Committee to oversee standards and arbitrate on complaints.
6 To offer practical industry-wide training and management development services.
7 To monitor and react to perceptions of the sector amongst key opinion-leaders.
8 To provide a forum for discussion on key PR industry issues.

9 To demonstrate the effectiveness of good PR in consultancy work.
10 To increase opportunities for members to develop new business.
11 To improve cooperation/relationships with fellow professional bodies in the UK and internationally.
12 To help members improve their efficiency, understanding, skills, professionalism and ethics.

http://www.prca.org.uk

Advertising Association

Most of the aforementioned bodies are members of the Advertising Association, even if their primary motivation is not pure above-the-line advertising. The Advertising Association acts as a collective forum within the communications industry and often acts on behalf of several member associations when there is a common good to be gained, for example in representing the interests of the UK advertising industry in all its parts to the European legislature or the UK government. The Advertising Association is a federation of 26 trade associations and professional bodies representing advertisers, agencies, the media and support services. It is the only body that speaks for all sides of an industry currently worth over £15 billion per annum.

Its remit concerns the mutual interests of the business as a whole. It operates in a complementary way with the vested interests of its members who have specific roles for their individual sectors. The AA speaks as 'the common voice' for all on:

● promoting public understanding of, and respect for, commercial communication and its role in promoting competition, innovation and economic and social progress in society;
● upholding standards and the principle of self-regulation;
● providing information, research and statistics about the advertising business;
● combating unjustified restrictions and outright bans on commercial communication for freely and legally available products or services.

The Advertising Association exists to provide a coordinated service in the interests of its wider membership, i.e. the individual companies that make up this large, diverse and competitive business. Its remit is 'to promote and protect the rights, responsibilities and role of advertising' in the UK. This is in line with Article 10 of the European Convention on Human Rights, which recognizes commercial freedom of speech as a right, alongside political and artistic freedoms of speech. The AA is a non-profit-making company, limited by guarantee, and funded by a combination of subscriptions, donations and revenue-raising activities such as seminars and publications.

http://www.adassoc.org.uk

Membership associations

These bodies have individuals as members, with the gaining of a qualification approved by the body concerned usually being the only way to obtain membership. Professional status for those who hold qualifications is enhanced by the work carried out by each of these bodies.

Communication, Advertising and Marketing Education Foundation – CAM – membership relies upon passing the CAM Diploma

The Communication, Advertising and Marketing Education Foundation (CAM) is the examinations board for vocational qualifications in the disciplines that make up marketing communication. Its Advisory Council consists of principal trade associations and professional institutes that, between them, represent all parts of the marketing communication business. It is from that industry-wide representation that the CAM syllabuses (on which the examinations are based) are developed. They are multi-disciplinary in their scope and the qualifications awarded reflect a breadth of knowledge and competence in all the key activities.

http://www.camfoundation.com

Chartered Institute of Marketing – CIM – membership relies upon passing the CIM Diploma

CIM is the professional body for marketing, representing 60 000 marketers worldwide. Their branch and special interest group networks aim to provide members with the opportunity to make contact with other professionals in all industry sectors and on every continent. They offer access to a wide range of professional services aimed at developing careers and aiding professional development.

Only members of CIM can work towards Individual Chartered status and call themselves Chartered Marketers. Just like Chartered Accountants, Chartered Marketers keep their skills and knowledge up to date. To help, CIM provides a continuing professional development (CPD) structure to keep marketers qualified, experienced, innovative and competitive. CIM is the only marketing body able to award chartered status to the individual. CIM was given authority by the Queen's Privy Council Office in the UK. The first awards were made in October 1998. In 1999–2000 the number of Chartered Marketers increased by more than half to over 3000.

http://www.cim.co.uk

Institute of Public Relations – IPR – membership relies upon passing the CAM Diploma in Public Relations, the IPR Diploma, a PR Degree or holding another recognized qualification in public relations

With over 6000 members the Institute of Public Relations is the largest professional body for PR practitioners in Europe. It represents the interests of people working in public relations, offering access to information, advice and support, and provides networking opportunities through a wide variety of events, seminars and training workshops. The aims of the IPR are to:

● provide a professional structure for the practice of public relations;
● enhance the ability and status of its members as professional practitioners;

- represent and serve the professional interests of its members;
- provide opportunities for members to meet and exchange views and ideas;
- raise standards within the profession through the promotion of best practice – including the production of best practice guides, training events and seminars, and a continuous professional development scheme.

http://www.ipr.org.uk

Market Research Society – MRS – membership relies upon holding the MRS Diploma or another recognized qualification

The MRS represents the professional interests of 7000 market research practitioners. The Society sets qualification criteria for admission to its various grades of membership. It issues a Code of Conduct and oversees compliance with the Code. Supplementary Guidelines are also issued on specialist dimensions of research practice. In addition to professional accreditation, MRS members receive access to publications and information services, career development via training and CPD, and a wide range of conferences, seminars and meetings geared to special interests. As the Society has members on both the agency and client side of market research, as well as in the academic community, it is neutral and independent of each of these 'constituencies'. It is the lead body in coordination of the Market Research Industry Liaison Group, with the British Market Research Association (BMRA) and the Association of Users of Research Agencies (AURA). It also leads the Marketing Market Research Initiative, which aims to foster conditions that enable market research to flourish, and to promote the identity and value of market research to business, government and the general public.

http://www.marketresearch.org.uk

Most of these bodies have a great deal of involvement with the development of qualification syllabi and the monitoring of standards of practice and ethics within their respective fields. Once again, a great deal of their work is actually administering decisions made by committees made up of members.

Summary of Chapter 1

Within this chapter we have covered the following:

1 Overview

In this section the aim is to gain a real overview of how and where marketing communications fits into the overall picture of marketing and marketing planning. The three main sections are:

a. *Understanding marketing planning*

This is an overview of the key steps in planning – whether it be marketing planning or, indeed, marketing communications planning.

The role and importance of auditing as a part of the planning process, as well as setting objectives, selecting strategies, building implementation plans and the importance of monitoring activity are also dealt with.

b. *Getting back to basics – minding your Ps and Cs*

This section looks at the traditional seven Ps of the Marketing Mix through fresh eyes, as this is where the author proposes the adoption of the seven Cs when addressing marketing and marketing communications planning.

This is an important insight into the basis for planning truly customer-orientated marketing and marketing communications programmes.

c. *How communication might work – some theories*

This section looks at some of the respected theories of how the process of communication works, from an academic and even psychological viewpoint.

2 The business of communicating

In this section the focus is on how the business of marketing communication works within the UK today. With a historical perspective, and by referring to many of today's leading trade association websites, this section should clarify the working relationships found in the modern business.

a. *The development of communication methods*

This section contains an overview of the historical development of today's communication methods.

b. *The business of communication today*

This section addresses how clients, service suppliers and the media interrelate in today's business environment. It introduces the concept of the Triangle of Reliance.

c. *Business relationships today*

This section introduces a part of the text, which will later deal in detail with how to find, brief and manage service suppliers.

d. *The business that looks after itself*

This is the section of the book that gives readers an insight into how the business is run: by explaining the roles of many of the leading trade and member associations, the reader should now better understand how the industry oversees its own people.

Self-test questions and opinion development

These are not exam questions, nor are they meant to represent the sort of question you might expect to face anywhere else. They are designed to help you check whether you have understood the content of this chapter. All you have to do is read the questions, give them some thought and maybe jot down some notes on what your response might be. Not all the questions will have factual answers – rather, they might encourage you to think about a topic or an issue and formulate an opinion based upon what is now, hopefully, a better understanding of the topic.

- What are the key questions that have to be asked and answered in any planning process?
- What are the seven Ps of the marketing mix?
- What are the seven Cs of the marketing mix?
- What is the relationship between the Ps and the Cs?
- What does AIDA stand for, and in what way is it relevant to understanding how communication might work?
- Who do you think understands better how communication works: a psychologist, a sociologist, an advertising agency account executive, a market researcher, a marketer?
- Why do you think mass communication developed at all, and why is there now such an emphasis on one-to-one or one-to-few marketing communications?
- What is the triangle of reliance, and how do you think it might change in the future?
- Name three media trade associations and explain what they do and why they do it.

Extending knowledge and understanding

You are encouraged to undertake the following activities to further your knowledge and understanding of the topics covered in this chapter in the following ways.

1 Visit at least five of the websites listed. In order to be able to assess how well the websites communicate with their target audiences do the following:

- draw up a list of potential target audiences;
- assess how easy it is to navigate the site;
- assess how well both visual and verbal communication techniques are used;
- give comparative scores to the sites;
- track the sites over at least three months to see how live they are kept.

2 Make sure you hunt out copies of the following trade press from *now on*! You might be able to get them free if you are a student, or may have to beg them or borrow them from someone else's desk – however you get them, get them! Usually you have a choice between the paper version and an online version – which, without subscribing may give you just a very little, or really rather a lot! Check out both the printed *and* online

versions if you really want to get and stay up to date with issues that really matter in the world of marketing communications!

As you work through the book you will find that different chapters refer to different areas, but all will have their own trade press and it's not worth waiting until you get to the chapter to sort out what can be a lengthy ordering process, so here goes with a list of at least the major titles you should look for and their website starting points so you can begin the process:

Marketing	http://www.marketing.haynet.com
Marketing Week	http://www.mad.co.uk
Campaign	http://www.campaignlive.com
	(advertising magazine)
Media Week	http://www.mediaweek.co.uk
PR Week	http://www.prweek.net
Precision Marketing	http://www.mad.co.uk

Planning your marketing communications

2

By the end of this chapter you should:

▶ have a clear understanding of the stages in marketing planning;
▶ have a detailed insight into auditing in the widest sense;
▶ have a clear idea of the issues that arise specifically when dealing with communications planning;
▶ know why communications audits matter and know how to do them;
▶ understand what communications objectives are and know how to go about setting them;
▶ have a better understanding of some of the most popular methods for setting a budget.

An overview of planning

It is worth starting here with an overview of the whole picture. Marketing communications planning and implementation will be most effectively carried out if it is tackled with a clear set of objectives, over a set timescale, using the right tools for the job and with cost-efficiency at its core. That means you need to understand how to organize promotion, the nature of the tools available and how to use the tools of planning in this field. This is the point we have now reached: you should have a better idea of how the business of promotion works, how the minds of consumers work, how promotion aims to reach the psyche of the customer generally and how specific tools aim to do that individually and as a planned whole.

Let's begin by taking a look at where marketing communications planning fits into the overall picture.

The specifics of marketing communications planning must fit into an overall corporate planning framework, which allows all those involved to see how their functional responsibilities work with those of others. As you read more and more widely, you will realize that many authors develop their own visual and mnemonic aids to describe the planning process. What follows is my own memory jogger, which I drew up after looking at a whole range of texts and study notes.

I think that it is best for every student of marketing, promotion and marketing communication to develop such an overall understanding of the process that they can build their own little sketch to remind them of the overall picture. You should read around the topic and develop your own memory aid.

As you can see, Figure 2.1 shows that it is an appreciation of the interrelationship of the elements that is essential. However, in order to be able to decide upon where we want to go we have to establish where we are, what opportunities exist for us, how the rest of the marketplace is operating and how the overall environment might allow us to exploit the chances that are available for us to take.

| **Figure 2.1** | *The stages that lead to the selection of promotional tools* |

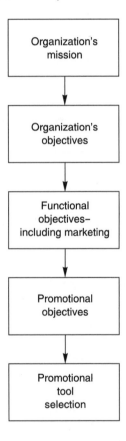

The key questions that have to be answered by the process of planning are listed below, and can be summarized as SOSTCA (MMMMM). This model can be applied to any level of planning – business, divisional, marketing or marketing communications. The same questions always have to be asked and answered, and these headings could usefully become the headings with, say, a marketing plan or, indeed, a marketing communications plan.

Situation	Where are we now and how did we get there?
Objectives	Where do we want to be?
Strategy	How will we get there?
Tactics	Our detailed explanation and justification of activities.
Control	What will be measured, when and how will it all be managed?
Action	A calendar of specific events
(MMMMM)	What should be shown on the calendar of activities: i.e.
	Men – exactly who will be responsible for the activity?
	Money – the cost.
	Minutes – exactly when the activity will take place?
	Measurement – what information will be gathered to measure what, when?
	Management – shows when management meetings will take place.

Where are we now and how did we get there? The marketing framework

There are many paths that can be followed. The process of auditing to discover the full truth of present circumstances must be carried out throughout the range of functions, but our focus needs to carry us towards marketing communications (marcomms) planning and implementation via an understanding of marketing planning, so we must look at what is often called the *marketing audit*. I have developed my own system, which is useful both in practical terms as well as in being relatively simple to visualize and memorize for examination purposes. My process for establishing a true picture of where you are now is called the 4U Audit – that will, I hope, always work '4U'!

Figure 2.2 illustrates how the corporate environment nestles within the outside world 'U's of your direct and indirect competitors, the micro-environment and the macro-environment. What do I mean by each of these terms?

Note that you need to use terminology in an acceptable way, so here are some commonly used terms that might help you with this process:

Direct competitor – this is an organization that offers a direct alternative to your product/service in a way that is very close to your own, e.g., Cannon Cinemas and Odeon Cinemas; MacDonalds and Burger King. Customers can choose between two different cinemas or two different fast-food burger bars. This is direct competition.

Indirect competitor – this is an organization that offers an indirect alternative to your product/service in a way that is different from your own, but serves the same essential purpose on the part of the customer, e.g., Blockbuster Home Video and Odeon Cinemas; Pizza Hut Home Delivery and McDonalds. As you can see, in each example the customer will still be either entertained or fed, but has chosen a very different way of getting his or her entertainment or food. Taking the cinema example,

| **Figure 2.2** | *The 4U Audit* |

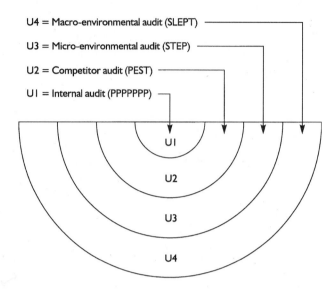

U4 = Macro-environmental audit (SLEPT)
U3 = Micro-environmental audit (STEP)
U2 = Competitor audit (PEST)
U1 = Internal audit (PPPPPPP)

be aware that other indirect competitors would include a huge range of other leisure and entertainment pastimes.

Micro-environment – all those external factors not directly related to your competitors, but which form a part of the environment within which the whole market operates. An example would be the general change in eating habits towards more healthy options: this is happening and you must note it. It is measurable from existing data or research that you might wish to commission, and it will affect not just your marketplace as, say, Pizza Hut, but the whole social attitude towards fast food versus salad bars, for instance. Many micro-environmental changes come about because of pressures brought to bear by direct and indirect competitors or by interest groups, e.g., the activities of various groups against McDonalds' farming methods or the fat content of their burgers. With care, you can 'deal with' the problems and opportunities thrown up by a study of the micro-environment.

Macro-environment – this is not just encountered when looking at other countries with an eye to entering their marketplace, although it does have a specific significance in such cases. If you are a fruit juice bottler, a cold winter in Florida can raise the price of orange juice concentrate on the world market to such an extent that you have to develop new recipes that use less of the expensive orange concentrate and more of other ingredients such as mango juice, passion fruit, etc. Politics here means the widest political climate of a country or region, whilst in the micro-environment it could mean more localized political issues.

Let us look more closely at how the 4U Audit works in practice (see Figure 2.3).

Using the 4U Audit – the factors to assess when auditing | **Figure 2.3**

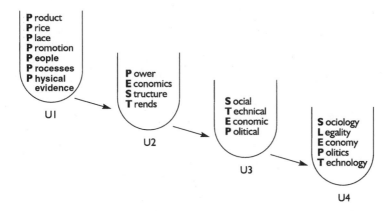

P roduct
P rice
P lace
P romotion
P eople
P rocesses
P hysical
    evidence

U1

P ower
E conomics
S tructure
T rends

U2

S ocial
T echnical
E conomic
P olitical

U3

S ociology
L egality
E conomy
P olitics
T echnology

U4

U1 internal audit (PPPPPPP)

This means that you carry out a full assessment of your internal abilities. The focus on a marketing audit means that it is useful for us to look at the marketing mix in great detail, so, once again, the seven Ps have their uses. By assessing against each of the seven Ps (Product, Price, Place, Promotion, People, Processes, Physical evidence), you will have a framework that will force you to address all the key issues relating to either the single product or service involved or the whole range of products/services under consideration.

U2 competitor audit (PEST)

Look at all your competitors, both direct and indirect. The focus here is on seeing all your competitors as pests, or as throwing up challenges that you will need to meet. Thus, the mnemonic PEST really does become memorable. Just go one step further and remember what each letter stands for in *these* circumstances, and you'll be well on your way to showing that you understand what needs to be investigated to build up a full picture.

In this instance P stands for *Power*, which means assessing and quantifying the power held by each player in the marketplace (perhaps market share, number of passengers carried, etc.).

E is for *Economics*, not in the huge, textbook sense, but in terms of which competitor has what type of financial standing within the marketplace.

S is for *Structure*, which means that you must analyse the structure of the marketplace via the products/services offered by both your direct and indirect competitors, looking at how the position has arisen and assessing what lessons can be learned from this. Once you have a structural picture of the market, develop a similar picture of the customers within the market.

T is for *Trends*, which need to be analysed historically if they are to help in the future – you need a sound basis for prediction here. Certain trends will be well established and therefore easy to track, e.g., more leisure time, higher levels of disposable income, baby rearing fashions, etc., others will be more difficult because they are just beginning and might not, therefore, yet be seen as trends! If you are heading up a record company, the trend for Britney Spears sound-alikes and look-alikes might grow or die, so you need to be able to predict the next trend – will it be Irish rock, acoustic playing, heavy rock?

U3 – micro-environmental audit (STEP)

Look at the micro-environment as offering the opportunity to STEP all over your competitors and really succeed by becoming top of the pile! STEP as a mnemonic will allow you to focus on the correct areas to ensure that you are taking on board all points that really matter.

S is for *Social* factors, which must be studied in depth. With a micro-environmental audit for, say, teenage fashions, the micro-S would focus on the social tendencies of the target audience, i.e., the teenagers themselves, looking at how they often spend time as members of groups or gangs, how their fashion sense is heightened by what their pop idols wear or don't wear, etc.; whereas the macro-S (see below for more detail) would focus on how many teenagers of what ages lived where and how teenagers in general differ from their predecessors and try to stand out. Thus the micro-S and the macro-S are slightly different.

T is for *Technical*, which, if we follow through the above example, would allow us to look at what machinery/equipment/fabrics are available for teen fashions now, and how they can be made relevant. Can we make clothes more quickly, from lighter weight/cheaper fabrics if they are only intended to have a short lifespan (as opposed to classic-style sweaters made by us for the upmarket, middle-aged female, where quality and longevity matter, not fashion)? So in this section we look at the technical features that we can control.

E is for *Economic* factors. How much can teenagers afford to spend on clothes in an average month? How many work on Saturdays? Has this changed? What about pocket money? Do more teenagers now get paid for doing chores, or do parents still pay for clothes and thus retain responsibility for selecting them? These economic factors are specific to the micro-environment.

P is for *Political*, which does not necessarily mean party political, although some politicians specifically court popularity with teenagers who are still not old enough to vote, because they want to be sure they will be the choice of the next generation of voters. If we stick with the teenage fashion theme, then it can be said that teenagers are certainly politically aware and have opinions, but that they might see politics in a different way, not in the party structure of the day. You would need to assess this and be aware, for example, of the impact of 'green' politics on today's youth.

U4 – macro-environmental audit (SLEPT)

This refers to those factors that will, frankly, happen whilst you have SLEPT. They are the factors about which you can do nothing, but of which you need to be as aware as possible, and which you need to watch like a hawk to try to predict how they might affect the future success of your product/service.

S is for *Sociology*, in the *big* sense! The sociologists, not the market researchers, will study the sociology of a locale, region, country or continent in the first instance. Often linked to historical factors, you must study the sociology of your target audience's geographic and demographic location. If you look at Eire versus Northern Ireland, although two very small populations share the same small land mass and a great deal of common history, you will find that some products choose to show themselves as having the same market position, relative to competitors, in both the north and the south, but that Southern Irish actors are used in the Eirean TV commercials, whereas the commercials shown in the north are exactly the same as those shown in England, Wales and Scotland. This is to make the products seem more 'Irish' and thus more socially acceptable. Some might say that this is a political point, but in reality it has become sociological. See the notes on politics, below.

L is for *Legality*, which must be checked but cannot be changed, unless you change whatever is illegal about your product/service or advertisement. It might be that you are facing new food labelling legislation, or that the law on who you can and cannot mail has altered. Laws can affect marketers and promoters in many ways, and as the person planning a promotional programme your audit will focus mainly on laws relating to all types of promotional activities. Up-and-coming changes in legislation that might adversely affect your business (e.g., tobacco advertising being banned) can be planned for and even lobbied against.

E is for *Economy* in the *big* sense. We are not just looking at single markets here, we need to look at the bigger picture: in times when money is very tight, promoting money off standard product lines can win customers, when an emphasis on continuing high levels of quality might keep some loyal customers but is unlikely to attract new business. Similarly, when levels of disposable income are higher than usual in certain demographic sub-groups, they attract the attention of the marketer. Currently we are seeing an enormous growth in the number of over-50-year-olds with a reasonable level of pension income – the 'wrinkly' pound is attracting the efforts of many marketers, such as tour operators for example, who are tailor-making products and services for this affluent age group.

P is for *Politics*, but, again, in the major sense rather than just the domestic party political sense. The politics of any country totally colour the outlook of its people, even if this is covertly rather than overtly. In terms of international marketing and promotion, it is quite obvious that the political 'climate' of a country or region is a vital factor to be investigated, but it is no less important in terms of domestic marketing and marcomms planning.

T is for *Technology* in the broadest sense, in terms of looking at the capabilities of a region (e.g., Minitel in France affecting the uptake of the Internet) or the lack of them (e.g., reliable telephone connections in Albania). The availability of constant power systems is necessary for so many applications that just a simple break can create chaos. The technological climate of an area must be investigated as must all the others. Will you take technology forward, or will you rely upon what exists? Will you need to build a technical infrastructure, or will you use what is there?

Where are we now and how did we get there? The specific marketing communication issues

Once you have agreed your marketing position, your marketing objectives will follow, as will an agreement about your marketing strategy.

We are interested in the P for Promotion or the C for Communication. So we will now turn to the planning process for marketing communications within the marketing planning process. It might be that a part of your overall marketing auditing will involve your marketing communications activities and their results – they certainly *should* be covered. But you actually need to consider the very specialized nature of marketing communications auditing as a separate entity.

Communication audits – what are they?

A Communication Audit is an investigation that will allow you to discover the answers to the following questions:

- what are you already doing in terms of your communication effort?
- how, exactly, are you doing it?
- how long have you been doing it for?
- what have the effects of having done it been?

These might seem to be perfectly obvious questions, but you might be surprised that some organizations not only rarely ask these questions but that even more never bother to dig beneath the glib, simplistic answers to the questions that it might be possible to produce at an instant's notice. There is no point making assumptions about the effect of marketing communications activity – this is dangerous and will always work against you.

The other warning point is that it is *not* enough to ask those who are doing it about what they are doing – you must get out there and ask the recipients of your marketing communications about how they feel about it. You might be sending your customers what you think is a great series of informative letters, individually addressed, carefully tailored and sent at key moments in the purchasing calendar – your customers might think you are wasting money sending them letters they don't want, don't read and could well do without because they find them irritating. You would only discover this if you actually asked them – so do! This would be an example of the sort of thing you would do as part of a Communication Audit but, as you can imagine, a real audit that is to form the basis for important future planning and decision making needs to be a formalized, professionally planned business exercise, rather than just a piecemeal investigation into effectiveness.

Communication audits present an objective report on the communications of an organization. An audit can be widely focused, covering all stakeholder groups, or more narrowly focused on one or more groups such as customers, employees, investors, the community, etc. It can also be limited to one or more specific communication programmes.

In today's rapidly changing technology-driven environment, organizational communicators are challenged to be more flexible, responsive and innovative in meeting both the immediate communication needs of the organization and anticipating future needs. An audit today must address this dual challenge.

A communications audit is akin to a medical check-up or financial audit. It is a thorough and systematic examination to determine what is functioning well and what is not. It will often provide guidance and direction on how communications can be improved. Its primary purpose is to determine the degree to which communications with specific groups are effective, useful and valuable in supporting and advancing the organization's strategic objectives. Findings of an audit may result in minor or major changes in communications strategies and the ways in which communications are planned and implemented in the future.

So how do you do a Communications Audit?

Audit methods, completion time and costs vary depending upon the audit's scope and the organization. Each organization has its own communications needs, goals and climate. It has a unique culture, history, dynamics and competitive and financial environments. An audit for one organization will be quite different from that for another. That said, there are some commonalities. The audit process unfolds in several stages.

I – planning and design

This involves getting samples of *all* your marketing communications from every part of the organization – a mammoth task, and one which might be made easier by the marketing communications department keeping at least two file copies of everything it creates, or knows is being created, within the organization.

You might think it makes sense to gather all of your external communications, and it does, but don't omit your internal and partner communications too.

Thus, you might be putting out the call for literature from Istanbul and staff letters from Iver, making sure you have staff newsletters from the plant in Cologne as well as from the plant in Coventry. Whatever it takes, you must gather a total pool of *what* you have been doing. Whilst a big job, this is pretty straightforward when it comes to advertising, photos of exhibits, literature and even websites – but what about the results of your press relations efforts? Well, you can gather the clippings, get the feedback from the assessment services you might be using, etc. And, as for internal letters etc., well, you might have to be content with a cross-section, plus a list of times/dates when such documents were sent, and to whom.

It could take months to do this, so don't leave it until the last minute, and don't let it stand alone as an activity: by always planning ahead you can make sure you have a sample gathering system in place all the time so you are continuously collecting materials, thereby making this a process, not a one-off huge job! You could then be getting on with your 'Effect Research' at the same time although, again, this should be a part of an ongoing process.

The planning and design stage defines the audit's scope and goals, the population involved, communications to be audited, audit methods to be used, timeframe and budget. The audit plan is often developed through interviews, discussions and collaboration with a variety of senior managers within the organization and the auditor or audit team.

II – research and measurement

Many organizations spend a great deal of time and money finding out what their external marketing communications budget has achieved for them, but never carry out research into the effectiveness of their internal communications. Therefore, they never discover that they are having to spend millions of pounds telling customers that they will deliver better service when all they really need to do is communicate more effectively with internal audiences about what they expect from them in terms of service delivery!

The lessons here are clear – if you do it, you must evaluate the effect of it! It really is that simple. It applies to issues such as print, where it might seem that this print job is too small to research, as is that one, as is the next one – then you get to the end of the year and find you have spent £500 000 on print in total, without any evaluation at all!

Of course, auditing and evaluation cost money, so don't expect to get them done for free. But even if you put aside a small percentage of your *total* budget at the start of the year for this purpose, you will find you have a much better idea of what is working and what isn't – so you can spend your money more efficiently next time, even if it didn't work well for you this time.

Research and measurement begins with informal exploratory research and often moves to formal, scientific methods of gathering information. The two informal, exploratory research methods used most often are in-depth interviews and focus groups. The formal, scientific measurement method used most often for primary source research is a survey. Analysis of existing databases of information (prior surveys and other databases) is sometimes used to add further dimension to the audit findings. This is known as secondary source research.

Depending on the goals and design of the audit, research and measurement of some or all of the following may be involved: face-to-face communications and the grapevine; flow patterns among individuals, departments, divisions and leadership; publications in print, video and audio plus other audiovisuals; large group meetings and events; memos and written communications; leadership and manager-based communications; electronic communications such as e-mail, voice-mail, intranets; and feedback systems.

In addition to communications media, patterns, flow, channels and technologies, a communications audit examines content clarity and effectiveness; information needs of individuals, work groups, departments and divisions; non-verbal communications and corporate culture issues; and communication impacts on motivation and performance.

You need to be sure you are auditing those areas upon which people can be most affected by communications: peoples' knowledge, understanding and perceptions; opinions, attitudes and beliefs; issues, concerns and feelings; needs and preferences; abilities; intentions; and behaviours.

III – analysis and reporting

The final phase is analysis and reporting. After examining all the information gathered in the research and measurement phase, an analysis is conducted to determine how well the communications satisfy the needs of the organization and the stakeholder groups today and how well these communications will serve changing needs in the operational future (1–2 years).

Conduct of a communications audit is usually performed by outside consultants because of their professional experience, expertise and objectivity. In addition, an independent third party's guarantee of confidentiality often produces a higher level of trust from employees and other stakeholders in in-depth interviews, focus groups and surveys. This often produces more open, candid, real world information than that which can be acquired by in-house research efforts. This is especially true when an organization is in the process of transformation.

When would you perform an audit?

Though it is always advisable to audit an individual communication's effectiveness on an on-going basis as an integral part of the communications cycle, broader communication audits are essential when an organization is undergoing change – for example: major expansion, merger or acquisition; reduction of personnel; new functions or business lines are undertaken; external circumstances are forcing changes; and when there is an acquisition of new technology – especially if it is information or communications technology. Benefits of an audit:

A communications audit well done will produce a clear understanding of how communications are really working and the degree to which they are satisfying needs. From this flows a number of possibilities: improved productivity and competitive advantage; better use of existing and future communications and information technology; more efficient use of time; discovery of hidden information resources; improved morale; and a more vibrant corporate culture, among others.

Where do we want to be?

So, once you have found out where you are, and have analysed how you got there, you can decide where you want to go. You will set your objectives. In a marketing plan these will be marketing objectives, such as capturing 21 per cent market share, or increasing volume sales by £2 million, for example. But we are considering marketing communications, so we have to consider a different type of objective.

What is your communications objective? Unless you can answer this question you cannot begin to plan or implement a communications programme. So let's start at a logical point: what could your objectives be? There is no such thing as a definitive list, but here are some reasonable objectives for marcomms:

- sell direct to consumers;
- create direct sales leads for your sales force;
- support your sales force in the field;
- create product awareness;
- inform/educate about product uses;
- stimulate product trial;
- remind existing users;
- reassure existing users;
- encourage extra sales within a timeframe (short term);
- retaliate against competitor presence.

The specific reason *why* any of these might be your objective must be considered, and will depend on the circumstances you either find yourself to be in, or find you are given by the examiner. Care should be taken when setting any objectives, including promotional objectives, with the very useful mnemonic SMARTT coming into play, which is explained in Figure 2.4.

Once you have decided on your objectives, your aims, then you can decide your strategy. This means selecting from your toolbox the right promotional tools to allow you to get the job done. By weighing the advantages and disadvantages of each of the promotional tools that this text has dealt with you will develop an overall pattern for your promotional programme. Then you can decide on tactics: the weight to be given to each tool, how, over time, each will be deployed to balance your promotional achievements. Look back to the ways in which certain tools are good at certain jobs, reassess in your mind how timescales can affect effectiveness. Of course, all of this activity has to be paid for somehow – so let's look at getting the money sorted out!

Budget setting

Marketing budgets may be broken down into an operating-costs section, a product-development and research section, and a promotional expenditure section. Organizations vary in their budget-setting framework, and there is no right or wrong way for overall budgeting to be calculated in this broad sense – it will depend on the business and, often, on historical methods.

		Figure 2.4

Specific	All objectives must be drawn up precisely – this means they relate to specific, detailed end results and are not merely vague statements of intent.	
Measurable	If an objective is not quantified it cannot be measured – if it cannot be measured, how will you know whether or when it has been achieved?	
Achievable	What is the point of setting sights so high that goals are unlikely to be achieved? It is demotivating and reflects poorly on the whole organization.	
Relevant	This means ensuring that objectives are relevant to the overall thrust of the business – don't undermine all your other efforts, use the right tool for the job.	
Timed	Objectives must be achieved within agreed timescales – be it by the end of day three or within the next 48 months.	
Targeted	You will target different sectors of the market with different objectives – don't just set 'blanket' objectives.	

When it comes to the promotional budgeting, budgets may be set against a product, a product range, a brand, a brand group, a business unit, a division or an entire business. Once again, you will probably find that, until you reach board level, there is little you can do to influence this framework. That said, when it comes to a specific budget there are many ways to decide the amount to be spent upon promotion.

The arbitrary method

This means you pick a figure by hunch and work within it! Yes, you're right, it sounds odd and is largely based on the experience of the person picking the figure. This method has little in its favour, but should be mentioned if only because so many organizations still seem to rely on it. An alternative is simply to work within the budget handed down from on high, without putting any work into arguing for a different figure based on another budget-setting method. To be fair, many promotional campaign managers, whatever their title might be, find themselves having to work within this sort of framework. It at least has the advantage that you know an amount of money is being made available for promotion, but it has little else to recommend it.

Percentage-of-sales methods

These look either at the past performance of a product/brand, etc., or at its predicted future performance. There are some problems here. First, what percentage do you spend? Second, if you are working on historical performance you are not recognizing changing market forces, and if you are looking ahead your estimate is dependent on the accuracy of your forecasting. What percentage to use can be addressed by examining industry averages. But then, are you an average performer within the industry, or do you want to rise above this?

When looking backwards in time at past performance you are at least setting a figure in line with sales levels you know were achieved last year, but can you achieve them this year? Are you aiming to maintain market share or increase it? If you had a poor year last year, should this year's promotional budget suffer because of it? Will your competitors be spending the same? All in all, although this is a very popular method of setting a budget, it can hold you back and can be misleading.

When looking forward you need to be pretty sure that you are going to meet your sales targets, or you will be overspending wildly. Indeed, overspending early in the period because of poor forecasting can lead to one of the worst possible positions – results coming in show you will not hit targets, so promotional budgets are slashed and you end up not only with little or no promotional presence towards the end of the period, but an incomplete effect achieved by what you spent to start with.

The unit percentage method

This means you carry out detailed costings analyses on each unit produced and add in a percentage to the selling price that is to be allocated directly to promotion. This has a built-in problem in that you still have to decide what percentage to add, as well as being directly tied into sales levels, which might be highly seasonal.

The competitive parity method

This has merit – it means that you look at what your competitors spend and match or exceed this, depending on your position in the market. This method can be very useful if you are entering a new market, when what others spend can at least guide you. But no two marketing mixes are the same, and who is to say that the promotional mix chosen by competitors will be the one that is best for you? Also, if you miscalculate your competitors' expenditure you can totally miscalculate your own budget!

The objective-and-task method

Sometimes also called the *target-sum method*, this method at least does not get bogged down in the questions that all the previous methods ask, i.e., how much should we spend? Rather, this method approaches budget-setting from the other direction by asking how much it will cost to achieve given objectives. Here you begin by deciding what you want to achieve, design the best promotional plan to achieve those objectives, cost the whole programme and use that figure as your budget. This sounds as though it is the perfect way to set a budget, but even this is not perfect, as you might well exceed what the product/brand can, in reality, afford. Not only this, but, because all markets are so dynamic, whilst it is fine to set overall promotional strategies in place ahead of time, you really do need to retain flexibility of both implementation and budget spending over time.

The composite method

This means using several budgeting techniques all at the same time and is, in truth, the approach most often adopted. A mixture of the arbitrary method with a nod in the direction of a percentage of sales, usually under the auspices of a set figure but with some recognition of the task in hand, is often used by organizations who operate in the real world, rather than in the academic textbook!

There really is no such thing as a perfect, single method of setting a budget. Look at the situation in hand and discuss the alternatives, deciding which is the best, given the circumstances. What you should be able to do is at least have an idea of the comparative merits and demerits of each method, and be able to apply them to any situation the examiner gives you.

Summary of Chapter 2

In this chapter we have covered the following.

Planning your marketing communications

This chapter gives an in depth insight into how all planning works.

a. *An overview of planning*
   The introduction of the SOSTCA (MMMMM) planning framework, which leads into the rest of the chapter.

b. *Where are we now and how did we get there? The marketing framework*
   This section allows a detailed insight into the whole auditing process. The unique 4U Audit for the total marketing auditing process is introduced and what communications audits are and how to do them are discussed.

c. *Where do we want to be?*
   This section addresses the issue of what types of objectives can be set as marketing communications objectives.

  d. Budget setting

  This section takes a look at the key ways in which budgets *can* be set, as well as their strengths and weaknesses.

Self-test questions and opinion development

These are not exam questions, nor are they meant to represent the sort of question you might expect to face anywhere else. They are designed to help you check whether you have understood the content of this chapter. All you have to do is read the questions, give them some thought and maybe jot down some notes on what your response might be. Not all the questions will have factual answers – rather, they might encourage you to think about a topic or an issue and formulate an opinion based upon what is now, hopefully, a better understanding of the topic.

- What does SOSTCA (MMMMM) stand for?
- What is the SLEPT of the 4U Audit? What does it mean to marketers?
- What is more important – auditing or setting objectives?
- What stages are there in carrying out a communications audit?
- Who do you think should be involved in a communications audit, either for the organization you work for, or for one that you know?
- Name three different types of communications objectives, with three examples from current communications campaigns for each.
- Write notes on all the possible ways that a well known manufacturer of a leading brand of soap powder could set a marketing communications budget, with the most likely method first and the least likely method last. Why are they in that order?
- If just spending a lot of money on marketing communications always worked, then all the dotcoms that ever launched with multi-million-pound budgets would now be famous and doing well. So what do you have to do within your communication planning to make sure it's successful, other than just spend a lot?

Extending knowledge and understanding

You are encouraged to undertake the following activities to further your knowledge and understanding of the topics covered in this chapter in the following ways:

1 For an organization of your choice (preferably your own or that of a relative/friend) try to find out what its stated marketing communications objectives are, or have been in the past. Are they good? Are they useful? Or are they 'woolly'? How does the quality of marketing communications objectives affect life in the real world?

2 If you want to see how things work in the real world, try some web surfing – often a good guess at a product's name, plus '.com' within a search engine will get you to your favourite brands. For example, just by entering 'coca cola.com' into the Lycos search engine I found myself able to go to a fascinating site – the Coca Cola Enterprises Inc website – just take a look for yourself: this is a great website that takes you through the whole production process for Coke, that gives you an insight into the whole marketing process and tells you about their ethics.

Find this site: http://www.cokecce.com

When you have visited this site, then go to the consumer-facing Coke site.

Find this site: http://coca-cola.com

In what ways are the sites different? What do you think are the reasons for the differences? Does it make sense for Coke to have two sites like this? What do you think are the communications objectives behind each? What will Coca Cola be measuring for each site to judge whether it is a success or not?

3

Above the line communication methods

Learning objectives

By the end of this chapter you should:

► understand the difference between above and below the line media;
► understand the commission system;
► be aware of the meaning of many general media planning terms in use every day when planning above the line media campaigns;
► have a detailed understanding of all the key attributes, planning criteria, research, strengths and weaknesses of television, radio, press, out-of-home and cinema;
► understand the difference between intermedia decision making and intramedia decision making.

What exactly is 'above the line' media?

Above the line refers to all media upon which a commission is paid. It refers to television, press, posters, cinema, radio and certain applications of electronic media and direct mail. The term 'above the line' is a traditional term that goes back to the times when advertising agencies would send their bill to their client with a list of media upon which they had already received commission at the top of the page and, then, below a line drawn across the page, a list of all the other activities they had carried out on behalf of their client for which they were yet to receive payment. Thus, 'above the line' and 'below the line' were born as terms referring to the different media.

How the commission system works

The commission system is another tradition in the media that grew through practice. It actually refers to a discount on advertising space given by the media owner to a recognized agency or media-buying shop. It works like this. Media owners find it beneficial to deal with the 'bulk buying' centres represented by agencies and media shops. This means they are able to have smaller sales forces and a concentrated sales effort, rather than having to keep in touch with all potential advertisers direct. Media owners are therefore prepared to offer a discount to these bulk purchasers, the percentage of which will vary from medium to medium, but which is generally about 15 per cent.

Whilst the media owner will grant this discount to an agency, they will not do so to a client direct, although normal sales-driven discounting does, of course, occur in all situations when necessary. Thus, whilst the client is charged for 100 per cent of the cost of the media space by the agency, the agency pays the media owner 100 per cent less their discount. The agency pockets the difference – this is their 'commission' (see Figure 3.1).

The commission system | **Figure 3.1**

WITHOUT COMMISSION

Client	**Media**	**Agency**
Client wants one full-page advertisement in national daily newspaper	Newspaper sells one page of space direct to client company	Agency designs and produces copy and artwork to appear in newspaper for client
⇩	⇩	⇩
Client pays £20,000 + £2,000 Total = £22,000	Media owner charges client full cost of page, e.g. 100% of £20,000	Agency charges client full cost of creative, production and repro, e.g. 100% of £2,000

(Future pages using same creative cost client £20,000 each time)

WITH COMMISSION

Client	**Media**	**Agency**
Client wants one full-page advertisement in national daily newspaper	Newspaper sells one page of space to agency for use by advertiser/client	Agency buys space for client, designs and produces copy and artwork for client
⇩	⇩	⇩
Client pays £20,000 to agency	Media owner charges full cost minus 15% commission to agency, e.g. 85% of £20,000	Agency charges client full cost of page, e.g. 100% of £20,000, keeping 15% differential to cover costs of creative and production

(Future pages using same creative cost client £20,000 each time and agency pockets £3,000)

COMMISSION PAY-BACK

Client	**Media**	**Agency**
Client wants one full-page advertisement in national daily newspaper	Newspaper sells one page of space to agency for use by advertiser/client	Agency buys space for client, designs and produces copy and artwork for client
⇩	⇩	⇩
Client pays 85% of £20,000 plus true creative and production to agency, £17,000 + £2,000	Media owner charges full cost minus 15% commission to agency, e.g. 85% of £20,000	Agency charges client for space 'at cost', e.g. 85% of £20,000, and charges client a pre-agreed rate for creative and production, e.g. £20,000

(Future pages cost client £17,000 each time *if* full 15% passed on to client by agency: actual % is discussed by agency and client prior to any contractual agreement being reached)

Some clients prefer to deal with their agency on a commission-only basis, where the agency keeps all the commission on media purchasing, and finances all other work carried out on the account from this commission. Other clients prefer the agency to pass the discount on to them, paying the agency only the exact amount that they have paid for the space, with all the work carried out on the account being charged for separately on an itemized basis. Many client companies have developed a system where they use a mixture of both methods, with a portion of the discount being passed on to them and with a variety of methods of charging for services rendered by the agency being employed.

Indeed, with the introduction of media shops, and the splitting of the media planning and buying functions away from many full-service agency accounts, together with the pressure of the recession meaning that clients have increasingly wanted every pound they spend to produce a tangible and measurable result, the use of commission-only payment systems has all but disappeared, with either a straight fee basis, or a mixture of fee and commission becoming the norm in the client–agency relationship. Indeed, figures from the Advertising Association show that more than 50 per cent of accounts are now handled on a split commission/fee basis in the UK.

General aspects relating to media planning

The major above the line media are television, press, radio, posters and cinema. The growth in the availability of 'other electronic' media will also be dealt with but, to be honest, this still remains a largely peripheral medium.

- *Intermedia decisions*: decisions to be made between media, e.g., should you use television or press?
- *Intramedia decisions*: decisions to be made within a medium, e.g., should you use the *Daily Telegraph* or *The Times*, having decided to use press instead of television?

All media decisions must be made in the light of the actual situation. Factors to consider are:

- target audience;
- budget;
- timing;
- nature of product/service;
- nature of task (e.g., launch, build loyalty);
- historical activity;
- competitor activity.

Because there are so many variables, it is impossible to say something like: 'If you are launching a new brand of draught lager you must use television advertising'. If anyone ever says to you, 'Of course we want to use *x* medium', you must be the one who stops them and asks 'Why?'.

The word *why* can be the most useful in advertising campaign planning, as in all promotional planning. There are also some other definitions that you should understand, so here's some jargon explained:

Target audience: the audience you aim to reach with your advertisement. The number of members of the audience may be thousands or millions, and you will develop your cost per thousand (CPT) for reaching them by dividing the media costs by the number you reach.

Reach: the percentage of the potential audience you reach, or cover, with your advertising. The same as *cover*.

Frequency: the number of times this audience sees your advertisement. Equates with OTS (opportunities to see) and OTH (opportunities to hear). It is an average, not a specific.

Ratecard: the rates published by media owners for the medium they are offering for sale.

Burst advertising: the term used to describe a short, sharp, heavy burst of advertisements, where a large 'share of voice' within the chosen medium is the aim. This type of high-density advertising usually occurs at the start of a campaign and at intermittent periods thereafter. The aim is to gain maximum awareness and impact in a short space of time.

Drip advertising: the term used to describe an ongoing low level of advertising activity. Used to keep the product/service in the audience's mind.

Each medium has two types of characteristic: its media characteristics and its creative characteristics. Think of it this way. The media characteristics refer to those aspects of the medium relating to how it reaches what type of audience, i.e., the factors that influence the choice of, quite simply, a blank space. The creative characteristics refer to those aspects that involve what you then do, creatively, with that blank space, or empty airtime. Of course each set of factors will affect the other and, in turn, influence the choice of medium.

In an advertising agency, because all members of the account team are well versed in their own specialism, say the creative aspects, that does not mean that they know nothing about the other aspects, such as the media characteristics. Through discussion and teamwork a media selection will be made, with the account handler steering the discussion by introducing useful little pointers such as the budget available!

Whenever we look at above the line media selection it is tempting to ask which comes first – the creative considerations or the media considerations or, indeed, the budget, historical performance, etc. Just like the chicken and egg question there is no right answer. Team discussions leading from briefing sessions mean that the balance of influence will be different every time. Try not to get bogged down in 'what is more important' at this stage, therefore; rather, concern yourself with gaining an overall understanding of the points for each medium that would need to be considered – all around.

Now let's take a look at each of the above the line media in turn.

Television

Overview

This is a powerful medium with which we are all familiar. Different time segments have different viewer profiles. Indeed, each television programme will have a different viewer profile, with similar types of programme having similar types of profile. Indeed, the companies that have won the franchise to broadcast are in the business of buying, making and broadcasting programmes that will attract a certain type of audience – an audience they believe will be a saleable commodity to advertisers. That said, all those who currently hold franchises did have to put forward proposals in their franchise bids that showed the Independent Television Commission (ITC) that they would not simply run programmes designed to attract 'lowest common denominator' audiences, or just the very lucrative B, C1 or C2 housewife to whom most fast-moving consumer goods (fmcg) marketers wish to speak.

Thus, with careful planning and the purchase of specific timed spots on television it is possible to reach almost any type of viewer in the UK. Bearing in mind that about 98 per cent of the UK population own at least one television set, you have an almost unique opportunity to enter the sitting rooms of almost everyone in the country. However, because television can be an expensive medium to buy and produce advertisements for, it might not be the most cost-effective method of reaching your target audience. And cost-effectiveness is one of the key factors in planning media selection. It just is not good enough to say 'We want to reach lots of people so let's advertise on the telly', though you might be surprised at how often that conversation can be heard around a board table, where television is seen as the panacea for all advertising problems.

Creative characteristics

Television is a very flexible medium creatively, offering:

- sound, vision, movement;
- the ability to demonstrate;
- slice of life opportunities;
- 'serialization' opportunities, e.g., Nescafé Gold Blend advertisements;
- lots of entertainment opportunities.

But even television has its problems:

- you cannot smell a television commercial;
- unless the viewer responds, there is no sampling opportunity;
- commercials are transient and can easily be missed;
- zipping (fast-forwarding commercials on video-recorded programmes) and zapping (changing channels during the commercial break) are also problems, but unquantifiable ones!

Using the framework of the medium itself is possible, so many television commercials are treated almost like mini television programmes, with the expectations we have as viewers of anything we see on television being met: some commercials are mock news programmes, some are mock chat shows, and so on. So the conventions of the medium as a whole are capitalized upon by the creative teams developing advertisements for the medium itself. Why is this? Well, a viewer will feel comfortable when viewing a commercial that meets their expectations but, equally, this means that many creative teams specifically aim to fight against the conventions in question. Some commercials are designed to challenge our expectations of what a television commercial should be – a commercial for a bank that is all text in black and white with no sound track might actually catch our attention more than one with a more 'conventional' approach, purely because it is so out of the ordinary. Of course, that sort of creative treatment would need to match with the bank's overall proposition to the marketplace, or else there would be a problem.

This is a key point: whatever the creative characteristics of any medium, they should only be used insofar as they meet with the overall campaign aims and objectives and live with the integrated promotional programme.

Thus, with television, whilst so many creative possibilities exist, the creative treatment should be a part of a synergistic approach to campaign planning.

Media characteristics

This is a field full of terminology that needs to be explained, so here are some essential television media terms.

Impacts – an impact is the actual exposure of an advertisement to a member of the target audience, i.e., one person seeing an advert once. They are a vital measurement as they are used to calculate cost per thousand and, in turn, station average price. They might also be referred to as impressions or messages.

Station average price (SAP) – the currency against which the majority of business on ITV is negotiated – the same as cost per thousand. SAP is the average CPT that a particular station has sold its airtime at over a particular month, as follows:

gross revenue ÷ station impacts = station cost

Station average price can be further calculated to give SAPs for particular demographics, e.g., men, ABC1 adults, etc.

Dayparts – There is an agreement between the agency and broadcaster that will stipulate when adverts are shown. The day is divided into segments and each segment is allocated a percentage of rating delivery, e.g.:

09:30–17:15   25 per cent
17:16–19:30   35 per cent
19:31–23:00   30 per cent
23:01–26:30   10 per cent.

(N.B.: a 'day' lasts from 06:00 to what is termed 29:59, i.e., 6 o'clock the following morning, i.e., 03:00 on Monday = 27:00 Sunday.)

TVR (television rating) – each TVR represents 1 per cent of a specified audience, e.g., 40 housewife TVRs; 1000 TVRs, all adults. Whilst you cannot reach 100 per cent of an audience, you can reach less than 100 per cent more than once, so TVRs are actually an expression of both cover and frequency. The TVR is used by the broadcasting industry to measure the audience for a programme or a commercial break. It is done by comparing the audience to the population as a whole. If, for example, a soap opera achieves a 'Housewife TVR of 30 in Yorkshire', this means that 30 per cent of all housewives in the Yorkshire region watched an average minute of that episode, while the other 70 per cent watched another channel or were not watching television at all. TVRs are calculated for each minute of all channels measured. Programmes and commercial breaks take their TVRs from the average TVR for the relevant minutes. TVRs are not to be confused with 'channel share'.

Channel Share or Share – the percentage of the viewing audience watching one channel rather than any of the others, over a given period of time, e.g., a channel share of 37 per cent for ITV in September means that of all the individuals watching television in an average minute in September, 37 per cent were watching ITV and the others were watching other channels or their VCR. The calculation is made minute by minute, and an average taken. Channel share is sometimes referred to as 'audience share', 'share of viewing', 'percentage share' or just 'share'. It should not be confused with TVR.

Overlap – used to describe that point of an ITV region able to receive the signal of more than one terrestrial commercial channel.

Gross homes – all those homes able to receive an ITV region's programmes. Overlap homes are counted two or three times.

Net homes – overlap homes are allocated to one region only.

Revenue share – the percentage of all ITV advertising revenue that one regional contractor commands.

Flow – an analysis of the audience for the five terrestrial channels, 'other' and VCR playback. It shows how many viewers, at each minute, were watching the same channel as in the previous minute, those who were watching another channel or their VCR the previous minute (i.e., they have joined the programme) and how many who were watching the channel the previous minute have changed to another channel or their VCR (i.e., have switched out). It also shows who had their set on the previous minute and have now switched off, or vice versa. Used by broadcasters to construct competitive schedules.

The ownership of television broadcasting companies is changing as this book is being written – the ITV Network website is a great place to visit to find out what is going on and being planned for ITV (http://www.itv.co.uk).

Currently, it is possible to buy television airtime from a mixture of sales forces that work specifically for a television company, or sales houses that represent a number of companies – but even that is a constantly changing situation.

Buying and selling airtime

Airtime is usually sold on a spot-by-spot basis with three commercial breaks per hour. Only 7 minutes of advertising per hour is allowed, rising to 8 minutes at peak times (18:00–22:30). Airtime is sold in metric lengths, with 30 seconds being the most common. The laws of supply and demand apply in this market, and television companies operate on a pre-empt, auction system. This means that the highest bidder wins the spot in question, unless the original purchaser pays what is called a 'non-pre-empt premium', which safeguards their right to the spot. The actual rate will depend on the buyer's judgement of the size and nature of the audience, with the ratecard being the starting point for negotiation. Television airtime buying is not for the amateur! The following gives you some idea of the current comparative cost indices for television airtime, with 100 for 30 seconds being the norm:

60 seconds: 200
50 seconds: 167
40 seconds: 133
30 seconds: 100
20 seconds: 80–85
10 seconds: 50.

As you can see there is a 'penalty' for buying short periods of time – bear this in mind if you are putting forward plans for 'top-and-tail' 10-second spots that appear at the beginning and end of a commercial break. They are a good idea creatively and can add real impact to a campaign, but they cost a lot!

The actual cost of airtime and the specific structure of ratecards varies from contractor to contractor, so it is impossible to generalize.

The other factor which means that a ratecard can only ever be used as a starting point is the way in which either discounts are offered or surcharges are added. Television companies like to get new advertisers onto their channel, or encourage test marketing in their area, and thus they offer discounts other than the usual commission arrangement. Alternatively, they levy surcharges in order to allow the media buyer to ensure the position in the break they want, etc.

When planning television campaigns it is not just the spot cost that must be considered but also the overall aim of the campaign. Burst advertising, as a general rule of thumb, would employ 400 TVRs over 4 weeks, utilizing a cross-section of airtime. A ball-park figure for this level of activity would be £1.2 million that, over the course of the month in question, would allow the advertiser to reach their audience as follows:

82 per cent of the adult population (i.e., 35 725 000 adults) would see the advert at least once. This is known as one-plus cover.

40 per cent of the adult population (i.e., 17 427 000 adults) would see the advert four times or more. This is known as four-plus cover.

Coverage of the population would grow very quickly initially, with frequency, rather than cover, building more the further through the month (and the accrued TVRs) you move.

| **Figure 3.2** | *Approximate coverage and frequency guide (assumes ITV/C4 80:20 split)* |

No. of TVRs	1+ coverage	Average frequency/OTS
100	50	2.0
200	67	3.0
300	75	4.0
400	80	5.0
500	83	6.0
600	86	7.0
700	88	8.0
800	89	9.0
900	90	10.0
1000	91	11.0

Drip advertising is sometimes used by well-established brands, or brands that have been launched recently. Again, as a rule of thumb, about 50 TVRs per week would be bought. The cover and frequency of TVR packages have been calculated for you, so all you have to do is refer to the appropriate table (see Figure 3.2). Do remember that the length of a television spot (60 seconds or 10 seconds) does not affect its TVR.

Research

So what are you buying? One of the oft-quoted concerns with television advertising is that it is expensive, with anything less than a £500 000 expenditure on airtime really not making much of a dent in terms of TVRs. Thus, the research that shows planners and buyers what they are planning and buying is vitally important.

The Broadcasters' Audience Research Board (BARB) is the main television industry source of audience data. It is owned jointly by the BBC, ITV, Channel 4, Channel 5, BSkyB, Flextech and the IPA. It commissions professional research suppliers to measure how many people are watching television (audience measurement) and their enjoyment of programmes (audience reaction). The ITC subscribes to both services.

BARB's Audience Measurement Service provides estimates of television viewing on a minute-to-minute basis of all channels received in the UK. The sample of 4485 households is constructed to be representative of 17 ITV regions and 12 BBC regions. An Establishment Survey of some 40 000 interviews per year is conducted on a rolling basis to provide the profiles of the television households for panel control purposes and to provide a pool from which new households may be recruited to the panel. The activity of television sets, VCRs and cable and satellite decoders is monitored electronically, and all permanent residents in panel households and visitors declare their presence in a room while a television is on by pressing an allocated button on a special handset. Throughout each day the meter system collects viewing information and holds it in a memory store. Each night the data from all the panel households is automatically transferred to the data processing centre via phone lines, and results are available daily. Under contract from BARB, RSMB Television Research Limited is responsible for the Establishment Survey, panel control, panel maintenance and quality control, while Taylor Nelson Sofres is responsible for supplying and installing meter systems, data collection and results processing.

Other facts recorded are the individual viewer's age, sex, social class, marital status and ethnic origin, plus the number of television sets in the household, whether a video recorder is owned, the work status of the housewife, the work status of the adults and the adult terminal education age. The sample is disproportionate and weighted results are produced in both electronic and printed forms.

The main panel for BARB was set up in the early 1990s to fulfil a number of objectives, namely:

- *To measure guest viewing more accurately.* Guests in or out of home viewing, accounts for some 10 per cent of television viewing. Until recently, guest characteristics were taken as those of the average audience at the time of viewing. The new system allows true guest viewing to be measured at the time of viewing.
- *To measure video usage, recording and playback*, using a system called 'fingerprinting'. When a transmission is recorded the videotape is marked, when it is played back it can be recognized. This is referred to as 'time-shift' viewing, and the ability to measure this means there are now two television currencies: 'live viewing', i.e., the viewing that took place when the programme was broadcast; and 'consolidated viewing', i.e., live viewing with all time-shift viewing added.
- *To obtain a larger sample* allowing more accurate measures of smaller audiences. As the number of UK television channels grows, so television audiences are likely to become more fragmented. In theory, advertisers will want to target more discrete audiences rather than merely mass markets. Thus, the new panel samples disproportionately large numbers of 'desirable' audiences.
- *Boundaries of taste* – In summer 1997, the ITC began to place a series of questions in BARB's special questionnaire booklet each week. Respondents were asked to identify anything they had seen on television in the preceding week that they judged to be 'outstandingly good', and what it was. They were also asked if they had seen anything, including advertisements, of which they personally strongly disapproved, to identify the item and note reason for disapproval. The final question was 'do you think it was wrong for it to have been shown?'. Since 1998, the BBC and BSC have shared the results of these questions and have published the findings quarterly since 1999.

Other television options in the UK

Satellite and cable

These forms of viewing have been widely available since 1989. Subscribers must buy or rent a dish or box to be able to receive any programmes, and then must also buy a de-scrambling device in order to be able to watch specific channels. Once the satellite is set up viewing can begin – many mainstream hours of viewing are free, but movie channels, for example, usually have to be paid for on a monthly subscription basis.

Both forms of getting broadcasts into the home offer the advertiser more opportunities to talk to potential customers. Although research is available on these media, and therefore there is knowledge about who an advertiser would be addressing, ratecards are even harder to stick to in this field as, since it is a comparatively new medium, there is still an enormous amount of negotiation going on! Discounted rates, special deals and packages are the norm, so it is difficult to give any price guidance.

Digital television

Digital television is now rolling out across the UK too. The trade press is full of stories about the difference that digital TV will make to the UK, the main thrust of digital being the fact that very high resolution programming can be delivered to a household by request or as the result of the household having elected to purchase a channel. This gives viewers a huge choice (thousands of channels can enter the home) and gives the channel owners the chance to know exactly who is viewing what.

What is digital television? Digital television is a new, more efficient method of transmission that can squeeze several television channels into the space currently used to carry a single analogue channel. This will create opportunities for many more new channels and programme services. Eventually all television services in the UK will be transmitted digitally.

What does it mean for viewers? By using digital technology, around 200 channels, perhaps more, are possible. Digital also offers other advantages to the viewer, such as wide-screen pictures, CD-quality sound and near video-on-demand (where a film is shown with different start times on several different channels so that the viewer can choose a convenient time to start watching). Interactive services such as home banking, home shopping and connection to the Internet are being made available digitally through the television set.

How does it work exactly? Digital television has two main building blocks: picture production and transmission to the home.

- *Picture production.* Television pictures comprise a successive series of picture fields changing at 50 times per second that, if directly converted to a digital signal, would require 216 million bits of information per second. From frame to frame much of this information is repetitive and therefore redundant. A more sophisticated approach uses computer analysis to predict changes in motion between frames and keep, as information, only the unpredictable portions. A further process, DCT, is able to reassemble all the remaining information, making it easier to identify only the wanted detail. All other parts are discarded. At the receiving end the essential information is decoded while the previously discarded detail is reproduced. When these two elements are brought together again a picture is formed that has virtually no loss in quality. A typical picture now occupies only about 3–6 Mbit/s, a reduction of about

1/50th from the original 216 Mbit/s. This form of compression, known as MPEG-2, has become a world standard.

● *Digital terrestrial transmission.* Current analogue signals using the PAL System I standard reach about 99 per cent of the UK population via a network of some 1200 transmitter sites. Each site uses four frequency channels to transmit the BBC, ITV and Channel 4 services. Channel 5 has a smaller network of transmitters. Only a limited number of frequency channels are available for the transmission of UK television services. Analogue transmissions use these 8 MHz wide-frequency channels to provide a single service but the ITC has found a way of inserting up to six services in the same space. Known as multiplexes, six of these channels can, using digital techniques, be interleaved between the analogue channels. They are to be broadcast from 81 transmission sites where the first four multiplexes will reach about 90 per cent of the population and the remaining two some 75 per cent. Digital transmissions are much less liable to interference such as ghosting and electrical noise. Although at a much lower power than analogue transmission the service can be received on existing aerials and portable reception is possible.

Overall, the big question is whether more and more TV channels will increase the size of the TV viewing audience, or will it merely allow for keener targeting of much smaller audiences? If we look at North America we can see that the more channels that exist the thinner the audience is spread, with advertisers who want to talk to mass audiences having to buy space on a wide range of channels – so this proliferation of channels might be bad for an advertiser who wants to reach 'the housewife', for example. On the other hand, with smaller, much more carefully targeted audiences available, some channels can sell keenly targeted space for a relatively low total cost, so it might be possible for a single insurance broker to afford to advertise on a Female Money Management programme on a Family Money Matters channel, for example.

Radio

Overview

The first commercial stations, London Broadcasting Company (LBC) and Capital Radio, went on air in London in October 1973. Nineteen stations were on air across the UK by 1980. For the first 20 years of its life it is probably true to say that commercial radio was undervalued as an advertising medium by client companies and advertising agencies alike, unlike in the USA where commercial radio existed long before commercial television.

However, the late twentieth and early twenty-first centuries have seen radio come of age as a UK medium. This has been helped by three key changes in the radio industry:

1 national commercial stations have made national radio advertising campaigns easier to buy;

2 advances in planning and buying via Radio Joint Audience Research (RAJAR: see following research section for full explanation) and IMS (one of several computerized campaign planning systems) make it easier for advertisers to get what they want;

3 the birth of the Radio Advertising Bureau (RAB) with its mission to 'improve the climate of familiarity and favourability towards commercial radio amongst advertisers and their agencies' has led to an increased level of promotion for radio as a medium.

Commercial radio developed dramatically during the 1990s and is now attracting more advertising revenue than ever before. Commercial radio recorded its highest ever quarterly revenue figure at £145 million across October to December 2000. This was up 10.9 per cent year-on-year, boosted by a 17.1 per cent increase in revenue from national advertisers; airtime revenue from national advertisers took a 73.8 per cent share of the total for this period.

The full year 2000 saw commercial radio firmly establish itself as a £½ million medium – total revenue grew 15.4 per cent year-on-year to reach £536 million. Again, demand amongst national advertisers was particularly high with revenues growing at the faster rate of 25.7 per cent. Finance (+20.8 per cent) and government institutions (+51.4 per cent) were the fastest growing product sectors, although retail was, unsurprisingly, the highest-spending category across the October–December 2000 quarter.

The majority of money comes into radio stations via the straightforward sales of airtime, or 'spots'. Licensees (the companies with the franchise rights to broadcast) set their own levels of 'minutage' (the amount of advertising minutes within an hour), which is usually about nine minutes per hour.

The radio medium is controlled by The Radio Authority and its trade body is the Commercial Radio Companies' Association (CRCA). There is a layered set-up for the various stations, comprising national, regional and local stations. The four national stations on air at present are:

Classic FM: the first official national commercial station in the UK began broadcasting between 100 and 102 FM in September 1992. Its popular classic format targets ABC1 adults aged between 25 and 40.

Virgin 1215: an AM frequency, which was Richard Branson's first foothold in the radio market. Launched in April 1993 the station has an adult-orientated rock format. The signal, like all AM broadcasts, is particularly weak during the hours of darkness in most areas, and in some built-up areas during the day. London was a particular problem, which is why the Radio Authority awarded Virgin a London-wide FM licence which allows them to broadcast the same output as the national station, with split commercial breaks (thus, advertisers can target London, the rest of the UK or both).

Talk UK: the last national licence awarded, again broadcast on AM, however not as successful as the two previously mentioned national stations. Talk tried to attract different audiences to different programmes,

Typical commercial radio station layered structure (e.g., Birmingham)

Figure 3.3

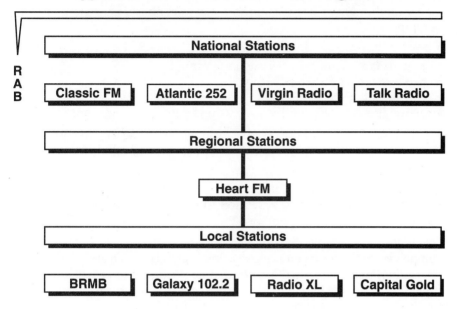

Typical Local Structure - Birmingham

in the same way television does. However, radio listeners tend to tune into the station, not the individual programmes.

Atlantic 252: transmitted from the Irish Republic on long wave, Atlantic was launched on 1 September 1989 and reaches most of the UK. Pressure from advertisers and agencies forced the station to be included in the RAJAR research (see later notes on RAJAR). It is an all-music station aiming at 15–34-year-olds.

Creative aspects

Radio can take your potential customer to a desert island with the sea lapping gently against the shore for a fraction of the cost of sending a filming team on location to shoot the scene, because radio takes the listener's imagination to places, rather than their eyes. There is an increasing amount of research evidence that the way people consume radio (and radio advertising) is very different from the way they consume other media. For a start, the vast majority of people listen because they are doing something else. Radio is merely an accompaniment, and acts as a 'personal climate controller' for the listener. Unlike traditional TV viewing, there are few expectations of positive entertainment. Also, radio has no pictures.

They call it 'the intimate medium', and this makes sense – people listen on their own, in their personal spaces, and they are loyal to the stations they choose (this already sounds more like magazines than TV). The texture of radio also seems to be different. People don't see radio as aspirational, they see it as human and genuine in nature. It speaks with a very human voice.

In a recent research study, people projected the nature of Radio-Land as being *warm, caring, earthy, jolly* and *real*. They projected TV-Land by contrast as being *glamorous, callous, shallow, sunny* and *false*. Immediately this calls for a different approach: how can you impress the consumer when your orthodox advertising techniques – glamour, polish, aspiration – simply don't apply?

Radio can:

- create sound pictures in the audience's mind;
- take listeners anywhere, cheaply;
- grab the attention with music;
- remind listeners of your TV advertising by using the same music/voices.

It is the responsibility of the creative team within the agency to ensure that these advantages are exploited, but one must bear in mind the following disadvantages:

- radio cannot show a product;
- radio needs high levels of repetition to ensure memorability;
- radio has to rely totally upon sound.

The Radio Advertising Bureau has a vested interest, on behalf of the commercial radio companies, in ensuring that it is the creative benefits of the medium that are focused on, rather than the disadvantages. The RAB is funded by a levy on all commercial radio advertising and has as its task the promotion, through better understanding, of the radio medium. Its stated aim is 'to guide national advertisers and their agencies towards effective advertising on Commercial Radio'. Its messages do, therefore, focus on both the media characteristics and the creative characteristics of the radio medium and they have an excellent web site full of facts and insightful case studies. Find them at http://www.rab.co.uk.

They have made an enormous difference in the way in which advertising creativity on radio has been viewed, and their promotion of the concept of Sonic Brand Triggers (SBT) is one example of this work:

Sonic. SBTs use sound, but there are brands triggered by other senses:

- visual: e.g., company logos, little red telephone (Direct Line), jar for Nescafé; most contemporary brand triggers are visual;
- taste: e.g., the taste of the Burger King Whopper;
- smell: all identifiable perfumes do this.

Some brands work in more than one sense – in the cases of Intel and Direct Line, their brand identity evokes in both vision and sound (and both evoke each other – you hear the tune, you see the visual).

Brand. There are many familiar sounds out in the real world that consumers do not relate to any particular brand – many TV advertising theme tunes seem very familiar but what was the brand? Sonic triggers can become linked to brands over time through repetition; they can also lose their brand linkage over time, through lack of repetition (e.g., the Haddaway track 'It's my life', which used to be tightly linked to Tampax advertising).

Importantly, SBTs elicit a response of some kind, rather than just existing for their own sake; the responses vary – making the consumer feel something, think something, know something, be reminded of something, feel closer to something, associate with something (or associate something with something else) . . . an SBT that doesn't trigger a response clearly needs development.

SBTs vary in the way they evoke the brand. While some, like the British Airways theme, are very 'soft sell' and evocative, others are much more urgent and persuasive. Some are linked to the brand by association (Papa and Nicole), where others are explicitly linked to the brandname (PC World) – the latter style is typically less subtle, but offers a very short route to an effective SBT. So an SBT is something that works in sound (words, music, noises) to trigger a response in the consumer relating to a given brand and is widely used in radio advertising. Why are they so important? SBTs are important for four reasons:

1 *they allow unmistakable branding* – consumers famously don't care which brand an advertisement is for – a SBT implicitly confirms the identity of the brand (ads where the brand is not recalled are of questionable value);
2 *they go in 'under the radar'* – they allow an advertiser to deliver a branded 30-second message without requiring the attention of the listener; SBTs are recalled easily, even by those who felt they were paying little or no attention;
3 *they can operate continually at the emotional level* – most SBTs are musical and evocative rather than verbal and hard-sell; this allows them to be repeated continually, gradually adapting the consumer's brand perceptions;
4 *they can create 'virtual TV'* – many SBTs are created initially on TV (example: Diet Coke's '11:30 Diet Coke break') and these can often be successfully adapted for radio, with consequent benefits in terms of increasing frequency and campaign longevity.

There is also always a big question about how effectively telephone numbers work within radio commercials. There appear to be three principal roles for telephone numbers in radio ads:

Short-term direct response only
It is common for exclusive music compilations, e.g., 'Call now – this album is not available in the shops', to major on the memorability of the telephone number, as there is no other way for the listener to access the product. These ad campaigns live or die by the number of people who actually call up and order the product – they have no longer-term goal.

Brand response advertising
This type of advertiser – the biggest category on radio – includes a telephone number to offer access to those listeners who wish to respond directly, but recognizes the fact that most listeners, most of the time, are not (or not yet) in the market for the product or service advertised.

Examples would include Direct Line Insurance and The Carphone Warehouse: both advertisers receive measurable direct response as a result of the radio advertising, but both know that this is only a fraction of the true effect of the advertising. They are building up awareness amongst the listeners who will be coming into the market at various points over the coming weeks, months and years.

Advertisers like these rely on the fact that radio is *not* the only link to the brand – they also have directory entries, websites, outbound call centres, brochures, salespeople, ambient media, stores, ads in the print media, etc. (in fact, Direct Line have often left out a specific phone number and guided listeners towards their directory entry). Typically, the telephone number of advertisers like these is not the main hinge of their radio commercials, but it's there, clearly spelt out, for anyone who is sufficiently motivated to want to ring straight away.

Other/emotional

A third category of advertisers is apparent on radio – these brands include the telephone number mainly for emotional reasons. For example, one of the regional electricity companies includes its customer care number mainly to reinforce the impression that they are committed to this service ethic. One of the major financial institutions plays a similar tactic – they appear to be highly accessible to the customer, though in fact they expect very few calls in response.

It is probably true to say that this 'accessibility' impression also applies to the brand response advertisers in Category 2.

Media characteristics

Once again, this is an area full of terminology requiring explanation – here are just some of the terms used in the radio business, together with brief explanations of their meanings:

RAJAR: Radio Joint Audience Research.

TSA: total survey area. The marketing area of a service, used as a basis for audience measurements.

Listening: recorded in terms of 15-minute segments and defined as at least 5 minutes' listening within a particular segment. (Between midnight and 06:00 listening is recorded in 30-minute segments.)

Average audience: the average number of people listening in any time segment.

Total hours: the total length of time spent listening to radio, or to a station, by the population group being measured. Calculated by summing every 15 minutes of listening.

Average hours: the average length of time spent listening to radio, or to a particular station.

Share of audience: the percentage of radio's total audience that is listening to a particular station.

Share of listening: the percentage of total hours of radio listening that are accounted for by a particular station or demographic group.

Cumulative audience (reach): the number of different people listening during a specified period of time. The cumulative audience is the potential group that can be exposed to advertising on a radio station, and is usually expressed both in actual numbers and as a percentage of the population.

Reach: the number of different people who are exposed to a schedule of advertisements.

Impacts (gross impressions): the total number of exposures to a schedule of advertisements; *not* a measure of the number of different people exposed to a commercial.

Radio ratings: impacts expressed as a percentage of the population group being measured:

impacts × 100 ÷ population = rating

Frequency: (opportunities to hear – OTH) the average number of times the audience reached by an advertising schedule is exposed to a commercial:

gross impressions ÷ reach = frequency

Gross rating points: impacts expressed as a percentage of the population being measured. 1 rating point equals 1 percent of the population.

Cost per thousand: the basic term used to express radio's unit costs. Most frequently used to compare the cost of 1000 impacts on different stations; it is also used to compare the cost of reaching 1000 people via different media:

schedule cost ÷ impact (in 000s) = cost per thousand

Planning and buying radio airtime

Basically you can buy exactly what you want! You can have one spot, run once on one local station or very heavyweight campaigns on national stations and bought on national networks too!

Computer aided planning

Computer aided planning, such as the IMS planning system, means that campaigns can be planned very fast and very simply. Commercials can be input to the system either manually by studying the RAJAR diaries, or by computer by way of 'optimization': a schedule can be 'optimized' by inputting certain criteria, such as the reach required, the level of frequency that you want to achieve, the cost per thousand desired or the budget. The computer mouse is used to click on the 'optimize' window or button, which results in the computer scheduling slots to give the best-performing campaign within the budget.

National stations

Campaigns will be planned using RAJAR data to reach the right number and type of people at the right time, and for the right cost. A computerized planning system such as IMS might be used, or the station itself might put together a proposal for the client that includes a mixture of traditional spots plus sponsorships or promotions.

Commercial radio packages

Local commercial radio stations have collaborated in the setting up of ease-of-purchase packages. The packages are branded under the name National Network Radio (NNR) and aim to simplify the buying of airtime aimed at specific target markets. In addition to NNR there are several opportunities for advertisers to buy into programmes or features that are broadcast across a large number of local radio stations. The environments that advertisers can buy into include the chart show, news, sports programmes and traffic reports. These packages provide the benefits of being associated with local programming and the convenience of a single point of purchase, as they are available from all the big sales houses.

Research

Background

To sell airtime against competing media, such as press and TV, the media owner will want to know how many people listen to the service(s). Not only so that the agencies and advertisers know how many people their campaign will reach, but also to decide the rates for certain commercial spots at certain times of the day or week.

Radio audience research underwent a big change in 1992, when the system used since 1977, called the Joint Industry Committee for Radio Audience Research (JICRAR), was replaced by a new service, RAJAR, or Radio Joint Audience Research.

RAJAR

RAJAR is the audience research system used by the UK radio industry. Since its launch in 1992 there have been many developments in the radio broadcasting industry and, in 1996, it became clear that a new methodology would soon be needed to cater for the increasing number of stations from which listeners could choose. The new methodology was launched at the beginning of 1999 and the first results were reported in June 1999.

RAJAR is jointly owned by the British Broadcasting Corporation (BBC) and the Commercial Radio Companies Association (CRCA). RAJAR was established in 1992 to provide a single source of radio audience data for all radio services in the UK, both BBC and commercial radio stations. It replaced two separate services – the BBC Daily Survey, which was conducted for BBC Radio, and JICRAR, which was conducted for commercial radio stations.

There is no doubt that the creation of RAJAR has greatly improved overall confidence in radio as a medium over the years since 1992, principally because it provides a single accepted measure of radio listening. Much has changed since 1992 and the radio market has become, and will continue to become, increasingly complex. The number of national services has grown from seven to nine stations and regional and local services have increased from 130 to over 250 stations. The period has also seen rapid growth in many more specialist services – ethnic, specialist music, speech based and so on. Stations and advertisers are demanding more timely information and in ever greater detail. And the arrival of digital radio and the plethora of possibilities it offers are soon to take effect.

Currently there are over 250 national, regional and local BBC and commercial radio stations in the UK. These stations, in turn, create over 500 unique areas because of the way in which stations' transmission areas overlap. Each of these 500 unique station areas must be surveyed. Every week, more than 200 trained interviewers place radio listening diaries with more than 3000 different and carefully selected respondents. Respondents can be any one aged 4+ living in private households. Each respondent is interviewed and shown how to record and complete a seven-day diary of his/her listening habits. At the end of the week the diaries are collected by the interviewer and returned to the research company where they are electronically scanned and checked. The data is then ready for processing and analysis. Once processed, the radio audience data is published and is available, in print or electronically via the Internet, every three months.

The new method of surveying radio audiences differs in three principal respects to the previous system:

1 *Personal repertoire diary and station cards.* Key to the new method is the personal repertoire diary for recording listening habits. The diary element has been retained from the previous system, but in a radically different format, so as to deal with the increasing number of stations coming on stream. The new personal repertoire diary is more user-friendly in design. It is less cluttered and also simpler to complete, as it allows each respondent the opportunity to create his/her own personalized station list against which to record listening habits. An essential part of the new diary is the station cards. Each respondent is shown a pack of cards representing every possible station in his/her area at the beginning of the interview. While sorting through these station cards several times, each respondent is asked to select the stations that they might listen to during the week. This process ensures that all radio stations listened to, no matter where they may be heard, are listed in the respondent's diary. There are also additional spaces so that other stations can be added subsequently if necessary.

2 *Individual diary placement.* The introduction of the new personal repertoire diary means that *each* respondent must be individually briefed on how to complete the diary and assisted (by means of the station cards) in selecting his/her station list. As a result the new survey method relies on only *one* respondent per household. Restricting the diary placement in this way has the benefit of eliminating any potential skew that can arise out of shared listening between household members. This has the advantage of increased sample reliability and more robust data.

3 *Continuous reporting*. The new method reports listening on a rolling basis, which will improve the overall efficiency in building individual station samples during the year. Under the old system a different selection of stations was reported on in each quarter. Now *all* stations' listening figures are reported every three months, with audience data being refreshed with the most recent data.

Research is conducted by IPSOS-RSL.

Radio stations and sales houses use the information in RAJAR to plan their ratecards, whilst advertising agencies and all media planners and buyers use RAJAR to help them plan their campaign activity and make sure they are paying a fair CPT.

Press

Overview

You need to be aware that the UK press scene is so busy that there is no such thing as 'press', other than in the very broadest intermedia decision-making sense.

We can break up press into a couple of broad categories, with some subdivisions:

- *Newspapers* – including daily nationals (e.g., *The Telegraph*), weekly nationals (e.g., *The Observer*), daily regionals (e.g., *London Evening Standard*) and weekly regionals (e.g., *Western Mail*), daily locals (*Swansea Evening Post*) and weekly locals (*Bromley News Shopper*), plus daily (e.g., *International Herald Tribune*) and weekly internationals (e.g., *The Economist*).
- *Magazines* – consumer magazines: weekly (e.g., *Woman's Weekly*) and monthly (e.g., *Tatler*); interest magazines (e.g., *Biking Times*) that are often monthly, bi-monthly or even quarterly; business magazines that might be trade press available on the news-stand or for a subscription (e.g., *Marketing Week*) and might be weekly, monthly or quarterly; and professional journals that again might be weekly, monthly or periodic but which are only available to what is known as a 'controlled circulation' – very often you have to be a member of a specific institution to receive the publication in question (e.g., *Marketing Business*, which is the magazine received by Members of the Chartered Institute of Marketing).

Each publication will have its own specific reader profile etc., but there are some general creative and media characteristics that we can look at here.

Creative characteristics

The press is, of course, a printed medium, but has the advantages not only of allowing for advertisements to appear as a part of the print itself, but also the additional option of including an insert.

Let's consider the creative characteristics of the printed medium:

- long copy is possible, with the possible retention factor for lists of stockists, telephone numbers, etc.;
- colour is available in most publications – if you want it and are prepared to pay for it;
- couponing is possible;
- creatively inspired 'runs' can be taken, e.g., a series of advertisements in one issue building a story;
- samples can be attached, e.g., perfume, face cream;
- specially designed advertisements that are of specific relevance to the reader who has chosen *this* publication have a high impact.

However:

- reproduction is out of the advertiser's control (except for inserts);
- the editorial environment might prove less than suitable, depending on the news that day;
- demonstration, other than by sample, is impossible;
- there is no sound or movement available.

Technological developments mean that now it is more cost-effective than ever to use CD-Roms as cover mounts or inserts, that new ways of inserting different types of materials into magazines are being developed all the time, and that this is an area where short-run printing methods and the massive reduction in set-up costs for print publications means that we are likely to see the continued proliferation of new titles for ever more specific and focused target groups.

Media characteristics

In the UK there is a huge variety of press available, offering the advertiser and the media planner many opportunities for reaching specific groups of customers or audience segments. A good publication has a personality that attracts certain readers, whilst repelling others, and advertisers select publications that reach their desired group. Let's look at the various sections of the press available to us.

Newspapers

About 65 per cent of the UK population read a daily national newspaper, 28 per cent an evening paper, 72 per cent a national Sunday newspaper, and 72 per cent a free local weekly paper. Newspapers have a short life-span and aim to have general appeal based on their news stories, editorial stance and the other forms of information and entertainment carried within their pages.

We are fortunate in the UK to have one of the most diverse ranges of newspapers in the world, with the 'Wapping revolution' making newspaper production much cheaper than in the past and allowing publishers to reach more reader segments. That said, the investment required to set up a newspaper, even with editorial and print separated and the advance of technology, is huge. That means that publishers have to work hard to attract a readership that is appealing to advertisers.

National daily publications break down, generally, into:

- quality: *Daily Telegraph, The Times, Guardian, Independent, Financial Times*;
- midmarket: *Daily Mail, Daily Express*;
- popular: *Sun, Daily Mirror, Daily Star, Daily Sport*;
- special interest: *Morning Star, Sporting Life, Racing Post, Lloyds List.*

Be aware that the capacity for offering regional advertising within the national dailies is growing, and it will be interesting to see to what extent the regional press will be affected, and how their owners will fight back.

Consumer magazines

The key characteristic of consumer magazines is their flexibility in reaching keenly defined audiences. They range from high-circulation general titles (including colour supplements in national newspapers) to small-circulation special interest titles. Three out of four magazines sold are weekly titles, with the largest sectors (in terms of circulation) being television listings and female interest magazines. Rapid growth in the male interest sector has taken place over the last couple of years, and might be set to continue.

There is a huge number of titles. The best way to get a feeling for the range and circulations available at any one time is to check *BRAD (British Rate and Data)*. Usually rates are set annually; however, the firmness with which the ratecard is adhered to by sales people will be determined by the prevailing business climate. Experienced media buyers, with a lot of business to place either in one publication or with one publishing house, can still get huge reductions on the published ratecard prices, sometimes up to 50 or 60 per cent.

Euromagazines

A good example here would be *Hello!* magazine, with the emphasis on converging life-styles across Europe. Bear in mind that pan-European advertisers seek pan-European advertising opportunities, and they want to reach the same market segment in each country. The German publishing houses have been particularly successful in 'exporting' titles to other European countries. On today's news-stand *Elle, Marie Claire, TV Quick* and *Hello!* are all examples of how the Euromagazine has really begun to come of age.

Business magazines

These are trade, technical and professional journals. Generally speaking, trade publications (e.g., *Marketing Week*) are available in most large newsagents, technical publications (e.g., *Plastics and Rubber Weekly*) need to be ordered, subscribed to or are received on a controlled-circulation-list basis depending upon job title, whilst professional journals are usually received free of charge as a membership right for those who belong to a given professional body or can, again, be bought by subscription (e.g., *Marketing Business*, the journal of the CIM).

The number and range of business publications serving any one sector will tend to be determined not by the number of people buying the magazine, but by the value of the advertising market. For example, solicitors have one major weekly publication, the *Law Society Gazette* with a circulation of about 60 000, but dentists, who number about 17 500 in the UK, have six major titles. Why? Well, there are more advertisers wanting to talk to dentists who buy supplies, equipment and services than want to talk to solicitors whose purchasing needs are very much smaller. This is what rules the market in terms of titles available and the rates charged for advertising.

Usually, business magazines pay a 10 per cent commission to agencies, rather than the usual 15 per cent. Once again, ratecard prices are the starting point for negotiation, and good seasonal discounts can often be negotiated. Sometimes monthly titles only publish 11 issues per year because of seasonal dips in business, often during the summer.

Some general press media terminology

SCC (single column centimetre) – the basic unit of advertising space in newspapers, with the usual minimum size in display being three column centimetres.

Classified – advertising only in sections, usually sold by the word and set by the publication.

Display – any advertisement that is not sold as lineage (as it is in classified). (N.B. display advertisements can appear in classified sections.)

Semi-display – paper-set advertisements given a rule around the edge to make it stand out from the rest of the classified advertisements with which it appears; sold by size of space, not by the word.

Spot colour – single colour added as a solid colour; helps advertisements stand out in all sections.

Horizontal – refers to a broad-appeal publication, usually weekly, where high circulation is the aim; e.g., in the building trade, *Building* magazine carries weekly editorials of interest and relevance to builders' merchants, architects, local authority specifiers, construction engineers, etc.

Vertical – refers to a narrow-appeal publication where the aim is coverage of a given interest group, however low that might make the circulation; e.g., in the building trade there are titles of interest specifically for builders' merchants, architects, local authority specifiers, construction engineers, etc.

Research and information

The Audit Bureau of Circulation (ABC) is a key body in terms of establishing press circulation figures. It is a non-profit-making company with a membership of advertisers, agencies and publishers. Its purpose is to verify and certify circulation figures on an independent and audited basis. It provides the circulation figures that are used as currency within the marketplace by publishers and planners, and it is now estimated that well over 90 per cent of press advertising expenditure is placed in publications that have ABC-audited circulations.

ABC provides audits for every class of publication: national newspapers (monthly); paid-for newspapers and magazines (twice yearly); specialist consumer and business titles (generally annually). ABC also offers other services:

- *VFD (verified free distribution)* – an equivalent certification for free circulation publications.
- *EDF (exhibition data forms)* – a verified system of monitoring exhibition attendance.
- *MDF (media data form)* – can be appended to an ABC certificate by a business publication to contain a statement on quality of recipients.
- *ABC Profile Audit* – ABC's own analysis of a business magazine's readership profile.

The NRS

The NRS (National Readership Survey) is a non-profit-making but commercial organization that sets out to provide estimates of the number and nature of the people who read UK newspapers and consumer magazines. Currently the Survey publishes data covering some 245 different publications.

- It provides editorial and other interested parties with an up-to-date description of the readers reached by individual publications.
- It provides the publishers of newspapers and magazines with the data they need to sell advertising space.
- It provides advertisers and their agencies and media specialists with the (same) data they need to plan and buy advertising space.

Thus the NRS provides a common currency of readership research data for newspapers and magazines, using a methodology acceptable to publishers, advertisers and their agents. It operates at all times to the highest professional standards, in a manner that is cost effective and sufficiently flexible to take account of change and the needs of its users.

On behalf of its subscribers, NRS Ltd commissions specialist research companies to collect and process the required data. A contract is periodically put out to tender and interested companies are able to submit competitive bids. The current contract, which now runs to December 2001, is held by Ipsos-RSL Ltd, who have a long history of running the Survey. They successfully competed for the next contract, which will run for a minimum of four years from January 2002 to December 2005.

The funds needed by NRS to operate and to pay for the research are provided by the three industry associations whose members are involved in buying and selling national press advertising space. Members of the International Publishers' Association (IPA), Newspaper Publishers' Association (NPA) and Periodical Publishers' Association (PPA) pay an annual subscription to the relevant association, in return for which they gain access to the research data. Each association then makes its contribution to the funds needed by the NRS. In addition to these funds, the NRS generates about one-third of its income from the sale of data to organizations who are not members of these bodies.

The survey method

A multi-stage pre-selected probability sample is drawn from the Postcode Address File (PAF), and each year a total of some 38 000 adults aged 15 years or over are personally interviewed, at home. Each interview lasts an average of 36 minutes. The interviewer uses a laptop computer to conduct the interview, inputting the respondents' replies as the interview progresses. This use of Computer Assisted Personal Interviewing (CAPI) technology helps to produce a consistent interview and allows for rapid processing of the data.

In the first stage of the interview the respondent is given a set of cards (approximately 50), each of which has five or six typewritten titles of newspapers or magazines set out on it, and asked to select all cards that contain at least one title the respondent has read or looked at for at least two minutes in the past year.

The selected cards are then used again. On the reverse side of each card is a black-and-white version of each title in its own style and typography (a mini-masthead). The interviewer systematically works through each card, asking the respondent if they have read each title within the past 12 months. For those titles read in the past 12 months the interviewer then asks when was the last time that the title was read, and how often the title is read. The answers generate recency and frequency data, respectively.

Recency data are used to estimate Average Issue Readership (AIR). A respondent is classed as a reader only if they have read a title within its publication interval. That is to say, to be counted as a reader of a particular daily newspaper, then on the day of the interview they must claim to have read it yesterday; to be counted as a reader of a particular weekly publication, they must have read it within the last week; of a monthly, within the last month; and so on. If the respondent claims to have read a title longer ago the answer is still recorded, but is not counted in the AIR estimates published by the survey.

Frequency data are used to calculate reading probabilities for each title, which can then be used to estimate cumulative readership, across a number of issues of a single title, across a single issue of a number of titles, or both.

After this readership part of the interview has been completed the interviewer begins a series of other media-related questions, including Source of Copy for publications read, and exposure to other media (cinema, radio and television).

The third section of the interview is the Classification section, in which the respondent is asked the age, sex, marital and occupational status of each member of the household, in some detail their own occupation and, if they are not the chief income earner in the household, the occupational details of the person who is. Occupational details are important, as they are used to determine the social grade of the individuals in the household and social grade is a powerful discriminator in areas of behaviour.

The fourth and last section of the interview then asks questions about the respondent's lifestyle, covering a number of aspects: motoring, holidays, possession of certain household durables, academic and other qualifications, investments and financial activity, and income.

The last question asked is if the respondent would be willing to be interviewed on a market research survey again, should they be approached. In spite of the length of the interview, and the personal nature of some of the questions, over 80 per cent of respondents say they would.

Fieldwork is continuous over the year, running at some 3150 interviews per month. Each monthly sample, and the annual sample as a whole, is weighted by sex, age, region and social grade, to ensure the profile of the sample reflects the profile of the total population.

The annual interviewed sample of 38 000 adults makes the NRS one of the largest programmes of continuous readership research in Europe. It was the first in the world to introduce, in July 1992, the broadscale use of CAPI technology.

The data produced by the survey are published in a number of formats. Hard-copy volumes are published twice a year: Volume 1 is issued in August, covering the previous 12 months July to June, and Volume 2 in February, covering the previous 12 months January to December. These volumes contain some 220 tables each, and primarily give the Average Issue Readership figures for all of the publications covered. Readership is reported by all adults, with subgroups covering sex, age, class, region, a large number of other demographics and exposure to other media. Volume 3, also published in February, gives data on the duplication of readership between publications.

In addition to these volumes, subscribers also receive monthly bulletins of basic data that update the volumes. The data in these bulletins cover the most recent 12, 6 or 3 months for different publications, depending on the size of their readership and the frequency of their appearance.

However, this hard-copy publication of the data, though substantial, is limited in the amount of detail it can deliver. NRS Ltd has therefore authorized a number of computer bureaux to offer subscribers special analyses of the NRS data, via which subscribers can specify whatever cross-tabulations of the basic data they wish. NRS supplies these bureaux with quarterly updates of the entire database on tape and receives from the bureaux a royalty on each analysis that is conducted.

Heavy users of NRS data who commission frequent special analyses through these bureaux may find it advantageous to take out a Special Analysis Licence, which would enable them to load the quarterly data tapes onto their own PC systems. Licence holders are able to conduct any number of their own analyses without payment of further royalty fees.

You can find out more about NRS on their website:

http://www.nrs.co.uk

Joint Industry Committee for Regional Press Research (JICREG)

The purpose of JICREG is to allow media planners to deal with regional press as they do with other media. Launched in 1990 it has greatly changed the way in which regional and local press advertising is planned, bought and sold. It has become the main currency used by advertisers, agencies, regional press publishers and their sales houses.

JICREG readership data is generated by applying readers per copy (RPC) figures to circulation breakdowns at postcode-sector level. The RPC figures are generated either from market research, undertaken to strict JICREG guidelines, or by using JICREG models. These models have been developed following detailed analysis of all available research and are regularly updated to ensure that they continue to reflect current research findings. The amount of research being undertaken by regional and local newspapers is on the increase and currently accounts for 62 per cent of total readership. Five years ago the proportion of titles with RPC figures based on actual research was barely one-third. Today the figure is nearly one-half and still rising.

JICREG data is incredibly complex, with hundreds of data fields on over 1000 titles. A major recent development – jointly funded by JICREG and the Newspaper Society – was a sophisticated electronic system for checking data that publishers supply for inclusion on the Newspaper Society database.

JICREG software, 'JIC-in-a-box', is a Windows PC system that enables the entire JICREG database to be stored on a local PC or network and provides quick and easy access to the entire JICREG database for any area. Subscribers may now also access the full JIC-in-a-box system on the web via JIC-in-a-box Online. Non-subscribers may also access JICREG newspaper readership data at location level *totally free of charge* on JIC-in-a-box Online. This service now includes the facility to export readership data to spreadsheet applications, such as Microsoft Excel, for offline viewing and analysis.

More can be discovered about the JICREG offering at their website:

http://www.jicreg.co.uk

Cinema

Overview

Cinema advertising is definitely impactful. You sit in the dark with only the big screen to look at, the sound is all around you and you truly experience the commercial.

Cinema has been experiencing a massive renewal in the UK in recent years, with more people attending more cinemas for bigger-than-ever movies! Cinema exhibitors now focus on comfort and service for the cinema-goer. The improved and enhanced facilities, such as advance ticket-booking, parking, comfortable seating, as well as wine bars and cafés, have had the effect of attracting ever-increasing numbers of affluent, double-income, working professionals to the cinema.

The fact that cinema exhibitors are able to screen two or three major releases at one time has resulted in more frequent visits to the cinema. Almost one-quarter of the population (23 per cent) go to the cinema once a month or more. Cinema-goers are now making an average of eight visits a year against six visits five years ago.

With broadening audiences and a significant increase in frequency of visits to the cinema, advertisers can now target various socio-demographic groups in far shorter (6 week) windows than was previously possible.

Creative characteristics

The true creative characteristics of cinema are:

- high impact, lots of memorability;
- able to make advertisements 100 per cent relevant to the film-going experience;
- able to make advertisements 100 per cent relevant to a particular film;
- often able to run a longer version of a television commercial;
- sound, vision, movement and demonstration are possible;
- tie-ins with leaflets at the cinema, or even samples, is possible;
- because it can be local or national, you can tie-in local dealers of a national network, e.g., Ford dealers;
- can be interactive, e.g., award-winning campaign for British Airways by Saatchi's that used an actress in the cinema audience to converse with an actor on screen.

But there are some drawbacks:

- it is difficult for people to take down contact details;
- coupons, etc., need to be arranged with the cinema, or you cannot use them;
- the way that cinema is used creatively totally depends on the budget: cheap commercials can look very cheap when compared with the quality of the movie itself!

If you want to find out more about how creativity can affect the effectiveness of cinema advertising it might be worth visiting the following websites, where you can find case studies:

http://www.pearlanddean.com
http://www.mediasales.carltononline.com

Media characteristics

There has been a significant increase in cinema attendances from 72.6 million in 1986 to 142.5 million in 2000 (source: Cinema Advertising Association (CAA)), with estimates for the year 2001 standing at 148 million, for 2002 at 154.7 million and set to continue to grow throughout the next few years. There are currently 3012 cinema screens in the UK (2000 figures).

The audience comprises 67 per cent 15–34-year-olds (with 52 per cent male/48 per cent female split), with 66 per cent ABC1s and 34 per cent C2DEs (source: CAA/NRS January–December 1999). People are not only visiting the cinema in greater numbers, they are also visiting more frequently; with 23 per cent of the population now going once a month or more. Cinema-goers are now making 4.0 visits per year, compared with 2.6 in 1987. Cinema remains the most popular leisure activity for under 35-year-olds, the second most popular for ABC1 adults and third most poplar across the population as a whole.

Changes in the traditional calendar of film release dates – historically concentrated in the summer months – means that cinema is now a highly attractive advertising proposition all year round. Major films are now just as likely to be released in January or February as in the traditional summer months. *Titanic*, for example, was released in January 1998 and admissions for that period (January–March) were the highest for over a quarter of a century.

Even though the picture for cinema is very rosy, you should still note that it is difficult to build cover and frequency through this medium: true, the core audience can be difficult to reach in other ways, but you still need to look at a 28-week campaign to build a 65.9 per cent cover (source: CAA/NRS).

There are two contractors covering 99 per cent of all advertising screens: Pearl and Dean, and Carlton Screen Advertising Ltd, with Carlton Screen Advertising Ltd holding the rights to the vast majority of sites. These two bodies negotiate with the cinema owners for the right to offer the advertising time for sale. Contracts are usually re-negotiated every year, or whenever cinema ownership changes.

Planning and buying cinema advertising

There are several ways to plan, and then buy, cinema advertising. Owing to the power of Carlton Screen Advertising Ltd they tend to set the patterns, with Pearl and Dean having to put together their own packages. The most common length of commercial is 30 seconds. Key methods of planning and buying are:

Screen by screen (or line by line): every screen in the country can be bought individually and each screen has its own weekly rate, with minimum exhibition being one screen for one week. The weekly rate would cover one 30-second commercial running prior to each pro-gramme shown on that screen during the week.

Audience guarantee plan (AGP) or Audience Delivery Plan (ADP): the name depends on whether you book through Carlton Screen Advertis-ing (AGP) or Pearl and Dean (ADP): where screentime is booked by Incorporated Society of British Advertisers (ISBA) region using a fixed CPT and a seasonal admission base. The rates vary from region to region. This option offers a cost-effective method of covering mass audiences, gives the advertiser a guaranteed admissions target, allows screentime to be scheduled in advance and, because the admissions are independently audited monthly, in arrears, you can sometimes gain some extra coverage!

Packages: various types are available – art cinemas, Disney, Children's Club, film by film. The advantage here is that the advertiser has complete control over the environment within which his advert will appear and this, thus, allows niche targeting of audiences. Two packages are aimed at children, highlighting their importance as a cinema audience: Children's

Club has a higher percentage of young children, with a slightly more downmarket profile than Disney, where there are obviously more accompanying parents. Accordingly, costs will differ.

Premier: this is a niche plan that specifically targets the core 15–34-year-old audience. An advertiser's ad would not run during films aimed at attracting an older or younger audience. This pack delivers 60 per cent of network admissions and allows guaranteed audience levels with a fixed CPT and non-pre-emptible space (see TV notes). Rates vary (see AGP notes).

When planning cinema advertising, bear in mind that alcohol advertising needs to be treated with care: it is acceptable for 15- and 18-rated films, but will only be shown with U-, PG- and 12-rated films if the audience profile projection indicates that less than 25 per cent of the audience will be under 18 years of age. Also, Alcohol Proscribed Film Lists are issued regularly.

Research

There are three main quantitative sources of cinema research:

1 *Gallup admissions monitor*: this piece of research is carried out on a continuous weekly admissions audit basis. It provides data for the AGP/ Premier campaign packages. It is carried out on the basis of simply counting torn tickets (80 per cent of sample) and a more in-depth questionnaire to a representative sample (20 per cent).
2 *CAVIAR* (Cinema and Video Industry Audience Research): this analyses who watches which films, where, when and with whom. It is the piece of research sponsored by the CAA and it provides a means of predicting likely audience profiles for forthcoming attractions. This, obviously, aids planning a great deal.
3 *IMS*: coverage and frequency evaluation using data from NRS (see 'Press'), TGI and CAVIAR. What this allows is an analysis of combined media schedules, e.g., cinema plus TV, based on cross-analysed data.

Qualitative research studies are also carried out. Refer to the web addresses for Carlton Screen Advertising and Pearl and Dean to see more research first-hand.

Outdoor

Overview

Outdoor is more than just roadside advertising hoardings: it comprises roadside, transport (buses, trains, tubes, taxis and stations), bus shelter, shopping precinct and other peripheral sites such as street furniture, parking meters and dustbins. 'Outdoor' is used to refer to all these types of advertising opportunity, as well as the world-famous one-off sites that we see at, for example, Piccadilly Circus. Outdoor attracts over £300 million worth of advertising expenditure annually across this range of sites.

There is also a 'sub-section' of outdoor that is now often referred to as 'out of home' advertising. It refers to the sort of advertising opportunity that exists in many strange places: the handle of a petrol pump, the floor of a supermarket, the inside of a shopping trolley – all are out of home, all allow for very focused messages because of the situation, but none are likely to form the main pillar of an advertising campaign and all are areas about which it is difficult to obtain hard information on rates and data.

For the purposes of this text let's stick to the 'main line' media choices that can be made in this field – but in reality it is always worth checking out the small campaign ideas that can make a real difference to the success of getting a message to an audience.

The outdoor market had an estimated value of £595 million in 1999, with a 6 per cent of total UK above the line advertising. It was the fastest-growing sector at +13 per cent for the second half of 1999 *over* 1998 (all advertising = +7 per cent for the same period).

Creative characteristics

- Sites are excellent for short copy with bold images.
- No sound, movement or demonstration is available, so the words and pictures have to work hard to gain attention in the urban landscape.
- Closeness to point of sale means messages are often reminders of other media messages.
- Coupons are not possible, nor are samples, but phone numbers can be used, especially easily remembered Freephone numbers.

However, in the outdoor scene more than most, the creative characteristics alter for different types of site. For example, sites positioned across the track on railway or London Underground stations can utilize long copy very effectively, as can in-taxi posters; the illusion of movement and demonstration can be given by using the Ultravision style of site that revolves and shows three faces to the motorist sitting at a junction; and so on.

Media characteristics

Different-sized panels attract different advertisers because they tend to be positioned to reach different audiences. The main panel names and sizes are as follows:

6 sheet – these measure 1.2-m wide and 1.8-m high, of which there are 65 000 sites.

48 sheet – measuring 20-feet wide by 10-feet high, of which there are 32 000 sites.

96 sheet – these are two 48-sheet sites next to each other, measuring 10 feet by 40 feet, making what is often referred to as a 'supersite'. There are 3000 of these in the UK.

Other – there are 20 000 other advertising panels in the UK that are not these standard sizes, because poster sites can really be any size and shape that is possible or desired: one-off supersites can be found, planning permission sought and the media world told about the specials that are available. Back-lighting, moving images created through light movement, holograms and real-life posters have all been seen from time to time.

This information comes from the Outdoor Advertising Association's website, which can be found at http://www.oaa.org.uk.

Planning and buying

This medium has the beauty of delivering very high cover and frequency figures for relatively low cost per thousand, and can be used either as a narrowcast medium, with campaigns planned to reach a small audience very frequently, or as a broadcast medium, gaining huge coverage of the public.

It is possible to buy just one site or 4000, one bus side or 1000 and, with most campaigns being bought in blocks of 2 weeks or 1 month, longevity of message is guaranteed, as is geographical targeting. The most common way to buy posters is by package through a specialist, although it is possible to buy line by line, or site by site, from contractors direct. Prices vary a great deal on a site by site or even package by package basis.

Poster specialist – a media planning and buying company that specializes in planning and buying only outdoor campaigns, often on behalf of agency media departments or even media dependents/independents. Their income is an extra 5 per cent commission granted to them by the poster contractors above and beyond the normal 10 per cent granted to recognized agencies.

Poster contractor – the company that holds the lease or owns the poster site that is for sale. They erect, post, maintain, market and sell poster sites, usually through their own sales force, with a large percentage of their sales being made through poster specialists, although the larger companies increasingly market direct to agencies and clients.

Research

POSTAR

May 1996 saw the launch of POSTAR, the most up-to-date form of poster audience research. POSTAR Ltd represents both the buyers and sellers of posters in the UK, and aims to keep updating its data constantly: it was launched in place of the previously planned OSCAR II.

POSTAR tells the media planner how each poster site is located and positioned, how many people pass each panel and *how* people see those panels. In order to provide this information the research designers have used computer-modelled traffic counts, a visibility study and a travel survey.

In order to estimate the traffic passing poster panels, local authority traffic counts for 10 000 poster panels were put through a neural network programme and modelled into up-to-date traffic estimates for over 100 000 panels across the UK. Local authorities could not provide pedestrian information, however, so NOP Research performed over 9000 12-minute pedestrian counts over 18 months at poster sites across the country. These were also fed into the neural networks so that estimates could be made. These traffic and pedestrian estimates will be updated annually.

Visibility Adjusted Impacts (VAIs) determine not just who passes a panel, and therefore has an *opportunity* to see, but how the likelihood of *actually* seeing posters is affected by such factors as panel size, angle, distance from the kerbside, illumination and clutter. An eye camera was used in this research, which aimed to establish exactly how we take in the urban landscape, rather than how we think we do. The adjustment scores given to panels are allocated for each panel type (6-sheet, 48-sheet and 96-sheet) and depend on the quality of each panel.

POSTAR's travel survey was set up to gain an insight into the demographics of the audience, rather than just their gross numbers. 7500 respondents were tracked over 80 000 journeys, allowing POSTAR to put together the information that allows them to work out the number of panels needed to achieve given levels of coverage and frequency for national campaigns, for ITV areas or conurbation campaigns.

Other research

Poster contractors often carry out both qualitative and quantitative research projects to assess the impact and value for money offered by outdoor advertising. It is worth visiting the contractors' own websites to find out what research they are publishing on their sites:

> http://www.maiden.co.uk
> http://www.jcdecaux.com
> http://www.moregroup.com
> http://www.primesight.co.uk
> http://www.scoreoutdoor.co.uk
> http://www.tdimedia.com

(These are the members of the Outdoor Advertising Association.)

Intermedia decision making

So, with an overview of all the main above the line media under your belt, how can you now start to plan the media you want to use?

Get back to basics:

- What is the nature of your target audience?
- What size budget do you have?
- What is the nature of your task?
- What is your timetable?

In an ideal world you would be able to select the right medium to reach the right audience the right number of times for your product or service to achieve your objectives. Usually, the small matter of budget limitations gets in the way, however, so you need to begin by working within the budget you have. Media planners deal with media budgets, a portion of the overall advertising budget and a portion that does not include production costs. That said, in terms of overall promotional practice you will need to consider production costs as an element of your total cost base.

Which medium is best? Which would complement this lead medium? How can you use this secondary medium to, for example, build further cover, or frequency, or to extend the advertising campaign at a price you can afford? Looking at the sorts of costs involved, what percentage of your budget will you use on each medium?

There are no right answers, only some wrong ones! Give the same budget, the same product and the same task to three different professional media planners and even they might disagree about which two or three media to use. What they will also probably disagree about will be the use of the specifics of each medium.

Intramedia decision making

Once the choice of medium has been made, then you need to choose within that medium. Which television channel, regionally, might be an easy one to answer – where is your product or service available? But should you use Channel 3 or Channel 4? What time of day? Buy TVRs or spot buy? You need to be able to put forward reasoned suggestions given the circumstances as they are. But, again, there really are no right answers, only some that will be able to be argued well because they are based on your knowledge and understanding of the situation and the media choices available. You will be even better armed if you have more than a passing familiarity with real, current advertising campaigns.

You also need to put forward a sensible plan of burst and drip advertising, as explained earlier on in this unit.

So, any media proposal should contain the intermedia plan, followed by the intramedia recommendations and the overall timed pattern of the campaign in a timetable format. Cover and frequency aims should be mentioned, as should the reasoning for the selection, given the task, audience, timing and budget.

Summary of Chapter 3

Within this chapter we have covered the following:

An in-depth look at all the above the line media, having established what it is that distinguishes above the line media from below the line methods.

1 General media issues

In this section we looked at what the commission system is and how it works, and how its existence defines what is 'above the line'. General media planning issues and terminology were looked at. What needs to be covered in a media plan was listed.

2 Specific media covered

All the above the line media were dealt with in detail:

- television,
- radio,
- press,
- cinema,
- outdoor.

For each medium, planning, buying, research, terminology and future development issues were dealt with in depth.

3 Inter- and intramedia planning

Both these parts of media planning were explained.

Self-test questions and opinion development

These are not exam questions, nor are they meant to represent the sort of question you might expect to face anywhere else. They are designed to help you check whether you have understood the content of this chapter. All you have to do is read the questions, give them some thought and maybe jot down some notes on what your response might be. Not all the questions will have factual answers – rather, they might encourage you to think about a topic or an issue and formulate an opinion based upon what is now, hopefully, a better understanding of the topic.

- What headings should be used in a media plan?
- Name all the above the line media.
- Why do you think the commission system still exists?
- Do you think it will still exist in ten years time?
- What are the main *media* characteristics of television?
- What are the main *creative* characteristics of radio?
- Who would you contact to plan and buy a poster campaign for you?
- Why do you think cinema audiences are increasing? What do you think would need to happen for them to increase even more?
- What are the main differences between planning and buying advertising space in a weekly business to business publication and a monthly, glossy women's publication? List the planning differences, the buying differences and the creative differences.
- What do you think is more difficult to do – intermedia planning or intramedia planning? Why?

Extending knowledge and understanding

You are encouraged to undertake the following activities to further your knowledge and understanding of the topics covered in this chapter in the following ways.

1 Build a portfolio of campaigns that use:

  - only one medium above the line;
  - two media above the line;
  - three media above the line;
  - four media above the line;
  - five media above the line.

2 Examine the ways in which the different media are balanced. What do you think is the weighting in terms of cost, coverage and frequency for each campaign?

3 Do any of these campaigns use *no* other below the line communication methods? Why is that?

4 Visit at least five websites, preferably one for each type of medium. Work your way around the websites to familiarize yourself with how the medium presents itself. Now put yourself in the position of being the manager responsible for selling each of the specific media that you have chosen. Thinking about how your competitors would sell themselves against you, how would you sell your medium (the medium, e.g., TV, and the specific media offering, e.g., GMTV)? Write notes as though you were going to present your sales case to a group of potential space buyers.

Below the line communication methods

4

By the end of this chapter you should:

▶ understand the role of created communications methods versus commissionable media;
▶ specifically have gained a clear insight into how sales promotions are planned and implemented, and understand their strengths and weaknesses in different circumstances;
▶ understand how sponsorship works in its many forms;
▶ understand the role of merchandising;
▶ be clear about how packaging fulfils a communications role;
▶ be clear about the role of direct marketing and direct communications, and have gained a real insight into how to plan, implement and manage a direct marketing communications programme;
▶ understand the role of the Internet both above and below the line.

Learning objectives

Overview

As the last chapter looked at commissionable media, so this one begins to look at created marketing communications methods, which are referred to as 'below the line' methods, and which can refer to *anything* that communicates your message, other than the above the line methods already referred to! If someone asks 'How many below the line methods are there?' it's rather like someone asking 'How long is a piece of string?' – in that the answer will always be, 'It depends ...'. And it depends on how many methods you want to invent, because the list of below the line, or created, methods can be as long as your imagination is wild!

From on-pack promotions to hot air balloons, from direct mail to electronic brochures, from an international sales force conference to a notice next to the coffee machine – all these are methods of communication that are *not* commissionable or already existing media communication methods, and that are, therefore, 'below the line'.

Since it would be impossible to look at all these methods in this book, let's stick to the main categories – but, when you are thinking of marketing communications method selection, always think beyond the obvious, always allow for creative thought, not just in *how* you say it but also in *where* you say it!

Sales promotion – what it's all about

Sales promotion can achieve many objectives – the main aim being to promote extra sales over a given period of time, within a given budget and with a given incentive to the customer to buy now, buy more or buy a particular brand. It is the concept of adding value to a product or service in given circumstances and making that product or service stand out in the customer's mind.

Incentivization – a big word that simply means 'buy me for this special reason'.

There is no end to the exact nature of the value the marketer can choose to add to the product or service involved. Indeed, the fact that it is such a creative field to work in is one of the reasons why so many practitioners turn to the world of sales promotions. That said, sales promotion must be viewed pragmatically – the purpose is to achieve desired and measurable objectives, as with all marketing communication and promotional functions. And don't think that sales promotions are restricted to supermarkets and fast-moving consumer goods (fmcg) products. The fields of services, business goods and consumer durables all now use sales promotions effectively. Also, be sure to question how much above the line advertising that you see has as its purpose the communication that a particular sales promotion is taking place. For example, how many posters do you see that tell you there is a particular on-pack promotion, or how many television commercials tell you about a special offer with a time limit? Very often we find out about sales promotion either at the point of sale or through the classic above the line media. Be sure you begin to analyse how much spend above the line is related to below the line sales promotions.

The sales promotion industry in the UK is worth about £5 billion per year, and it is growing faster than any other area of marketing services at the moment. Together with its sister discipline, direct marketing (the two are often linked), it is changing the way that marketers seek to win sales in today's increasingly competitive marketplaces.

The one thing to note about sales promotion, like direct marketing, is that it is a relatively new discipline, with few agencies having reached their Silver Anniversary yet! That said, those working in the agencies that offer specialist sales promotion services, which the marketer can choose to buy *à la carte*, do not view the topic lightly. Sales promotion gained ground in the early 1990s because it is a discipline that can provide easily measurable results against a given budget. With marketers needing to be sure that their promotional budget is producing actual results in the marketplace, the art and science of sales promotion has a particular appeal. It is not based on a 'finger in the wind', but on careful planning and budgeting. We will look at this later.

Now let's look at the techniques that can be used within the field. They break down into three key areas from the consumer's point of view:

1 *Free* – the consumer gets something free.
2 *Save* – the consumer saves something up to get something back.
3 *Win* – the consumer can win something.

Sales promotions are all variations on these themes.

Sales promotion techniques

Free

'Free' means just that – the consumer is being offered something for nothing. Now we all know there's no such thing as a free lunch, as do consumers. But in the field of incentivization the 'cost' of the free thing being offered might be as low as choosing a different brand to the normal one. The key techniques in this field are the four that follow, each of which has been analysed to allow you to consider the relative benefits to the marketer.

Free extra product

Giving away your own product is cheaper and less risky than buying in an extra gift, but packaging changes will be required to accommodate the 'Extra 10% of fizzy drink' or the 'Extra 100 g of washing powder', for example. There are several ways of offering free extra product:

- $x\%$ more in this pack, when the pack is enlarged and the extra amount emblazoned on the label;
- 3 for the price of 2, or 6 for the price of 5, where either an extra product is banded onto the original amount or a special outer is designed (this depends on whether we are dealing with, say, toothpaste or soap, or lager).

Free extra product is very common because it offers an instant incentive and reward to those who purchase the product now. However, it is of little value in encouraging those who have never tried the product to try it today – why would you want three of something rather than two if you think you might not like it?

From the marketer's point of view, the costs of the promotion are known and totally controllable because you produce x number of special packs and put them into your normal distribution chain, thus allowing for 100 per cent uptake. There is little chance of gaining new customers but a great chance of gaining share of sales in the period when the special packs are available.

The other great advantage from the marketer's point of view is that it allows loyal customers to receive a reward for their loyalty, without endangering brand perception by lowering the price.

Free in/on/with pack

Another instant incentive and reward for the consumer, this allows anything and everything to be given away free, from space ships in cornflake boxes to Air Miles. Depending on the type of packaging you use, you can place a gift inside, so long as it is safely packaged and meets any legal requirements for, say, food and hygiene regulations. The cost of gifts means that the sort of item found as a free gift is usually very cheap, explaining the popularity amongst children's breakfast cereal manufacturers of this method. It also allows for 'sets' to be made, encouraging consumers, especially children, to try to collect the whole range.

Character merchandise, where a cartoon/film/television series is used as the inspiration is particularly popular with children's products. Adults can be targeted by making sure that the gift looks less cheap and nasty by being relevant, e.g., plastic plant ties on a bottle of plant food, a knitting needle measurer in a large pack of wool.

From the marketer's point of view there is difficulty in predicting if the free gift will, in fact, increase sales solely because of the free gift. There is also the cost of the gift to be borne. Furthermore, not all marketers have the chance to put a gift inside their pack, so you might have to consider an on-pack promotion, e.g., a free emery board attached to a bottle of nail varnish remover. The nail file would need to be specially banded to the bottle but, as you can imagine, the likelihood of pilferage is high.

With-pack promotions, where the gift is held behind the counter and given out with the receipt of purchase, are gaining in popularity. This can be done at the till point, if well managed and the gift is small, or can be easily handled if the gift is associated with a traditional counter-based purchase, such as quality cosmetics or perfumes. Department stores lend themselves to this sort of promotion and, very often, the free gift will be of high quality (a branded make-up bag with small-sized contents) and even exclusive to one or two department stores.

In all three variations on this particular theme the marketer has the advantage of knowing the exact cost in advance and the consumer has an immediate benefit. This type of free-gift offer also has the advantage that, if the gift is sufficiently desirable in itself, the consumer may purchase the product for the first time in order to get the gift. Marketers must beware, however, that there is a fine line between finding a gift that has real appeal to the target audience, and dealing with wastage when, say, a with-pack promotion is not taken up as readily as hoped.

Free mail-ins

Usually linked to multiple proofs of purchase (POPs) such as, say, a ring pull, pack opening or bar code, this type of scheme has great appeal to the consumer only if the number of POPs required seems reasonable. *Slippage* is a term used in this sort of scheme: it refers to the fact that many consumers will begin to collect POPs, whilst relatively few will redeem. Slippage is valuable to the marketer – it means that extra purchases are being made within the timescale allotted, but redemption costs can be relatively low.

The balance between pack run/redemption rate/usage/POPs/time lapse is very difficult to calculate, which makes this technique risky. Careful analysis of other similar types of promotion is also difficult, unless they were within your own organization, as companies do not usually like to divulge the success of their promotions. Even with analysis of previous in-house promotions, a change in the weather, fashion or even news stories and scares can make or break a promotion.

From the consumer's point of view, it should be reasonable to collect the required items within the time allotted, and the gift should bear some value relative to the amount of money being spent. Thus, with ten fizzy drink ring pulls a plastic can cooler would be reasonable, and it would even be possible to collect enough over a couple of months for a set of six, whilst the purchase of a washing machine, car or several hundred pounds worth of goods through one retail outlet would be expected to bring a much greater benefit such as free or cheap air flights or holidays.

Even when the uptake of such flight/holiday schemes is high, in terms of sending in POPs to get the relevant vouchers, the marketer has yet another variable to deal with – how many consumers will actually go ahead and redeem the flight/holiday vouchers? There are famous, and infamous, stories about how over-redemption can result in chaos. True, the marketer can take out over-redemption insurance, but this is expensive in its own right, and it should be weighed in the balance against the budget size and the chances of exceeding the budget.

If free gifts are offered in this way then they must be truly free to the consumer. The additional cost of postage is allowed, but that is all. Packaging and handling costs must not be requested of the consumer. These costs will have to be borne by the marketer, so if the gift is heavy or delicate, the packaging and handling costs might make an otherwise attractive scheme very costly for the marketer. Also, where the marketer has to order gifts from manufacturers, the danger of over- or under-ordering is high – if those special branded coffee mugs are half the price in Taiwan, beware of shipping and manufacturing delays that could lead to irate consumers!

With all its plus points, and dangers, this is still a popular technique with marketers. When considering this technique make sure that the gift is one with which you as a marketer would wish to be associated and, with all the risks you will be taking, be sure to plan to allow for capture and future use of the information you gain about those who redeem. If consumers have taken the trouble to collect and redeem multiple POPs, you might find it worth storing the information they send you in order to talk to them again. The costs of such information storage and manipulation should be carefully weighed, and this option is likely to be favoured more when the expenditure level required by the consumer was significant, rather than merely the purchase of 15 packets of crisps!

Sampling

It really is difficult to beat the attraction of a free sample. There is no risk to the consumer and you are allowing them to form an opinion about your product or service based on the best possible type of information – their own experience. It is particularly effective if the product is new in concept as well as just being a new brand. Take instant white tea granules, for example. This is exactly the sort of product that will enter the marketplace with a huge job of work to do just to overcome people's prejudices about the *idea* of it, let alone anything else. How useful, therefore, to let potential purchasers try the product first, at no financial risk to themselves!

Of course, the way in which you sample will depend on what it is you wish people to try. Tea granules can be contained in sachets and distributed relatively easily on existing packs of an associated nature, e.g., biscuits. Samples can be distributed by mail, door-to-door, banded to an existing pack, inside an existing pack, cover mounted onto magazines, fixed within magazines, or even handed out at the point of sale. What matters is that you choose the method that suits the product and reaches the audience you need to reach, i.e., those who have not yet tried the product.

Be aware that miniature samples are expensive to produce, and you will bear negotiable costs whatever your method of distribution. That said, you might have to consider giving a full-sized free sample – a full can or pack of cook-in-sauce or a round-trip journey upgraded to Business Class on an airline.

The use of money-off coupons in conjunction with free samples is very popular. The coupon might be on the free sample or in the associated magazine or newspaper. This incentivizes the first actual purchase after the free trial, and again increases the chance of the customer committing to a new product.

Having to fill in a coupon to send off for a free sample might seem like a good way for the marketer to collect information on interested potential customers, but it can prove to be a huge barrier to uptake.

Save

Self-liquidator premiums

Self-liquidator premiums (SLPs) offer the customer either an exclusive item or money off a non-exclusive item when they send in x proofs of purchase (POPs) plus an amount of money. It is called 'self-liquidating' because the aim is for the promotion to be totally self-funding, with all costs of the gift/ postage being covered by the consumer.

The main problem here is that it is difficult to see what you could offer that would be so special that a mass of customers would be prepared to wait up to 28 days for it, having taken the time to collect the POPs in the first place! It is not very popular with customers, but seems to retain its popularity with marketers, which would indicate it must still be achieving some objective for increasing sales of products.

The risks to the marketer are high – again there is the problem of knowing what the uptake will be and the associated problem of knowing what levels of gift should be ordered. Gifts that serve little useful purpose other than to shout your brand's name will probably not be wanted by your customers, especially when they can probably buy a tee-shirt/sweatshirt/umbrella today, in the high street, for the same price and without it looking like a freebie!

So beware! This technique is probably best used in conjunction with another, such as running a competition or offering a free gift with an associated SLP. Always try to order goods in the UK, since you might find you need more and thus need a fast delivery time!

Never lose sight of the reason for a promotion – if the aim is to sell more product in a given time, be sure there is a very good reason for people wanting to buy now.

Money-off coupons

Consumers love them, marketers often hate them! Why? Well, a money off coupon is simplicity itself – as a customer you cut it out, take it with you when you shop and hand it over at the till to have an instant saving on . . . well, there you have it. The problem of redemption of coupons against the wrong brand or item is known as *malredemption*.

Sometimes it is a genuine mistake – the customer at the checkout really meant to buy Ariel instead of their usual Persil just to be able to use the coupon (this is know as *misredemption*) . . . and the girl at the checkout knows they stock Ariel and can't remember which big box went through 20 items ago. Some retailers are happy to let the system continue in this way. Few manufacturers are. The use of a bar code on the coupon that matches with the correct product can be used to reduce levels of malredemption and misredemption.

The Institute of Sales Promotion works with other interested parties to ensure that guidelines on the design of coupons are updated to recognize advances in technology or checkout practices.

Coupons were revitalized in the early 1990s with the introduction to the UK of the coupon booklet that is inserted into a national newspaper or magazine. This means that forecasting redemption rates has become extremely important, because a 1 per cent misforecast could mean that costings are wrecked. Also, bear in mind that money-off coupons need special security – they are as good as cash at the supermarket!

Most coupons in the UK are cleared through the Neilsen Clearing House (NCH). Retailers send the coupons there, NCH arranges payment to the retailer and invoices the manufacturer. NCH produces regular reports for manufacturers so they can monitor their products at all times.

Charities

Linking a promotion with a charity is fairly popular today – but you should never do this for altruistic reasons, only if the link is both relevant and in line with the overall aims of your organization or brand. The usual system is that either only the charity benefits ('For every pack you buy we will donate *x* pence'), or that both the consumer and the charity benefit ('Enter the competition and whoever wins gets £*x* and we give the same to the charity').

It is true to say that the larger, better understood charities are often selected as suitable, rather than the smaller, less well understood medical condition charities. This is because the marketer has to choose a charity that will immediately mean something to the consumer – their consumer. Tea bags linking with the RNLI, or biscuits linking with the RSPCA make sense, but shampoo linking with cerebral palsy could be seen as insensitive. Be careful!

Some of the larger charities do ask for a minimum commitment by the manufacturer before they will allow their name to be used at all, but at least these charities are geared up to provide the sort of publicity support the manufacturer would like. Charity promotions can be hard work, but do offer lots of opportunities for spin-off publicity. Do be aware that the thin line between support and exploitation must be trod very carefully, however, and that it might even be appropriate to reward consumers with at least some mark of having been involved, so you could link this sort of promotion with an SLP or a small free gift, for example.

One vital point for this sort of promotion is to set a top and bottom limit for the amount of donation involved – a runaway success could cost the manufacturer very dearly otherwise!

Win

Competitions

Yes, people do really win! But the perception of competitions by the consumer is often that there is little point in entering because it could never be them that would win the car/£10 000/holiday-of-a-lifetime. So entry levels to most competitions tend to be low, even when the prizes are big. Indeed, it is often better to offer a large number of small prizes rather than one big one, because people see their chances of winning something increasing.

However, the main reason that competitions remain popular with marketers is that the cost of the prize is known in advance and will not change, whatever the level of entries. This is a great advantage in that it offers budgetary control but allows the generation of extra sales by requesting, say, POPs to accompany entries.

The main area that the marketer has to be aware of here is the legal framework within which the competition must take place: the Lotteries and Amusements Act (1976) states that if the entrant to a competition has had to purchase something in order to enter (e.g., provide a POP) then there must be an element of skill within the competition. Enter the tie-breaker element – most popularly a phrase to be written by the entrant or a few questions that can be answered by most people with average general knowledge. This is how a competition differs from the next type of win category.

Free prize draws

These often sail very close to the wind, legally! A free prize draw must be just that – totally free to enter. No POP can be requested, no newspaper must have to be bought to obtain the bingo numbers within it, and so on. Plain-paper entries, i.e., an entry not on the official entry form that might be printed on the pack/in the magazine, therefore must be allowed.

A free prize draw has the advantage of budgetary control, as in competitions, but if no purchase is truly required it is very difficult to explain exactly how this type of promotion will increase sales! They do work, however, and yet are often the reason for court cases where the promoter has to justify just how free the entry is for the customer.

The Lotteries and Amusements Act is full of pitfalls for the unwary so, in reality, it is always best to seek specialist legal advice when you are planning to run either a competition or a free prize draw. Some large manufacturers'

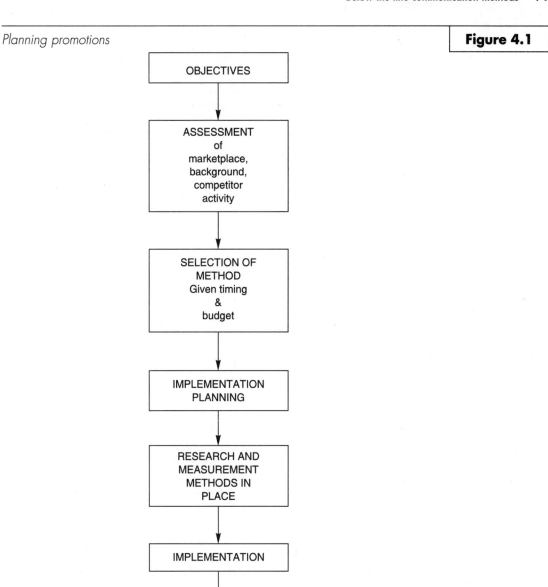

Planning promotions

Figure 4.1

own legal departments might have specialists within them, or alternatively the Institute of Promotion (ISP) can advise.

Planning to use a promotion

Now that we have looked at the main techniques involved, what sort of objectives can be achieved with them? Well, it is worth saying it again – be realistic when setting all promotional objectives, and be sure that your overall promotional programme (Figure 4.1) is planned to work as a whole, thus each promotional objective is more likely to be achievable. With sales promotions you might want to consider some of the following as your objectives:

- sampling/broadening customer base;
- line extension to new/existing customers;
- brand switching;
- forward/bulk buying;
- overcoming seasonal dips in sales;
- trade support;
- creating 'noise' on-pack or at point of sale;
- simply building volume;
- building loyalty.

Obviously, in an ideal world you would set your objectives and then your budget, but it is much more likely that you will have a budget figure and have to select the method that will achieve realistic objectives within that budget. Also, remember that you will have to sell the promotion into the trade as well as out to the consumer – there is little point in creating demand for a product that is not sufficiently well stocked!

Planning the right distribution method is vital:

- *On-pack promotions* (plus point-of-sale display material if possible) are the most powerful. Above the line advertising to announce the promotion can also help a great deal, and such programmes are known as *through the line*.
- *Leaflets in-store* are not popular with retailers. They have little space and even less desire to use it for your product. However, you might want to consider this if you are dealing with outlets other than the major high street fmcg retailers, e.g., with office equipment dealers.
- *Point-of-sale display material* is not even countenanced by some major fmcg retailers, and even those who consider it often require you to 'buy' it by offering them, say, discounts on goods. Try not to plan to use this method unless you are dealing with the non-major stores.
- *Door-to-door delivery* of coupons, leaflets and samples is still popular, and there are many companies that offer such delivery services.
- *In-store promotional women* (or men, depending on your target group) can hand out leaflets, samples, competition entry forms and so on, but again you might have to 'buy' space from the retailer with discounts, etc. Agencies providing such personnel vary in quality, so carry out careful research before hiring anyone.

Whatever method you choose for getting your sales promotion to the consumer, never forget that you have to include the retailer in your plans – even an on-pack offer should be promoted to and discussed with the retailer, rather than just despatching the new packs. Why? Well, other than the obvious point that if you are aiming to sell more then they need to stock more, be aware that some retailers are only interested in carrying exclusive promotions not available to their major competitor, e.g., Superdrug might be prepared to take 20 per cent more bottles of shampoo, only if Boots are not getting the same packs. Your retailer is your link with the consumer – treat them with care.

This raises another point. Should you use sales promotion techniques to the trade, even if you are not running a consumer promotion at the time? There is no right answer to this one, but you should consider the market within which you operate and find out whether discounts are sufficient to build a loyal relationship that gets you the best position at the point of sale.

The difference between a bribe and an incentive is very clear – the latter being totally above board. Competitions, not free prize draws, are very popular, as are small gifts that are relevant and useful, e.g., the pen with the logo at Christmas, the desk blotter with the logo in the spring, and so on. However, bear in mind that, currently, some gifts are taxable so, unless you want to arrange to pay the tax to the Inland Revenue on behalf of the recipient, you need to make gifts small and frequent, rather than large and annual – don't ever guess what the figure might be, always check with the Inland Revenue *at the time*!

You should also calculate the tax implications of all sales-force incentive programmes. Financial bonuses are an obvious choice, but make sure an expert checks out the implications of the sort of scheme that allows the upgrading of a company car, and so on. The rules change frequently, so the best advice is to check at the time. And don't forget that whilst overseas conferences and exhibitions might prove attractive to some, extra time off might prove more attractive to others! The website provided by the Institute of Sales Promotion is a valuable resource in this field, especially as it allows access to legal framework and an advice route. Find it at:

http://www.isp.org.uk

Sponsorship as a promotional tool

Sponsorship can be a very effective tool, if used properly and as part of an integrated plan of action. It really is one of the tools that benefits most from being used in conjunction with others. In this unit we will concentrate on two main types of sponsorship:

1 programme sponsorship, as dealt with by the Independent Television Commission (ITC) and by the Radio Authority (RA);
2 sport/art/other event sponsorship.

Programme sponsorship

The ITC is responsible for overseeing the sponsorship of television programmes, and the Radio Authority mirrors this function for radio transmissions. It is vital that this type of sponsorship is tightly controlled.

Television

The ITC Code has two key principles.

1 To ensure that programmes are not distorted for commercial purposes. A sponsor must not influence the content or scheduling of a programme in such a way as to affect the editorial independence and responsibility of the broadcaster.
2 To maintain a distinction between advertising and sponsor credits. This is to ensure that credits are not used to extend the time allowed for advertising.

The following are not allowed to sponsor television programmes:

● *political bodies*: these include any organization whose aims are wholly or mainly of a political nature (for a definition of a political body, see the ITC Code of Advertising Standards and Practice);
● *manufacturers of tobacco products*: this includes any company whose name is chiefly known to the public through its tobacco business, even though it may sell other non-tobacco products and services;
● *those who cannot advertise on television*: these are listed in the ITC Code of Advertising Standards and Practice.

Providers of the following are allowed to sponsor television programmes, but are subject to certain restrictions:

● *pharmaceutical products*: pharmaceutical manufacturers may not refer in their credits to brands that are only available on prescription;
● *bookmaking*: bookmakers (including companies whose principal business is bookmaking) may not sponsor programmes that include coverage of horse or greyhound racing or the results of such racing;
● *gaming*: gaming companies (including companies whose principal business is gaming) may not sponsor television game shows that closely resemble the gaming that takes place in bingo halls and casinos;
● *other restrictions*: no advertiser may sponsor a programme during which they would not be permitted to advertise.

The rules concerning sponsorship and product placement, for example, are complex and can change at any time. It is always best to check them rather than to assume you know what they are! A great way to do this is via the ITC's website, which is kept up-to-date:

http://www.itc.org.uk

Even when working within the ITC's rules it is still possible for programme sponsorship to open up exciting possibilities for the marketer. Thus, ensuring that not only the rules of the code but also the rules of promotional planning are also adhered to is the key issue.

Programme sponsorship can help you reach members of your target market who might be difficult, or much more expensive, to reach as a target audience being tackled by your above the line budget. A holiday tour operator might want to reach viewers of a game show that gives holidays as prizes, but know that their advertising budget is not sufficiently large to advertise in the breaks within the show. Sponsorship offers them a way to reach the viewers, with wrap-around sponsorship credits in return for a contribution to the costs of making the programmes as well as, possibly, the donation of holidays as prizes, for example. Of course, programme sponsorship does mean that the style, content and communication contained within the credits are limited to no more than a simple branding exercise, so should be seen as part of a wider promotional mix, but, that said, the chance is there to build massive brand awareness very quickly whilst using other media to communicate brand image and specific product or service messages in tandem.

Radio

The Radio Authority is the body that controls radio sponsorship within the UK. It has a Code of Advertising and Sponsorship Practice, which must be adhered to at all times.

Payment, or rewards in kind, can be made by the sponsor in return for its brand being announced at the beginning and end of a programme, as well as at 'appropriate' points during longer programmes, to ensure that the listener knows who the sponsor is. Sponsorships, like advertisements, have to be cleared ahead of broadcast.

The website has full details of the codes:

http://www.radioauthority.org.uk

Sponsorship of sports/arts/events

This is a different type of sponsorship and needs to be looked at separately. Any event can be sponsored – a football match, an athletics meeting, a horse race, a concert, a run of performances of a play, an exhibition of Victorian costumes. Alternatively, a person, team, theatre company, museum or football league can be sponsored. Each type of sponsorship will offer slightly different opportunities to the sponsor, so let's look at each option in turn.

Sponsoring an event

As mentioned above, any sort of event can be sponsored. It could be a total one-off, such as a specially organized pre-season football match, or an annual event, such as the Grand National horse race. Sponsors might choose to commit themselves to sponsoring an annual event for only one year or for any number of years they choose and which the organizers are prepared to accept. The nature of the sponsorship (whether huge amounts of money are involved, as in a golf championship where lots of prize money is offered, or small amounts for, say, a local football match) and the way in which the sponsor is linked to the event are still matters for discussion between the organizers and the potential sponsors. This puts the responsibility for deciding objectives squarely on the shoulders of the sponsor!

Once again, there are no right and wrong ways to use sponsorship. What you need is an understanding of the overall promotional programme and a clear understanding of why sponsorship is being used at all. The questions you need to ask are:

- Who will attend the event?
- Is this a chance for corporate hospitality?
- Will our competitors be using the event for hospitality?
- Who else will be exposed to the event? For example, will there be television coverage? Is there interest for press coverage? Radio? National press?
- How will I present myself to these other audiences? Include the name of the sponsor as part of the name of event? Put logo hoardings around the event site?
- Is this event relevant to our overall corporate/brand positioning? Does it add to our positioning programme or is it opening new vistas? How familiar with our name will those people be who are exposed to it?
- Who has sponsored this event in the past? (You will be associated with them in some way by those who are familiar with the event, and your sponsorship will be compared with theirs. Make sure you understand this historical perspective.)

Unless you can answer these questions you cannot decide how valuable the sponsorship will be to you, so you cannot even begin to discuss the financial side of the deal. You need a clear understanding of value to be able to say that a sponsorship is or is not worth £500 000 to your organization, for example. Even if the figures involved are small, say a few hundred pounds to be a sponsor of a local chamber of commerce exhibition to schools, you should still be sure that the money is being spent in reaching the right people in the right way with the right message!

Be sure that you sponsor the right event for you. A golf match for a distiller is very relevant; an oil company sponsoring a musical production in the West End of London might seem a bit off the mark, but then the projected audience profile might match the desired motorist profile that the oil company wants to attract onto its forecourts! It might be that your sponsorship forms an integral part of your overall corporate promotional programme, or it might be specific to one brand. Be sure you make the right choice.

Another point to make here is that it is the sponsor's responsibility to *check* that the organizer is planning to generate as much publicity for the event, in the right way, as the sponsor wants. Depending on the exact nature of the sponsorship deal struck, it might even be that the sponsor wants their own publicity machinery to be directly involved in the promotion of the event. It is this sort of detail that needs to be worked out beforehand, as there is very little point in arguing about it once the event has taken place and the opportunity has been lost.

Sponsorship of an individual

This is a slightly different form of sponsorship that revolves around a person, a yacht, a car, etc.

Your sponsorship could simply be 'in kind', i.e., you simply supply tennis racquets free of charge, or allow the person to use your gym or rehearsal facilities free of charge in return for your name being associated with theirs. There can, of course, be much more formal sponsorships: a formula-one racing car driver will be sponsored by an organization, always to be seen on race day wearing a baseball cap with their logo, whilst on practice days he might have another 'hat' sponsor.

Don't forget that 'an individual' might be a whole theatre group, whom you sponsor on an ongoing basis, with the group seeking other specific project sponsors on an *ad hoc* basis. Then, of course, you would need to negotiate the amount of connection you always receive compared with the amount received by their project sponsors. You might even want to ensure that x number of seats are available for you at every performance so that you can use the theatre as a hospitality venue, or even as a perk for your top sales personnel, or best-performing dealers.

Once again, be aware that you need a good match of relevance and, here especially, you might find ongoing hospitality potential, or you might find there is no scope for that sort of deal. By sponsoring, say, a yacht or a golfer, you are tying your reputation very closely to that of one item – a sinking yacht with your logo on the sail might not do your image much good, and scandal or unfavourable press comment is an ever-present threat with individuals. The only pointer here is to be sensible in your initial choice, and monitor whatever or whoever you are sponsoring. If something goes wrong that is nothing to do with your involvement, but your name is in some way associated with a calamity, be sure you have plans in place for how you would deal with this.

Overall, then, sponsorship can offer value for money and can boost your budget's ability to communicate with large groups of relevant people by associating yourself with something bigger than you could ever hope to produce alone. That said, it is still quite an underutilized resource in many organizations' promotional programming, so keep your eyes open for novel/impactful sponsorships.

Merchandising

This refers to the way in which, in total, a product is offered for sale. It covers everything from the packaging of the product (in terms of its outer packaging), to the way it is presented to the retailer for sale (whether the products are in trays that can be placed on counters as a part of the point-of-sale display, how the product stacks and stands on the shelving in the outlet), to any and all promotional items that may either be attached to it or form an integral part of the way it is offered for sale. In terms of, say, photocopiers being sold at office equipment retail outlets, in might even include such items as the training/user manual, samples of output from the system for customers to see/use, the development of an in-store 'try me out' system program to encourage the participation of the potential purchaser, and the literature that makes up the follow-up database building and after-sales service package.

The important thing to grasp when considering the field of 'merchandising' is that it needs to be relevant to the sales environment concerned and also needs to add to the appeal of the product or service, rather than be treated as a separate entity. Indeed, it will comprise many elements, with packaging and point-of-sale techniques being the key factors.

When you are a marketer who sells through retail outlets you will only be able to influence a certain proportion of the whole purchasing environment, a tiny part or a great deal of it depending upon the marketplace and the retailing situation within it. For example, let's say you are the UK distributor of a range of restaurant kitchen deep-fat fryers manufactured in the USA. You might find that you make many sales through catalogues or direct contract purchasing (to a fast-food chain, for example). There will be a portion of your sales, however, that will be made through the specialist retailers who offer commercial catering equipment for sale. How will you ensure that *your* deep-fat fryer has pride of place in the window display? How will you then ensure that it is always clean, free of grubby fingerprints, and well presented to potential purchasers? How will you ensure that your product will appeal as much as possible at the point of purchase without you having a sales person standing there looking over it 24 hours a day?

It is this type of merchandising question that must be answered every day by marketers. In this instance you could consider a package of eye-catching point-of-sale display stand-up cards with, perhaps, a holder for technical or performance criteria leaflets or range catalogue attached, together with a complementary cleaning kit for the retailer, frequent visits by *whichever* of your personnel happens to be in the area at any time, and even a 'best presented equipment' competition for retailers as an incentive to keep your product in tip-top condition would help too!

All aspects of offering your product or service for sale must be given attention; no detail is too small to be overlooked. Let's now focus on two key areas for attention – packaging and point-of-sale techniques.

Packaging

Packaging has to meet certain criteria in order to justify its position within the promotional mix. The outcome of meeting all your packaging requirements should be an item of packaging that protects and enhances the sales appeal of your product.

There is no definitive list of the attributes of packaging, which will vary from specific case to case, but here at least is a list of factors that should be considered:

How will it protect your product during transit?
Depending upon whether the product is frozen, to be shipped overseas, contains easily perishable goods or is very fragile, you will need to use different physical packaging solutions that allow the product to reach the retailer and the consumer in peak condition.

How will it display your product at the point of sale?
Will an outer pack fold over to make a display pack to go onto the counter (popular with children's confectionery) or will it show how delicious the

contents look when they are thawed, will it allow the customer to see the colour or texture or shape of the actual product?

How will it promote your product at the point of sale?
Will you use the pack to 'shout' at the customer with on-pack offers, recipe ideas and so on, or will you only use packaging in this way occasionally, with the normal promotional role of the pack being to draw attention because it is generally well designed/novel/traditional looking?

How will it protect your product after sale, but before consumption?
Your product needs to get from the retail outlet to the consumer's home. Will your pack allow this to happen without the product getting damaged, squashed, sliding around so that the presentation is spoiled? Will it be very heavy to carry? Does this matter? And when the customer is storing the product, will the packaging protect and keep it safe for them? Will it be easy for them to store part of the pack if they do not use it all at once, and will the product be kept at its best?

How will it affect the usage of your product by the consumer?
Does your packaging present itself as easy to open and use? Will it allow good delivery of your product? Is it going to make the job of presenting your product difficult for the purchaser?

How will it remind your consumer of your brand values?
Remember, if you want to continue the brand values you have established through the rest of your promotional programme right up to the point of delivery, you must ensure that your packaging does not let you down at the last minute. Even if your proposition to the customer was 'cheap and cheerful', they will still expect the packaging to perform all its necessary protection and delivery functions, as well as being easy to handle and open.

How will it encourage your consumer to buy again?
If all that is left in the boot of a car is the last drop of oil in a well-branded container, then the brand message will be right at the front of the mind of the purchaser when they re-purchase. This is the same for foodstuffs in cupboards, freezers and fridges, or office products and consumables of all types. The packaging is likely still to be an integral part of the product when it is being finished with/disposed of, so make sure it promotes your brand in a way that reminds the purchaser that it was, specifically, your brand.

How will it affect the environment when it is finished with?
This is an increasingly important question for the marketer to ask. In some countries, Germany for example, all packaging must now be recyclable by law. We have not reached that point in the UK, but most users of packaged goods are aware that packaging creates waste that can cause environmental problems. Your position might be to shout about environmental friendliness in all aspects of your product manufacture, and so packaging issues will be especially sensitive; or it might be that you simply want to highlight the fact that your packaging is recyclable, or even made from recycled materials. Technology means that many more packaging materials can be made from recycled products and be recyclable, or can just be recyclable.

Obviously, if you are in the business of selling windscreen wiper blades you will have a significantly different set of answers to the problems and issues posed above – in detail, that is, rather than in scope – than a marketer selling tea bags. Even the dealer mentioned earlier who offers deep-fat fryers for sale must answer these packaging questions, because the fryer that is sold in the retail outlet will probably be delivered from stock in packaging that needs to protect the item in transit and ensure that all parts are there when it arrives at its destination.

Some products are presented for sale with the minimum amount of packaging possible. For example, a range of towels and facecloths might have no 'packaging' as such, other than a swing ticket attached to them that has a price and a barcode on it. Why is this? Well, the best way to make this product appeal at the point of sale might be to let the consumer see and feel the product and, bearing in mind that most people would wash a towel before using it after purchase anyway, there is no need to wrap it up in a plastic/paper wrapper for display. Of course, this approach leaves the way open for the manufacturer of a different style of towel, with a different position in the market, to offer towels for sale wrapped in, say, a cotton drawstring sack, that can be reused as a laundry bag, where the drawstrings are used to hang up the product for presentation at the point of sale with just one unwrapped towel on display for selection purposes.

Packaging can set your product apart from its competitors; it can be the embodiment of the personality you desire for your product; it can draw the eye of the customer to your product rather than your competitor's. Indeed, it *should* do all these things, and if it does not then it is the marketer's fault that a great opportunity has been missed to give one final push to the product, not just to make this sale, but to ensure a consolidation of reasons for the next sale too.

The exact nature of the packaging chosen needs to be considered at the same time as the use that will be made of the packaging by the marketer and the consumer are considered. This might sound like common sense, but how often have you bemoaned the fact that a really good product is inconvenient to use because of the packaging 'solution' that the marketer has come up with? What about the really good idea of an individual portion of milk in one of those little pots – some of which are much easier to open than others, all of which are messy when they are finished with. How could you redesign the packaging for this product and make it user-friendly? What would be the advantage to, say, Unigate, of developing and offering for sale such a redesigned package?

Direct marketing

Direct marketing 'happens' when a client company (the provider of a product or service) decides to set up a direct relationship with the purchaser of its product or service. It may be that the provider, e.g., Nestlé, has a chain of distribution to deal with, i.e., retailers *and* end users. A direct relationship can be built with both types of buyer – the professional buyer who places huge orders on behalf of their retail chain *and* the end user who just wants one jar of coffee off the supermarket shelf.

The marketer within the client company needs to make the strategic decision to initiate and build this direct relationship, bearing in mind that the relationship must be managed to fulfil the objectives set for it. A key point to consider is that if direct marketing depends upon building a direct relationship with the customer then direct communications are the linchpin upon which direct marketing relies. Indeed, even in the pages of *Campaign*, a trade magazine seen as a traditional advertising title, there is increasing talk of 'direct communications' and the role played by this growing discipline within traditional, above the line advertising agencies.

Here we will consider various situations where direct marketing techniques can be used, how to choose the most appropriate method of promoting this relationship, then how to evaluate actual performance. There are few generalities in promotional planning, or indeed in the fields of marketing and marketing communications, but there are some key points to remember when considering the concept of direct marketing:

- all forms of direct marketing are growing very quickly; this can be seen to be mainly due to the fall in costs of computing time and equipment that allows financially efficient use of data;
- all traditional media can be evaluated in terms of their suitability for use in a direct marketing programme;
- keeping a customer is usually much cheaper than always having to find new ones, hence the growth in the practice of 'relationship marketing', a term that refers to the use of direct marketing techniques to build a long-term relationship with a customer and ensure you get the full lifetime value of their custom;
- since direct marketing only works to its full potential when you talk to *exactly* the right people in the right way at the right time, the cornerstones of planning a successful programme are research and testing.

Research and testing

The difference between research and testing is that while research tells you what people say they will do, testing tells you what they will do in practice.

- Research is cheap and fairly accurate.
- Testing is more expensive and more accurate.
- Roll-out is most expensive and most accurate.

Uses of research

Direct marketers have traditionally neglected research, because testing has rightly been seen as far more accurate. Research can be used to refine the test you propose to carry out. There is usually nothing distinctively different about research conducted by direct marketers. However, research uses direct marketing media, for example telephone and postal questionnaires.

Research may be used to check product acceptability, evaluate name choices, look at creative options, find out why results have been obtained,

| **Figure 4.2** | *The relationship between action and evaluation* |

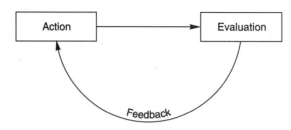

look at people's use of media (e.g., readership of direct mail, effectiveness of long copy). Research is inherently misleading because people have all kinds of reasons for misleading you, themselves, or both.

Testing

Direct marketing is a means of generating information. There is a slight difficulty in defining exactly what testing is in direct marketing terms. This is because it is possible to look at all direct marketing in terms of one long, continuous test; you never stop generating information and acting upon it. Direct marketing is a continuous process of generating and acting on information

Testing isn't unique to direct marketing, but direct marketing allows you to test very accurately. Compare this with classical test marketing and consider some of the limitations faced by the marketer who needs to produce a result that will allow him to predict how his product or service will do in the market as a whole.

First, direct marketing testing can be more accurate, because variables involved can be strictly limited. Second, direct marketing testing can be (not necessarily is) discrete, i.e., there is no competitive spoiling action. This depends on the medium or media being used. If you use direct mail, for example, your competitors are very unlikely to know what you are doing and are even less likely to be able to do anything about it.

What do you test?
- Test one thing at a time;
- test the most significant things first. The most significant things in any marketing activity are the seven Ps: product, price, place, promotion, people, processes and physical evidence.

Where you can only influence promotion, maybe because you are the marcomms manager not the manager responsible for the rest of the mix, the following list indicates the relative weight of importance you can attach to each part of the promotional process (Figure 4.3):

- *Targeting – 50 per cent.* Choosing your target audience is the single most important task.
- *Timing – 20 per cent.* Approaching your audience at the right time is your next most important task. The importance of timing needs to be

The relative importance of key aspects to be considered in the promotional process

Figure 4.3

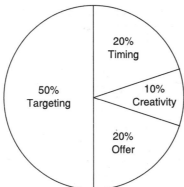

considered carefully when you are addressing direct marketing problems. For example, is it a matter of seasonality, such as children's toys at Christmas, is it a matter of a buying cycle, such as finding out when a car owner is likely to think about buying another car, or is it a matter of fitting in with the consumer's life, such as making sure a direct-mail pack with a leisure offer arrives at the weekend?

● *Offer – 20 per cent*. Why should the consumer do what you are asking him to do?
● *Creative – 10 per cent*. The creative part is the fun bit and the bit everyone can have an opinion about, so it is not surprising that many marketers spend far more then 10 per cent of their time getting involved with the creative aspects. In fact, the most brilliant creative idea in the world won't work if it goes to the wrong people. But remember that this list is concerned with response. Overall, the creative aspect may be of a much greater significance in terms of maintaining brand values.

Even among trained and experienced direct marketers statistics can cause problems. Many people talk in terms of rule-of-thumb quantities, and refuse to evaluate their results accurately. There are exceptions, of course. For example, established mail-order companies know how much a fraction of a percentage point is worth. Such companies are also used to thinking of customers/agents in terms of long-term profitable relationships.

Financial implications of testing

Remember that tests are not designed to make money but to buy information. Tests are the equivalent of test marketing; they tell you whether your marketing efforts will work or fail.

In many, perhaps most, of the tests you will look at the basic question is 'Will the cost per response/order from the results of this test justify going ahead or not?'. In order to answer this question you need to know:

● how good the test results are as predictors of what will happen on a larger scale;

- what the actual unit cost of reaching a wider audience is going to be, because this will affect the cost per response or sale.

You will usually meet this problem in the context of direct mail; it has a high unit cost and it is a good medium for testing because you know exactly how many people you are reaching. (Think about the difference between testing direct mail and testing television and press advertisements.)

If you are testing part of a list to see if roll-out to the whole list will work, analyse your responses using the roll-out cost per thousand, not the test cost per thousand. For example:

Test mailing quantity	10 000
Fixed costs	£10 000
Variable costs	£0.05/unit = £500
Total costs	£10 500
Unit cost	£1.05
Potential roll-out quantity	250 000
Fixed costs	£10 000
Variable costs	£0.25 (economies of scale) = £62 500
Total cost	£72 500
Unit cost	£0.29

Clearly there would be a great difference between the viability of reaching an audience at £1050 cost per thousand (CPT) and £290 CPT.

Types of test

This is not a definitive list. (Naturally you test the most significant things first. You may, at one end of the scale, be testing an entirely new product to a new market, whilst on the other you may be testing a change in a headline.)

- *Offer* – e.g., two for the price of one/50 per cent off/buy one, get one free.
- *Payment terms* – e.g., pay nothing for the first three months/payment with order/bill me later.
- *Size* – e.g., do you need a five-part mailer to pull more response than a two-part mailer, or did a large envelope get less response (maybe it didn't fit in the letterbox)?
- *Creative* – e.g., colour or mono, split copy.

The mechanics of testing

The point about testing is that you can only accurately test one variable at a time. If you think about that statement for a moment, you will see that there are several objections you could make to it. For example, there is a multitude of variables that go to make up, say, a mailing pack that targets a new product to a new audience; and these variables are, by definition, so interrelated that one could not test them all on their own.

In such a case, however, you might well wish to test what you believed to be the variable that would be most significant in influencing people's behaviour. It might be one of the seven Ps or another variable. If you change more than one variable at a time you cannot be sure which change has

Using retention to build business

Figure 4.4

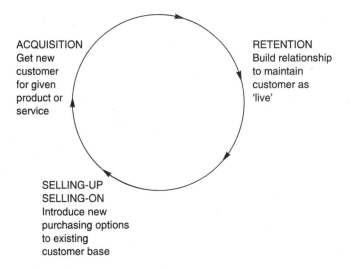

ACQUISITION
Get new
customer
for given
product or
service

RETENTION
Build relationship
to maintain
customer as
'live'

SELLING-UP
SELLING-ON
Introduce new
purchasing options
to existing
customer base

produced the change you have observed. Moreover, the audience itself is a variable; so if you want to test anything else, you have to expose a similar audience to each test. Here are examples of how you might do this:

- *mailing* – take a random sample list, split it into two;
- *press* – take an A/B split (or run inserts).

Financial planning – or how much is a customer worth?

Direct marketing, like all marketing, is driven by economics. In commercial terms, it is necessary to make a profit in order to survive. For historical reasons, not least direct marketing's evolution through mail order, response-driven advertising and direct mail, the economics of direct marketing have tended towards the calculation of immediate returns on investment. This is being overtaken by a more long-term approach that recognizes that it is increasingly worthwhile to invest in recruiting loyal customers and accepting a return on that investment over a longer time (Fig. 4.4).

Short-term financial planning, e.g., for a mail order advertisement, would need to cover:

- cost of promotion;
- cost of product;
- cost of distribution;
- cost of bad debt provision;
- any other costs (e.g., fulfilment house, insurance);
- profit.

This type of planning is the lifeblood of direct marketing because it enables you to see the cost and revenue implications of all activity. It provides the groundwork for long-term planning.

Long-term financial planning for lifetime value would cover:

- cost of recruitment;
- cost of retention, including database costs;
- profitability.

Marketing mix decisions for direct marketing

What are the differences between the criteria for research, development and selection of products for direct marketing and those for non-direct marketing (to coin a phrase)? The answer is that the question is really a red herring; all products can be sold using direct marketing. However, there are special areas of direct marketing that deserve some attention.

Off-the-page

This means selling goods through couponed advertisements in the press. Product choice has to take into account the characteristics of the methods of sale and distribution. For example, if you are planning to sell a silk dress you may find through experience that you need to use colour, that you need to buy at least A4-sized space, and so on, while this in turn will increase your selling costs. In addition, you may find that while you could sell some items off the page you could not afford to deliver them economically, e.g., because of prohibitively high transport costs or because of high insurance premiums.

Catalogues

Consider the attributes of a catalogue (business to business and consumer). How does it work? The best way to do this is to get hold of a catalogue or a number of catalogues and try to analyse the marketing objectives behind them. Try and work out what the target audience is and how the mail order company is positioning the benefits of buying by mail order. For example, you may find that the basic positioning is:

- *convenience* – shop from your armchair;
- *affordability* – payment by instalments;
- *exclusivity* – this is the only place these goods are available.

Some mail order companies are moving away from selling through agents and selling direct. Look at the points below and consider what the reasons for this might be:

- catalogue agents are generally C2DE, female, biased towards depressed areas and the north;
- catalogue agents have a low turnover. Typically, they sell to a small group of friends in order to earn enough commission to cover their own purchases;
- the mail order company has no direct contact with its end customers, and thus cannot build a relationship with them;
- recruitment and retention costs are relatively high;
- agents are paid commission on all purchases, but direct customers are not.

Product selection

Product selection is, as you would expect, absolutely crucial. Remember that, with very few exceptions, such as products that will be purpose built for each individual buyer, you will have to buy goods in advance. You will incur storage costs as well as the cost of the goods themselves.

If you are selling off-the-page in national press, you will have to take Mail Order Protection Service (MOPS) into account; you will have to satisfy the publication that you have sufficient stock to satisfy a reasonable level of demand.

Positioning

This is another red herring in terms of direct marketing, because positioning for direct marketing isn't any different from positioning for marketing in general. If you are marketing goods and services exclusively through direct marketing you should have no problem with maintaining consistent positioning. In some cases, where direct marketing is treated as being different from general or mainstream marketing, you may find that it is not always easy to ensure that the positioning adopted in direct marketing is consistent with that adopted by general marketing.

If a great deal of effort, time and money have been spent in positioning a product as exclusive and upmarket, for example, there will be a strong argument in favour of maintaining this positioning in all direct marketing activity, even at the expense of a short-term reduction in response. Pricing decision and policy for direct marketing is exactly the same as for general marketing. The differences lie in areas of pricing where direct marketing, because it gives more accountable results, can use techniques not available to general marketers. For example, direct marketing allows price testing where the media are appropriate, and therefore enables you to set the most profitable price (remember that this need not be the price that gets you the most sales).

In general, direct marketing gives you more control over pricing because it has a tendency to cut out middlemen. Having said this, remember the ways direct marketing can be used (e.g., Marks & Spencer, Next) to back up retail. Where, as a direct marketer, you are concerned with maintaining your loyal customers, you can use selective price differentiation to do so. For example, if you subscribe to a magazine such as the *Economist*, you will be offered favourable subscription rates if you renew your subscription for one year, and a better deal if you renew for two.

Loyalty will be a factor in your choice of initial price, too. For example, where the goods and services you are selling are paid for on a regular basis, as in the case of a magazine subscription or an AA membership, you can decide to offer a financial incentive to people who choose direct debit as the way to pay. This is because in practically every product field people who pay by direct debit will, on average, stay with you longer and earn you more profit.

Offer strategies

What is an offer? You may find it useful to distinguish between the proposition and the offer. The *proposition* is the main benefit your product or service claims to provide. Here are some propositions:

- Persil washes whiter (Persil).
- Let the train take the strain (British Rail).
- Guinness is good for you (Guinness).

The *offer* is the trigger, the immediate reason to buy. Here are some offers:

- Free trial.
- Easy terms.
- Pay less interest/no interest.
- Free gift for ordering.
- Free gift anyway.
- Sweepstake.
- No deposit.
- Nominal deposit.
- Temporary price offer (hurry up).
- Buy now, pay later.
- Sale.
- Two for one (plus variations).
- Stock clearance.
- Mystery gift (you have already won).
- More than one gift.
- Discount/gift for quantity.
- Discount/gift for buying within a certain period.
- Money-back guarantee (with variations).
- Buy-back offer (e.g., for stocks).

Be cautious when using offers. First of all, do you need one at all? The offer is designed to overcome sloth; don't give things away just for the sake of it.

Direct marketing is not about quick fixes. If you always use generous offers, especially money-off or premium offers, you can accidentally find yourself with a customer base of incentive addicts who will only ever buy if they are given incentives. Incentives cost money.

The best offers are, in general, related to your product or service and are more than just bribes. The thinking behind this is that, while people like bargains, they also realize that high price and high value go together. They are also likely to feel suspicious of products they are bribed to buy – the inference being that they are not good enough to sell on their merits.

Distribution system

First of all remember that distribution comes under 'place' as part of the seven Ps. The distribution systems used by direct marketing do not differ from those used by other marketers, except to the extent that goods ordered by phone or through the mail are distributed by post or by private courier services. In practice, in real life or in the examination room, you may be asked to consider how you would organize distribution systems to supply products from telephone or mail orders.

The term given to this part of direct marketing is *fulfilment*. It is used of any stage in direct marketing where a customer or prospect has responded to you and asked you to take some action – it may simply be a request for more information, or an order.

Here are some of the points you will have to consider:

● Will you handle fulfilment in-house or outside? (As with any other service, it is easy to be seduced by the apparent cost advantage of putting everything in-house, but you would then be saddled with costs all year round, not to mention any investment in equipment you would have to make initially.)

● What method will you use to get the goods to your customers? Consider product characteristics such as fragility. The alternatives are post/own delivery service (especially for business to business/outside couriers).

Future of distribution

Foretelling the future is best left to gypsies in tents, but here are some better-educated guesses.

Services that have traditionally been distributed by people (such as the man from the Pru calling, or the cashier at your bank handing out the money from behind the grill) will become less personal (face-to-face) and more interactive through terminals (e.g., cash machines – people prefer using these to human cashiers). Now that the Internet and interactive cable have arrived people don't actually have to leave their homes to transfer money, buy shares, order foreign currency or pay for goods, indeed there are websites dedicated to people who live in a room for a year just to prove you *can* live without leaving a room for a year!

As always, as far as consumer goods are concerned, lifestyles will dictate distribution. People with transport and busy lives will stock up in out-of-town hyperstores and use convenience shops or use the Internet or cable shopping. Door-to-door delivery has made an enormous come back and is set to grow.

More and more people work from home either all or part of the time. Companies will increasingly find it more cost effective to keep a small core of full-time staff and hire in freelances when they need them. This will mean that there will be a blurring of the distinction between consumer and worker in some areas and, therefore, a need to distribute things such as computer consumables to a wide number of individual sites rather than fewer central points. This is, again, just the sort of situation where the Internet and cable can thrive, but the distribution strategies must be there to meet demand.

Thus, whilst the Internet might impact direct marketing, it will be necessary for delivery systems to be available for the Internet to reach its full potential as a method of disseminating purchasing opportunities.

Media and communications strategies for direct marketing

Evaluating media for direct marketing does not differ from evaluating media for other purposes such as reach, CPT, effectiveness and medium for product (need to demonstrate, need for colour, etc.).

It is worth noting that direct marketing media selectors traditionally know how much airtime or space is worth in real terms (measured by the cost per response or cost per order generated) rather than in opportunities to see (OTS) or percentage of target audience reached – hence such things as per item (PI) deals (where the advertiser pays a set amount per response or per sale to the media owner). Traditionally, again, direct marketing media effectiveness is assessed by:

- front-end (response);
- back-end (conversion).

and increasingly also by:

- long-term profitability;
- retention costs.

The role that direct marketing communications play in doing the general advertising job of awareness and promoting the brand is now also having an impact on media selection.

What are DM media?

Any medium can be used for direct marketing purposes:

- direct mail;
- press;
- television;
- radio;
- posters;
- door drops;
- telephones;
- fax, e-mail websites.

What makes a good direct marketing medium?

It depends on what you are trying to do. For example:

- generating enquiries about a low-cost item would not necessarily demand a medium capable of transmitting a large amount of information;
- selling a high ticket item in one stage would need a large amount of information and persuasive content;
- if you need to have a form filled in and signed, you have to pick a medium that can deliver your form to the target.

Media applications

Direct mail

Direct mail is expensive, but is highly targetable, flexible and discrete. It is still the single most important direct-marketing medium and is used both for business-to-business and consumer marketing. However, it can be intrusive. 'Junk mail' is simply bad direct mail; it is usually both sent to the wrong audience and bad in itself (clumsy offer, creatively amateur). However, there are indications that the public does not distinguish between direct mail, which is more likely to be professionally done, and unaddressed door drops, which are likely to be done by amateurs. Much of what is called 'junk mail' probably isn't mail at all.

Telephone

This is the single most important direct-marketing medium in the USA. It is flexible, but is relatively expensive, highly intrusive and difficult to do well (because you need professional training, good staff selection, expert and continuing control – all of which cost money and tempt clients to cut corners).

It's okay for business marketing, as business people expect to receive sales calls at work, and see it as part of their job. Because of its obtrusiveness as a medium, it is less good for consumer marketing, unless you are talking to existing customers and can be seen to be providing them with opportunities that non-consumers do not get.

Press

With the press you can use space (insertions) or loose-leaf or bound-in inserts (a slightly confusing use of terminology).

- *Space*: the use of space gives you the advantages of relatively short deadlines (except in, for example, gravure magazines), but limits the print area you have available, limits you in the use of colour (in local and national press) and control of reproduction quality. The press gives you a wide reach, and thus it is good for trawling for prospects and customers and through specialist interest groups cost-effectively.
- *Inserts*: whilst publications place restrictions on the size and weight of insert you are allowed, overall you still have more scope for creativity, as your choice of colour is limited only by your budget. You have control of production quality, and you can achieve economies of scale by printing large numbers of inserts to go in different publications. In general, inserts pull in better than space.

Door-to-door

Door-to-door marketing can be very effective because it is extremely economical in terms of unit cost. It is targetable up to a point through Acorn, Pinpoint and Mosaic, or through distribution with selected freesheets (e.g., *London Living*). It is cheap to distribute and can be very cheap to produce. It has a very largely deserved down-market image, no personalization possible, and is surrounded by lots of clutter – it arrives with everything from double glazing to *Sun* bingo cards.

Broadcast

In many respects broadcast media are still the best way to reach a wide audience. Television allows demonstration of the product and has a high impact, although production costs tend to be very high and lead times very long. Radio reaches more closely defined target audiences and can be very quick and cheap to produce. Unlike television, radio is not subject to zapping, but radio is typically listened to while something else is being done

– it is a background medium. New media such as cable television will probably improve targeting and cost-effectiveness.

Electronic media

This is the real revolution in the field of direct marketing – the ability to communicate directly and even interactively with individuals via electronic forms of media.

The days of sending a fax in place of a mail-shot and seeing this as the height of electronic sophistication seem so far distant and so innocent in their naivety that we must bite the bullet and realize that what we see as state-of-the-art today will doubtless be overtaken by enormous techno-logical advances within a few short years.

The Internet allows direct access to recipients' homes, at the request of the recipient; touch-screen technology allows input direct from user to database and can send an 'order' to the marketer immediately; relatively cheap computer processing can allow the manipulation of huge amounts of data for a much smaller amount of money.

All these aspects of electronic communication, not just the Internet, have affected the way in which, and the speed at which, direct marketing *can* take place – but none of them change the basic concepts detailed above – none of them is a panacea!

How to get good, effective creative work

As with all forms of communication planning it is essential to define the objectives your communication has to achieve, then:

- write a clear brief and agree it internally and with the agency. The brief should include: current consumer perception, desired consumer perception, desired consumer action (e.g., buy off the page), required tone of voice, and any mandatory requirements (e.g., branding, legal);
- define your budget;
- when you review creative work, follow the dictates of reason, not the dictates of your heart;
- remember that the later in the process you change things, the more money it costs.

Remember, if it breaks the rules it is probably wrong! From time to time you will see in the trade press house advertisements for agencies that claim to throw the rule book out of the window; take these claims with a pinch of salt. There are lots of lists of rules that have cost other people a great deal of money to establish, and people follow them because they work. If you break them have a good marketing reason for doing so – merely being original is not a good reason.

Some rules:

- Long copy works better than short copy in most media (including broadcast) – as long as the prospect can absorb it, e.g., tube posters, where the audience has a long time to read, with supersites by motorways. The reason behind this is simple and the people who claim that their target audience does not have time to read long messages never seem to take it into account.

- If the person you are communicating with is not interested, he will make up his mind just as easily not to buy your product or service from a long communication as a short one. If he is a marginal case, the more real selling points you can put before him, the more likely you are to find the trigger that makes him decide to buy.
- If he is sold rapidly, he will either look at the rest of the selling points for reassurance or he will phone you or fill in the coupon straight away.
- Always put a letter with a mailing pack; apart from anything else, it is polite (this is especially important for business to business marketing) and a letter is a different animal from a brochure or whatever other material you are including in your pack – it does a different job.
- Always make your coupon easy to fill in and easy to clip out – diamond-shaped coupons in the middle of the page are likely to be a pain.
- Remember that the more commitment you ask for, the fewer replies you'll get, and vice versa; an obvious point, perhaps, but very important. The Next catalogue is a good example of the way you can use this to your advantage. Instead of sending the catalogue free, Next charge for it, not so much to recoup printing costs as to make sure only people with at least some interest in buying from it ask for one, thereby limiting wastage and increasing the perceived value of the catalogue.
- Catalogues seem to work best if they are a series of mini advertisements rather than a product book.
- Remember, too, that you can pick your positioning in your own catalogue – see if early right-hand pages pull better then other positions, for example. (Front cover, back cover, early pages and centre spreads in saddle stitched catalogues tend to do best.)
- Designing web pages is still in its infancy, and there really isn't a great deal of long-term research to work from. But what most research has pointed out is that you should have fairly simple graphics on your opening page, so that they don't take too long to download, that most people seem to be prepared to only go three clicks to the place they want to be and that, when they get there, they should be able to find the information/items/facts they want without having to hunt for them. There are a great deal of specialist agencies out there offering advice on designing for the Internet – as with all givers of advice, they should be vetted properly and you should look at the work they have already done for others.
- Above all, remember that your direct marketing communications do not just sell or fail to sell your product or service – they do the same for your brand and your company.

Fulfilment and back end marketing

What do we mean by fulfilment?

- Getting the goods to the customer.
- Getting the right goods to the customer – there is plenty of room for error (usually clerical).

- Making sure that the customer's credit is worthy (or cashing the cheque before sending the goods).
- Data collection and analysis – reordering of stock and management of cash flow as well as monitoring effectiveness of promotions, etc.
- Include customer relationship responsibilities – wrong products, faulty goods, late or non-delivery, etc.

What is the importance of fulfilment?

- You make money out of a satisfied customer; fulfilment is the way you satisfy customers.
- The fulfilment process controls cash flow and, through credit checking, the value of orders. It can make or break a mail order business. Remember that most failed businesses fail through overtrading.
- Accuracy of fulfilment is also vital from the point of view of the cost of wrong orders and returns (the cost of actual goods and the long-term cost of dissatisfied customers).

Customer relationship management built on care

Why bother to build a relationship with a customer? Why *is* customer relationship management (CRM) the buzz-word these days? Can you distinguish between customer care and marketing?

Let's be honest – customer care is not undertaken as an altruistic exercise. It is done to keep profitable customers and to enhance their value to you; it is therefore central to direct marketing. For example, customer care provides the opportunity to make a service better; telephone/postal research can identify specific areas of opportunity for you. Customer loyalty is profitable; it is therefore worth paying for. That's why it is worth building a relationship with the customers you already have!

There are two main areas of opportunity for CRM:

1 *General procedure*: create a programme of communications to maximize customer satisfaction – a two-way flow of information is necessary. A simple example from real life is a pizza restaurant that keeps children's names and dates of birth on computer and sends them a birthday card and the offer of a free pizza if they come in on their birthday, whilst certain financial services organizations dedicate millions of pounds to building computer systems that will allow them to track the whole relationship they have with a customer over many years, thereby allowing them to tailor their offering to the customer as their life-stage, and therefore requirements, alter.

2 *Special procedures*: one-off opportunities often occur on an individual basis, e.g., a customer complaint. It is possible to turn a likely loss of customer into an opportunity to increase loyalty, e.g., by having a policy of giving 110 per cent. Outgoing programmes can be tied in with your normal programmes of customer communication (newsletters, billing stuffers, promotional mail, outgoing telephone, etc.). Incoming opportunities (usually complaints) require well-trained unflappable people following clearly laid out general rules and with the option of referring the customer to someone with real authority, who can deviate from the rules, where necessary. There is little

An overview of fulfilment functions

Figure 4.5

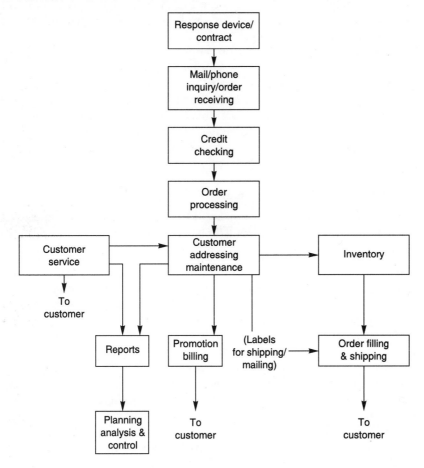

point in laying down rules for all special opportunities for customer care because, by definition, they will be different.

Every time you communicate with a customer you pay out money (Fig. 4.5). It makes sense, therefore, to use every opportunity you can to ask for another order. For example, bounce back with the fulfilment of an order by using a billing stuffer or sending an order form with a newsletter. Wherever the order comes from, whether face to face, on the Internet or from a printed catalogue, the opportunities for building the relationship with your customer appear at every stage.

When it comes to e-CRM, as one of the areas where there is most 'buzz' at the moment, the Internet is being hailed as a wonderful way to build better relationships with customers, because of the interactive nature of the medium. From the small organization that allows its customers to enter their own orders direct onto their website, to the multi-national fmcg giants, such as Proctor & Gamble, who have developed corporate and brand-specific offerings on the web to enable real interactivity between themselves and their customers, it *is* true to say that the web is being used in a way that no other communications medium has been used in the past – other than maybe the 'Man from the Pru' who was able to meet every customer face to face on a regular basis and *be* the real interaction between the company and its customers.

But even the largest organization forgets at its peril that interactivity cannot be forced, that websites will only be enjoyed as entertainment if they are entertaining, will only justify the housewife's use of time if she feels she gets valuable information or pleasure, and so on. So, although the technology is impressive, the basic rules remain the same – if you are planning to communicate with someone, be sure you know your objectives, be sure you understand the point of view of the audience and be sure to meet their expectations!

Managing a direct marketing plan

Managing a direct marketing plan is no different in essence from managing any other sort of marketing plan. The basic steps are:

- *Define your objectives.* These will depend on your function: as a client marketing director, you have to start with corporate objectives at board level; as a marketing manager you will have these defined for you; as an agency account director you will probably be given promotional or communications objectives. N.B., defining objectives means making them measurable – you must be able to use results to judge success or failure, and as feedback to plan the next stage in the process.
- *Budget for your activity.* In direct marketing this is likely to be a tighter control mechanism than in general marketing, e.g., £x per sale. Remember the various ways in which budgets can be set. A task budget is the best, but in real life you may not be able to get the budget controllers to accept this.
- *Plan your activities.* Use a critical path analysis that is as simple or complex as the task requires.
- *Feedback and control elements.* Even on discrete and simple tasks things that you can't control will happen to disrupt your plans. You must put into your plan either specific contingency plans ('Try plan B chaps') or allocate limited discretionary activity to the people actually doing the work.
- *Formal procedures for evaluating success or failure.* Everybody analyses causes of failure to the nth degree. You should also analyse successes so that you can repeat them.

Direct marketing services

Direct marketing agencies

These are advertising agencies specializing in direct marketing. They have the same structure and provide the same services as other agencies. In addition to the normal agency specialists, they may have a list or database manager.

Printers

In addition to the below the line work that printers produce for general advertising purposes, there are printers geared to producing direct mail.

Mailing houses

These will take the components of your mailing pack and put them in the envelopes, bag them, maintain the mailsort order, if required, and get them to the post office.

Fulfilment houses

These will hold stock, do paperwork and get goods to the customer. *Incentive suppliers* will, as the name implies, source and supply you with incentives such as carriage clocks and calculators.

Laser shops

These are another sort of printer.

Media shops

These are specialist brokers who buy media for direct marketing.

List brokers

These hold, look after or can arrange access to lists, and will arrange things such as Pinpoint or Acorn analysis.

Specialist computer bureaux

These will hold your data and do things such as de-duplication of your list against bought lists for you.

Electronic media

This term can be used to cover many different types of promotional method – from a moving electronic board at Piccadilly Circus to e-mail. Most people, however, think of the Internet when they think of electronic media. And because the Internet is, essentially, a direct form of communication but one that can be used also as a mass medium, that's why it is here!

The Internet can be used in several key ways to communicate both internally and externally and it can be used both below the line and above the line.

Below the line uses of the Internet

- *Internal communication*: by setting up web pages, sites and e-mail loops that can only be accessed by those issued with the correct password an organization can set up an effective tool for communication that is either purely internal or can allow access by, say, dealers and distributors. A purely internal site is called an *intranet*, and an area that can be accessed by, say, a dealer network, is called an *extranet*. More on this use of the Internet in the PR chapter, but this would certainly be classified as below the line communication, as no commission is involved on closed-site communication.

- *External communication*: with the right marketing strategy in place a marketer can use the World Wide Web to offer goods and services for sale worldwide – but that is the danger – not all organizations *can* deliver goods or services worldwide, so the whole marketing mix must be reviewed before this step is taken. This would be the use of the web as a channel of distribution, replacing say a catalogue for items that are then delivered by some sort of fulfilment service, or through which data can actually be purchased and disseminated, e.g., a research company offering research data for sale through its website, then giving the buyer a password that allows them to actually download the data in question. This would be using the Internet as a direct marketing method as well as a method of distribution.

Other than selling worldwide an organization can also offer information about itself, either freely or at a price to anyone with access to a terminal. It is essential that such home pages or websites are professionally designed and developed, otherwise they just end up as cyberspace leaflet holders, which is not really what the web is about. This would also be a below the line way of using the Internet, as, again, no commission is involved – you are, essentially, creating a communication method.

It is also quite common to use your own website to run 'advertisements' for your own organization. Early in 2001 reports from research companies specializing in on-line research indicated that on-line ads reached a record level of over 172 billion impressions during the fourth quarter of 2000, while top web media companies stocked 28 per cent of their sites with non-paid self-promotional ads. Apparently, entertainment and society websites ran the highest percentage of self-promotional ads (30 per cent) among ad-supported websites.

Another way of communicating via the web is to use e-mails. Recent surveys show that 65 per cent of companies spend 1–5 per cent of their marketing budget on e-mail marketing, with 22 per cent spending more than 5 per cent. Clearly, 87 per cent of companies see e-mail as important to their future marketing strategy.

Increasing by almost 100 million over 1999, by the end of 2000 there were 375 million Internet users worldwide – the majority utilizing e-mail. With the number of people around the world using e-mail growing exponentially, reports suggest that e-mail marketing will jump from a US$164 million industry in 1999 to a US$4.8 billion industry by 2003, and to an estimated US$7.3 billion in 2005.

This means that no marketer can afford to ignore the web as a potential means of either marketing communications or marketing.

Above the line uses of the Internet

Using the Internet to promote your goods and services through sites that already exist can be done in three main ways:

1 *Banner ads* are the web's equivalent of TV commercials. More specifically, they are rectangular graphics that are static, animated or rich-media in form. Banners typically link back to the advertiser's website.

2 *Sponsorship* is when an advertiser sponsors an entire website or section of a website. Sponsorship deals include banner ads, prominent logo placement, exclusives, content and promotions. In most cases, sponsorship allows for a direct link to the sponsor's website.

3 *Interstitials* are ads that open a second browser window. Commonly referred to as 'Pop-ups', they appear as static ads or 15–30 second multimedia commercials. Interstitials can also be used for customer research, such as surveys or running promotions, to communicate a detailed message.

On-line publications

Buying space in an on-line publication means calling the media sales people at the appropriate publication to buy space in a very traditional manner. Often space sales have been diverted to a specialist sales house. These are growing in number. The best way to check how to buy space, as well as deciding whether you want to advertise in a traditional manner, e.g., buying a recruitment advertisement, or whether you want to buy a specific link or area of the whole publication, is to visit the advertising sales part of the website in question: this will either give you the data you need or would point you to the right sales house for your needs.

Go to http://www.telegraph.co.uk for an example of how this works – there you will find the Electronic Telegraph site, the first on-line publication, which was launched in 1994, and you can then navigate to their advertising sales pages that will give you good visual examples of the sorts of spaces you can buy from them.

Buying space on other people's websites

Buying banner ads is undertaken through sales houses and companies that specialize in offering sites for sale that the owner of the site might not want to make available themselves because it wouldn't be worth their while.

With this sort of advertising you will buy space by the CPM (thousand hits per page). It is very hard to generalize about space costs, value for money or effectiveness. The Audit Bureau of Circulation is looking at ways to be able to standardize site-buying information – but it will be a tough job to get all parties involved to agree. Further reading of *Revolution*, a monthly magazine published by Haymarket Press, is advised, or you can visit their site at http://www.revolution magazine.com.

Summary of Chapter 4

Within this chapter we have covered the following:

We have looked at below the line media – or created communication methods.

1 Sales promotion

This section looks at how sales promotions work, what types exist and what they are good at achieving. By taking an in-depth look at all types of sales promotions and incentives this section introduces the concept of adding value to encourage either a trial, a sale or a building of loyalty.

2 Sponsorships

This section examines the different types of sponsorships available (programme sponsorship, event sponsorship, person/team sponsorship), weighing the pros and cons of each and looking at the sorts of issues that arise in the planning and implementation of successful sponsorships.

3 Merchandising

This section addresses the issue of the total way in which goods and services are offered for sale.

4 Packaging

This section considers the role of packaging.

5 Direct marketing

This is a comprehensive section looking at the difference between direct marketing and direct marketing communications. By considering the planning, implementation and management issues associated with both functions this section sheds light on the relationship between the two disciplines as well as distinguishing between them.

6 Electronic communication

This section considers both above and below the line uses of the Internet.

Self-test questions and opinion development

These are not exam questions, nor are they meant to represent the sort of question you might expect to face anywhere else. They are designed to help you check whether you have understood the content of this chapter. All you have to do is read the questions, give them some thought and maybe jot down some notes on what your response might be. Not all the questions will have factual answers – rather, they might encourage you to think about a topic or an issue and formulate an opinion based upon what is now, hopefully, a better understanding of the topic.

- What are the three major types of sales promotion?
- Your Chairman wants you, as marcomms manager, to organize the sponsorship of an art scholarship at an art college, and to make sure that his son is the first to be awarded the fund. Your company makes concrete sleepers for railway tracks. What possible pitfalls might you have to explain to your Chairman?

- How many different types of packaging can you spot for washing powder? Why are there so many? Repeat this process for carbonated drinks.
- For a website of your choice, record all the banner ads you see on it in one month. How many of them are well targeted? How many of them are well executed? Why?
- Pick an on-line publication (maybe something like *Revolution* that you should be reading anyway!) and study the advertisements that appear for one month. What makes them good/bad?
- What do you think will happen to the Internet as an advertising medium in the next two years? What about WAP?

Extending knowledge and understanding

You are encouraged to undertake the following activities to further your knowledge and understanding of the topics covered in this chapter in the following ways:

1 Go out and get two examples of each of the three major types of sales promotion; one for a service, one for a product. Examine how the promotions were set up, try to find out about them either through the company's own website or through trade press coverage. What were the objectives? Were they achieved? Was the creative good/bad/indifferent? Do you think there is a relevance and appeal to the target audience?
2 Pick a sponsorship of something – something that interests you ... maybe a football team, a singer, a concert, a school, a golfer ... and find out all you can about it through websites, the sponsor and the sponsored party. How well does it work? Could it work better? If so, how? If not, why is it so good?
3 Go into a supermarket and, rather than rushing along the aisles, take some time to study how many communication items go to make up the total merchandising effort, from signs to trolleys, to on-shelf displays. Make notes as you go. Now go to a competing supermarket and repeat the process. Back at home consider the different ways in which the stores handle their merchandising management. You could repeat this exercise for other retail outlets, e.g., Boots versus Superdrug, B&Q versus Homebase. Pay particular attention to the way in which the retailers make sure it is their personality that wins out over the personalities of the brands (which are often in both stores). How do you feel the merchandising managers for the brands try to keep control over the presentation of their brand?
4 Start to collect your direct mail. At the end of two months put it into two piles – that which you think was well targeted and that which was not. For the well targeted pile, split it into effective creative treatments and less effective creative treatments. Now assess why you have put the items into the piles you have.

5 Public relations – more than just a goodwill exercise

Learning objectives	By the end of this chapter you should:

By the end of this chapter you should:

- ▶ have a clear understanding of what public relations is;
- ▶ have a clear understanding of what publics are;
- ▶ be aware of how above and below the line communications methods can be used for public relations purposes;
- ▶ be clear about the different types of public relations efforts that exist;
- ▶ be aware of public relations planning methods;
- ▶ be clear about what needs to be contained within each section of a public relations plan.

Overview

Public relations (PR) as it is practised today is largely a twentieth-century phenomenon, although it has been practised sporadically since earliest times. Today, it is the Institute of Public Relations (IPR), within the UK, that we must look towards to begin to understand current practice.

The IPR defines public relations in the following way:

> Public relations is about reputation: the result of what you do, what you say and what others say about you.

> Public relations practice is the discipline that looks after reputation – with the aim of earning understanding and support, and influencing opinion and behaviour.

> It is the planned and sustained effort to establish and maintain goodwill and mutual understanding between an organization and its publics.

The key words in the above definition focus on the fact that PR is not something that just 'happens', but rather that it is something that must be planned and controlled. Also, it highlights the fact that PR has at its core the concept of understanding, rather than bald promotion. This does not mean that PR is not a valuable promotional method. Rather, it means that it is not a way of pulling the wool over people's eyes, but of communicating with integrity, of educating rather than persuading, of telling rather than selling.

PR is also more than an executive-level tool. As with all communication tools it must be planned for and integrated into the corporate communications programme at the highest level. It is a true management function and should be addressed by all departments of an organization, not just the marketing department.

One of the other unique aspects of PR is that it differs from advertising and many other forms of promotional communication in that, whilst advertising brings the product to the customer, PR brings the customer to the product. PR is a two-way communication process, whereas advertising tends to be a one-way process.

Another difference is that, whilst advertising is placed in the media by buying space and time, PR gets messages into the media through editorial outlets. Stories and items appear because of their value and interest and appear free.

PR is also likely to have much wider objectives than advertising. An advertising campaign may have the aim to increase sales by 10 per cent, while PR will have the aim to improve employee relations, customer relations and educate and inform the general public about an organization.

How does PR 'get done'?

PR consultancies

These can provide highly specialized, or merely general, technical and creative services and might be either an individual in the form of the personal consultant who will advise and then 'buy in' creative/technical services on behalf of the client, as required, or a group of specialists working in a consultancy that would be a 'full-service' consultancy. These people are able to advise because of their wealth of experience and training. They will have (whether an individual or a large company) a legal and corporate identity of their own, registered for the purpose of the business.

In-house PR departments

In-house PR departments may comprise one or many people, depending upon the nature of the organization and the type of PR in which it is particularly active. Small departments are usually made up of generalists, while large departments tend to use people who specialize in various fields, as required. It is often the case that small PR departments will use outside consultancies to help with specialist requirements, or at times when the workload is particularly heavy. In-house departments are manned by members of staff, who will be employed on a salaried basis.

In-house PR versus PR consultancies

Consultancies have the advantage of being able to distance themselves from the day-to-day problems of the organization, and may therefore be able to bring fresh ideas to existing situations. They also bear the costs of ongoing overheads for large numbers of specialist staff, or have sufficiently wide experience and large number of contacts to allow them to buy in the services required more effectively and efficiently than those within the organization itself.

In-house departments know the problems and opportunities of the organization better than most, because the information required to build understanding is at their fingertips at all times in the shape of their own internal files and their colleagues' own knowledge.

Some of the 'publics' of public relations

The publics of an organization are all those people who come into contact with it or who are affected by its activities (Figure 5.1). In order to understand their relationship with us, we organize them into groups and analyse their needs and wants and their opinions of us. An organization's publics vary according to its aims and activities, so the following list serves only as a general guide.

| **Figure 5.1** | *An overview of the PR communication process* |

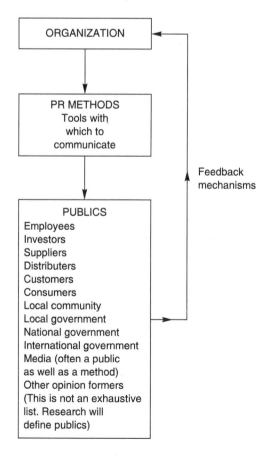

The press

The members of the press, i.e., journalists, editors, producers, researchers, etc.

Wants: news (not opinions, unless those of a VIP), facts, a fast response to their enquiries, information of 'interest and value' to their readers/listeners/viewers, an angle, exclusives.

The customer

The customer 'is always right', or should be made to feel so. A customer is known to the organization (dealt with face to face); a consumer is unknown to the organization (deals with intermediary); an end-user consumes or uses the product or service without making the buying decision.

Wants: service, quality/value, knowledge of the product/service (information), reassurance and back-up.

The investor

Shareholders, either private individuals or institutions, such as pension funds, building societies and banks. The financial market is closely associated, which trades in and advises on shareholding, such as stockbrokers, merchant banks, high-street banks and their city analysts. These act as city opinion formers, as do the financial press.

Wants: a good return on their investment, both as dividend and capital gain, information on how their money is being/will be used, prospects for the company/market.

The employee

Organized through trade unions or staff associations. May be shop floor, skilled, professional/technical, administrative, managerial. There are times when the potential employee becomes an important public, e.g., when locating a new factory or when skills are in short supply.

Wants: a fair wage and good working conditions (industrial relations), prospects, security, recognition, knowledge.

The government

Politicians and their administrators (civil servants, local government officials, Eurocrats). Politicians include MPs, MEPs and local councillors and their political parties. Government authority extends to bodies that enforce regulations, such as the Health and Safety Executive.

Wants: votes, to be kept informed about constituency/ward/department/special interest matters.

The distributor

Agents act on your behalf; dealers sell your product, taking a percentage of the price. Wholesalers buy your products and sell them on to retailers. They are the bridge between you and your consumer.

Wants: a good deal, back-up, encouragement, information.

The supplier

Other organizations that supply you with raw materials, parts, machinery and equipment, stationery, power, etc. (N.B., If your company is a supplier, your customer is a manufacturer or other organization.)

Wants: prompt payment, regular orders, knowledge of how their product is used.

Opinion formers

People and organizations that influence the opinions, attitudes or behaviour of others, e.g., politicians, newspaper editors, pressure groups, the community that is local to your factory or offices, Mr and Mrs Jones, doctors, religious leaders.

Wants: reliable information that allows them to form an informed opinion.

The role of research

The publics for each organization, and the PR situation, should be assessed before any PR plan is formulated. They should be 'brought alive' using demographic analysis and any personal experience of such relationships (we are all customers and employees). Remember, the headlines are guidelines only and each organization will have special publics (trade unions have members, charities have voluntary workers and donors, a football club needs good relationships with the police).

Because PR does really mean building a relationship with all your identified publics it is truly a management function, requiring top-level planning and co-ordination. However, there are also many executive-level tools that must be understood within this field. We will look at some of these next.

Methods of reaching publics

There is no right or wrong way to communicate with publics. Different publics might well be best reached by certain methods (Figure 5.2), however, so it is important to understand how these methods operate.

The British press

We are extremely fortunate in the UK to have an unparalleled range of national daily and weekly newspapers that have a strong editorial content and that allow the PR practitioner to target their messages. We have already seen the way in which the press targets specific socio-demographic profiles in its readership, thus allowing the publisher to have a saleable readership in terms of advertising. Despite the fact that the media relations programme that would be controlled by the PR practitioner does not buy space in these titles, it is of course still the case that the readership profile is of vital importance in the planning of PR coverage.

Figure 5.2

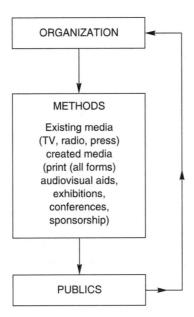

Regional and local newspapers allow the PR practitioner to communicate with geographically focused groups of readers, whilst consumer interest press or the trade press allow a focus on interest rather than location.

How does the press work?

By 'the press' we mean the people who gather, select and report the news. They include:

- *Editors*: these are the bosses. They are responsible for all the news (editorial) that appears in print. Their decision is final. On small or specialist publications, all information should be directed to the editors.
- *Sub-editors*: these edit material received, cutting it to length and/or rewriting it. They also write headlines.
- *Desk editors*: on larger newspapers, editorial responsibility for different sections of a paper (home news, overseas news, sport, etc.) is in the hands of desk editors. If your story is in one of these areas, it should be directed to the relevant desk.
- *Features editors*: these are responsible for the in-depth, longer stories that normally appear in the centre of newspapers. They are often looking for new feature ideas, so a story idea can be 'sold' to them. Some features are advertising features, which means editorial is dependent upon taking advertising space.
- *Feature writers*: these are journalists who write feature articles. They may work full or part time for the publication, or be freelance.
- *Freelancers*: these are journalists who are self-employed, either selling their story to publications or radio, or being commissioned, often by

features editors. They can be useful intermediaries when a story idea needs to be developed and placed.

- *Reporters*: these may be general news journalists (often juniors) or specialist reporters (especially on radio and television). If you telephone a newspaper you will usually be put through to a reporter first.
- *Stringers*: reporters who work for local papers or radio but who also feed important stories through to news agencies such as the Associated Press or national newspapers. If you think you are talking to a stringer, you are advised immediately to report up the line.

Other British mass media

Radio

Much local independent radio news is produced by Independent Radio News (IRN), a separate organization from the radio station itself that relays news to other stations. However, most stations have their own news editors, so check whether news should be directed to the station or IRN. Radio also employs specialist reporters who work for particular programmes or contribute to the news and cover such subjects as sport, women's interest and science.

BBC local radio stations have their own news editors, but often use the services of BBC Regional Broadcasting for their news and current-affairs programmes.

Radio interviews can be conducted live in the studio or by a reporter visiting you with a tape recorder or outside broadcast unit (OBU). In the studio, interviews can extend into 'phone-ins', in which members of the public ring in to ask questions of the interviewee. A 10-second delay is used, so that offensive remarks can be edited out, and the interviewer is at hand to control callers.

Radio also uses pre-taped news items, such as interviews, either produced by the station or supplied directly by outsiders. Freelance radio journalists can often be used to give a professional touch to pre-taped material by using commercial recording studios or equipment, but such material can be home produced.

Before being interviewed for a news item, prepare a sound bite. This is a 20–30 second section of the interview that can be edited out of the main interview for use in an overall story. It should contain your main message and stand on its own. This avoids the problems of being taken out of context and means that, if time is short, you can still get your most important point over to the listener.

Remember that radio is a background medium. People listen to it while doing other things, and so listeners are not hanging on every word you say. Repeating your main point is therefore acceptable. If you are giving out details of a forthcoming event, or of where listeners can gain further information, provide the presenter with the details in writing, so he or she can read it out a second time. It is always difficult for listeners to remember or take down information from a broadcast, so repeating an address, telephone number, location or date is common practice.

Television

With the increasing number of television channels available it is becoming more and more likely that there will be a televisual opportunity available via which you could reach one or more of your publics. Niche programming through satellite, cable and digital channels means that you can now reach very specific audiences, e.g., The Travel Channel, The Money Channel, The Cookery Channel and so on.

If you are invited into the studio you might find yourself being interviewed by the key presenter of the whole programme, who is often very knowledgeable about the subject being dealt with, often having worked in the field for many years. Usually these people are adept at putting interviewees at their ease and, if you have been invited in to speak on a topic or to comment on a situation where you are being viewed as the expert, then be assured that the questions you will be asked will be designed to elicit information that is helpful and interesting to the audience, If you are there to represent an organization, or even yourself, in a controversial situation, then it is likely that the questions you face will be searching. Yes, some interviewers can be aggressive, and some interviewees choose to respond in kind, but generally speaking, even if a question is asked in a less than pleasant manner it is best to respond in a level-headed way – there are some wonderful examples of interviewees being thought less highly of, or even losing their jobs, because they were not able to deal with an aggressive interview!

Whenever you appear on television it is best to remember that everything you do with your face and body will seem larger than life on the screen. So, if you are uncertain, or if you are advising someone who is uncertain about how they will feel when they are in front of a camera, the best advice is to get some media training before making any possible mistakes in public.

Generally speaking it is best to wear un-fussy clothing, no stripes, small checks or spots (they look strange on camera) and to avoid fancy jewellery that 'dangles' because any movement will be exaggerated on camera. The best advice of all? Seek advice from the producer and take it – they know what they want, they know what their audience expects and they are the ones who can ask you back again to talk about your next issue!

Created PR communication methods

Created PR material can refer to almost anything – from a corporate brochure to a hot-air balloon hovering over an open day at a police station. Here, some of the more common 'tools of the trade' are examined: print, audiovisual aids, photography and sponsorship.

Printed PR material

Essentially, since you are totally in control of printed PR material, it can be used for any purpose at all. As PR is about informing, printed material is often used with this aim – from one angle or another. That said, what is vitally important is that the PR professional controlling printed material understands print sufficiently well to be able to get what they want. Some of the functions of printed PR material might include:

- sales information;
- corporate;
- explanatory;
- campaigning;
- requesting (as in a questionnaire).

As the PR professional is in control of the function of PR material, so he or she is also in control of the nature of the material, i.e., what form it will take. The form selected should be that which suits needs best. Usually this will be fairly obvious. Don't forget that some groups of people will have special needs: e.g., leaflets about pensioners' bus passes should be in large print; direct mail to residents on a cosmopolitan estate should be multilingual, etc. The general type of formal decision could be one of the following:

- leaflets;
- direct mail shots (from letters to multi-part);
- catalogues;
- brochures;
- press advertising;
- news-sheets/newsletters;
- house magazines (internal/external);
- websites.

So how can you make sure that you get what you want? Here are ten key points for commissioning effective design:

1. First you must establish the use of the printed material/site.
2. Consider the type of printed material required (do not use the ubiquitous term 'brochure').
3. Establish the method of transmission.
4. Think of the length of print runs (these can affect design and printing).
5. Establish a rough budget and tell the designer how much is allocated for design (less 20 per cent).
6. Have an approximate idea of how pagination will work.
7. Don't let words do all the work.
8. Don't let pictures do all the work.
9. Give the designer as much information as possible (verbal, visual and written).
10. Give the designer a deadline (at least 2 days before you are to present the design).

A word of warning: present visuals first (people like coloured pictures) with only a copy outline to clients/principals, and leave the copy for final approval. Do not get copy approval first and then go to design, as this route takes forever and preconceptions are formed on the basis of the words only!

When you are getting a quote for print, the information you should give the printer in order for them to be able to put together a reliable price is:

- print run (number of pieces to print);
- number of colours (1, 2, 3 or 4 colour process);
- number of pages;

- ratio of copy to number of halftones;
- size (of page/sheet, with fold to final size);
- material (type and weight – designer to advise);
- finish (laminated/varnish);
- delivery (one address? Consultancy? Client?);
- run-on price per 1000;
- provide printer with at least a photocopy of the visual.

Give the same information to several printers to obtain competitive quotes based on the same criteria.

Audiovisual aids

These must always be:

- informative;
- convincing;
- reinforcing;
- illustrative.

Forms of audiovisual aid include:

- flipcharts;
- overhead projections;
- slides (carousel/pulsed tape);
- films;
- videos (including interactive);
- computer-generated material;
- websites.

The PR practitioner might choose to use audiovisual aids either as a presentation support or on their own. For example:

- press launch;
- employee relations and communications;
- projecting corporate identity;
- trade relations;
- training;
- induction;
- exhibitions;
- general information.

Different tools have different characteristics:

35 millimetre film

- Gives outstanding picture quality (large-screen cinema standard).
- Is costly.
- Is always preferred, if the budget permits.

Video

- Ease of editing and using special effects.
- Cheaper and quicker than film.

Slide tapes

This means the use of single or multiple projectors and a synchronized soundtrack programmed by computer to control the whole operation.

- Can be cheap.
- Optimum sound quality.
- Can be run unattended.
- Good for multilingual use.

PR photography

Photography that is submitted with editorial stories is, in fact, a form of 'created communication method' and the rule of thumb is that it has to be as good as that commissioned by, and included in, the media.

Many publications now want to receive photographs digitally or at least on disk. On the other hand, some still prefer to receive hard copy, i.e., actual photographs. If you are in doubt, call ahead to check that you will be sending what they want, or check in one of the directories that offers this information. Whatever the desired form of receipt of a photograph there are still some golden rules to be borne in mind when actually creating the photograph itself:

Ten golden rules for good PR photography

1 Use professionals *in that field* (e.g., use food photographers for food, studio photographers for studio set-ups, portrait specialists for portraits, and so on. Professional photographers, like all of us, have strengths and specialities, and do see the notes that follow).
2 Think visually from the start.
3 Direct the photography to get what you want.
4 Let the image fill the frame (or crop).
5 Ensure that the composition is tight.
6 Indicate scale (with something familiar, like people).
7 Show product being used (avoid 'product' shots).
8 Include action if possible.
9 Caption with the facts not the fantasy.
10 Look at photographs that are used in the media.

Commissioning PR photography

Also, it is useful to keep in mind the following checklist when commissioning PR photography.

- *Selecting a photographer*: working with a photographer should be very personal. It is a jointly creative activity and it is vital that you are both on the same wavelength in every way. There are several criteria for choosing a photographer; usually they are one of the following:
  - you already know him or her and have worked with him happily;
  - he or she has been recommended to you by someone you trust;
  - you may have seen and admired his or her work.

- *Working with a photographer*: if you have not worked with the photographer you have chosen, meet them or their agent and look at specimens of their work.
- *Briefing the photographer*: you always need to consider the following:
  - explain the nature of the photographs; editorial (magazine, newspaper, exclusive or general coverage), leaflets, local advertising, or whatever;
  - is it trade (emphasizing quality, finish and size) or consumer (establishing sales points)? What is the lighting and will it create the right mood, directing the eye?
  - is the session black and white or colour or both? Check proportions;
  - provide lists of names and designations of people or model numbers or products to be photographed.

- *Arrangements for the shoot*: considerations should include the following:
  - location of studio;
  - choice of background;
  - position of sun and other details.

- *Captions*: when photographs are being sent to the press in the hope that they will be published, it is vital that they carry an appropriate caption. Editors will have expectations that the practitioner should follow:
  - every picture must be captioned;
  - the caption should be affixed to the bottom of the reverse of the picture in such a way that it may be read from the front with the picture in view;
  - the caption needs a title to give a quick indication of what the picture is about. If the picture accompanies a news release, then the title should (in most cases) be the same as, or a shortened version of, the news release title;
  - few pictures will stand on their own without some indication of how their subject relates to the text of any accompanying news release. A lead-in can often be a direct quote from the first paragraph of the latter, since this gives the whole story in a nutshell. Double spacing of text is desirable;
  - after the title and lead-in, if any, should come a paragraph with the side-heading 'Picture shows ...'. This should say exactly what the picture shows – no more, no less. This is only part of the caption written specifically for that picture;
  - as in the case of the news release, the caption should similarly indicate the name, address and telephone number of the issuing organization. The month and year of issue should always be given; it may not always be necessary to give the day of the month;
  - the negative number should be indicated;
  - any copyright stipulations should be clearly stamped on the back of the print.

Exhibitions, conferences, seminars

Sometimes, all three happen together; for example, a major biannual pharmaceutical exhibition will provide the platform for an international conference and various specialist seminars all during, say, four days in Zurich. A PR professional's task is to investigate what already exists, assess whether it meets the needs and plan either to work within the existing framework or, as is often the case, go it alone. What follows here is intended to be a useful summary of points to consider.

Exhibitions

These are mainly trade and business to business, although some are consumer oriented (e.g., Ideal Homes Show, Clothes Show). They often run in a cycle thus (for each industry):

- biannual – large, international;
- annual – large, national;
- throughout year – regional/subsector of industry.

Always ask:

- Why are you taking the stand?
- What are the objectives?
- How long do you have to plan?
- What do you want to have achieved after having attended?

If your organization or product do not 'fit', organize your own exhibition. For example, you want to launch a new commercial boiler at a national exhibition. You are advised that it is not a sufficiently big new product to warrant attention. The solution is to set up your own exhibition of new and existing boilers taken (in a lorry) around regional commercial gas centres, with key specifiers and regional media invited by direct mail to their 'local' exhibition. The result is a high level of attendance, a high and detailed level of product knowledge is gained (across the range), good regional press coverage, *plus* ongoing trade-press coverage as new angles develop over the three months of the 'tour'. The cost is not much more than taking a medium-sized stand at the national exhibition!

Conferences and seminars

Exhibitions lend themselves best to *showing*. If discussion is needed, then it might be better to use a conference/seminar format, with some 'exhibiting' still being used in reserved areas (hotel foyer, coffee area, etc.). Conferences and seminars are used frequently in two key ways: internal or external.

External conferences and seminars are usually used to bring together dealers, specifiers, key opinion formers, etc., in an environment where information and views can be given and exchanged. Careful planning is *essential*, starting with deciding the purpose, desired outcome and guest list. Many specialist companies exist in the field of conference/seminar/event organization; it sometimes pays to use these experts because they will, for example, be used to planning 'spouse programmes', dealing with travel arrangements, etc.

Internal conferences and seminars are often used to bring together employees who might never otherwise meet! Also don't forget that, whilst it might be a vital element in saving a company, the 'loss' of staff *must* be dealt with carefully for the company to continue to function through its remaining staff, who at least understand the reasons for job losses.

Applications of public relations

Customer–dealer relations

Marketers need to identify, anticipate and satisfy customer requirements. Marketers use many techniques to enable them to do this, not the least of which is to establish *two-way* communication directly between themselves and their customers.

Examples of the role that a true PR exercise can play might be:

- Customer advisory services (e.g., Lillets, Elida Gibbs). These services allow customers to 'talk' to marketers in a very real sense.
- Informative literature, e.g., a brochure on 'towing and touring' supplied by a car manufacturer as a result of an enquiry from a motorist (not with the aim of selling anything).
- Running an on-pack competition asking for recipes using your product as an ingredient, with winners being published in a book and perhaps invited to cook their recipes on the cookery slot of a morning television 'magazine' programme, or for a women's magazine.

When it comes to dealers, the marketer is dealing with a vitally important part of the marketing mix – the P for place, i.e., the distributive outlets. The nature of the marketer–dealer relationship can vary enormously, with scale affecting the PR tools to be used. Generally speaking, however, again the aim is to develop a good, close, mutually beneficial working relationship. The PR tools that might be used here include, for example:

- literature for information/display;
- dealer 'training' packs or courses;
- dealer competitions, incentives, etc.;
- events, conferences, seminars, hospitality for dealers;
- exhibition support for dealers when *they* attend an exhibition;
- media relations support for dealers;
- simple 'advice giving' on any publicity matters for dealers;
- extranet access by password to a part of the corporate website that is exclusively for dealers/partners and might even allow orders to be placed on-line.

Employee and internal communications

All organizations vary in their make-up: a small company with two employees will obviously not need the same PR tools as one with 20 000 employees. That said, even when people work closely together, planned time away from the working environment can focus the mind wonderfully!

Before embarking upon any plan, therefore, some questions need to be addressed:

- How many employees are there?
- What types of employee are there? Do they all 'speak the same language'? For example, a wages clerk at a chemical plant might not know the first thing about chemistry.
- Where are the employees based – all in one place, spread nationally or internationally?
- What is the corporate structure – a single company, a group, a conglomerate, a recently merged multinational?

All these questions, and their answers, will help the PR professional decide the *objectives* of internal communication. Are we aiming to inform, educate, interest, reassure, get ideas, build loyalty? All of these? The next question is: How do we do this?

Media for employee relations

An organization can use all sorts of media for mass communication with employees. Some, to be effective, have to be established permanently, for instance a house journal cannot be switched on according to need, nor can a website or intranet. Other media, however, can be called into use on an *ad hoc* basis when required.

Examples in the 'permanent' category might include:

- annual reports;
- house journals;
- noticeboards;
- phone-in information service;
- intranet site.

Examples of those in the *ad hoc* category might include:

- corporate publications;
- exhibitions and displays;
- video;
- film;
- tape–slide presentations;
- personal letters to employees.

If starting from scratch, the communicator would list all the categories of information and evaluate the ideal media for each. This analysis would lead to identification of the 'permanent' media required.

Here are a few points to remember if you are planning to produce a newsletter (whether it is printed on paper, placed on an intranet site or both):

- Set goals for the newsletter by defining and getting to know the audience you're trying to reach. Don't try to be everything to everybody.
- Make sure a professional communicator, either an in-house staff person or an external resource, is charged with the responsibility for producing the newsletter.
- Don't 'preach' to the readership, its purpose should be to educate and stimulate a genuine dialogue between the company and its staff.

- Write to express – not impress. Use words that communicate your company's message clearly and correctly. Present material in short sentences and paragraphs. Avoid jargon that won't be understood by your entire audience.
- Establish a recognizable format and stick to it, so readers can become comfortable with the content as well as find information simply and quickly. Remember, familiarity is critical in developing readership.
- Develop a solid graphic design. Good design is essential in competing for the attention and interest of your readership.
- Use headlines and photo captions as a way to communicate key points in a story. They're often an editor's best tool in conveying important information.
- Don't make the mistake of cramming too much information into a newsletter. Readership surveys repeatedly demonstrate that readers want larger and more legible typefaces, so by providing less in volume, you may actually be able to communicate more.

Ideally, the communicator has the right permanent media for the current situation. However, the *ad hoc* media should also be kept in mind, with a clear plan of how to bring them into action if required. Letters are a very good and effective vehicle in an emergency, for example, as are staff meetings or cascaded management meetings, but they can sometimes be difficult to arrange at short notice, especially within a multi-national organization.

Increasingly, the idea of using an intranet to communicate internally is being hailed as *the* way to talk to staff. A word of warning: if *all* your staff have access to an intranet (a password-protected part of your Internet website) then it might just be the right way to talk to them. Very few organizations find themselves in this position – most have at least a portion of their staff for whom the Internet and the intranet are something they would not normally come into contact with, at least not as a part of their working day. There is some thought that, as home penetration of the Internet via digital television increases, the 'old-fashioned' house journal, which was often mailed to employees' homes, will be seen again in the form of an on-line magazine that is e-mailed to staff members at home – wherever in the world that might be!

That said, the web won't work as a communications tool for factory staff who have no access either at home or in workplace, will not appeal to, or even reach, many other groups for whom it is not a familiar technology and could cost you a great deal of money, with little effect, if you cannot encourage those who *do* have access to it to visit it! Like all communication methods and messages, your internal communications via intranet must be sufficiently interesting to the audience to encourage them to actually read them or, in this case, visit the site more than once and, indeed, on a pretty regular basis.

Gaining the reputation that it is 'an interesting site once you get there' is one way of encouraging people to keep coming back, but many organizations give their staff more proactive encouragements to visit their internal communications sites: collection schemes of points of some sort means that you can encourage people to visit every week for a particular time period if you reward them upon proof of, say, one visit per week for twelve weeks, for example. Research could throw light on what rewards/ schemes might work for a particular group – never assume that the same will work for everyone!

Political PR/lobbying

All organizations need to be aware of what is happening within government and parliament that might affect their business either directly or indirectly. What follows is a list of topics for consideration by all organizations and their PR practitioners:

- Current legislation (planned or rumoured) may affect the organization.
- The key personnel, government committees and quangos are involved.
- Special pressure points and how they can be exploited.
- When Green Papers, White Papers, Second Readings, etc., can be expected.
- How best to present your case at each stage in the process.
- Which politicians and officials may champion your particular cause, and what their standing is.
- How ministers and civil servants are likely to react to your proposals.
- How the consultative process really works, and how to influence it.
- How to persuade a select committee to listen to you.
- How to cultivate civil servants and understand their language.
- Where and how to apply indirect pressure (third-party endorsements, local press, opinion polls).
- How to get key words changed in a piece of legislation.
- When the House of Lords can help, and how to approach peers.

There are no right and wrong ways to ensure that your lobbying is perfect. There are many PR consultancies that specialize in this field because it is so full of pitfalls for the uninformed or the unwary. It really is worth using a professional who knows their way around this area, because they can, in the long run, not only save an organization time and money by already having the right contact in the right place with the right knowledge, but they should also be fully aware of the restrictions within which they are allowed to operate, which differ within the UK and the European legislature, and can therefore avoid embarrassing and possibly illegal mistakes!

Crisis management

'Crisis management' seems a misnomer, almost an oxymoron: a 'crisis' is something out of control, 'management' means control. Yet hundreds of companies and public utilities have plans worked out for the type of crisis that just might happen to them, so that a management procedure can be swung into action when disaster strikes.

Charities and voluntary organizations are particularly vulnerable to attack from the media when something goes wrong. Such problems are considered 'a matter of public interest' because the organizations receive public money and time and the money is for the disadvantaged. Possible disaster scenarios are:

- misappropriation of funds;
- high administration costs/low spend on cause;
- death, mistreatment or maltreatment of beneficiaries;
- withdrawal of a major donor or sponsor;
- criticism by doctors, professional bodies, MPs, etc.;
- patron problems.

In PR terms, crisis management means taking control of the flow of information demanded by the media and the public. If the organization undergoing the crisis is informative, open and honest with the media they will not need to turn to other sources (who may be the opposition) for information. Providing as much information as possible, as quickly as possible, will also prevent rumour and speculation. Thus, when planning media handling in a crisis, follow these rules:

- Tell your own tale.
- Tell it all.
- Tell it fast.

In a crisis the press come to you, rather then you trying to attract the press. The journalists and reporters that arrive and telephone are unlikely to be those whom you know and have been carefully cultivating. Pool reporters and home news journalists, who know nothing about your organization, will predominate and will have a negative, even hostile, attitude towards you. They must be provided not only with any news you have available, but also with general background information on your organization and its work. This should always be up-to-date and to hand.

If any members of the public are at risk, the press will give this priority – and so must you. In fact, the press can be co-operative in this matter, by getting emergency telephone numbers and advice to the public. They can also be the first to inform you of the crisis (the 3:00 a.m. phone call) and will be prepared to provide you with details, provided you call them back.

Remember that any reporter on the scene will be under extreme pressure on deadlines (with possible late editions being planned) and the 'hold the front page' syndrome will be noticeable. They will also tend to regard the story as their big break – a chance to get a by-line on the front page or to obtain the first live report of the story. So find out their deadlines and call them back/provide statements, etc., in time – and remember that the one who broke the story to you should be the first to get the information.

If the press don't get what they want from official sources, they will get it any way they can. This is why it is vital that all press calls and enquiries go to the PR office or crisis management team and to no others. Telephonists, receptionists and security staff must be briefed/trained to do this.

Finally, never say 'No comment' – the public will automatically assume your guilt and other people *will* comment. Remind your legal advisors that saying you are sorry is not an admission of liability. Announcing an inquiry and promising to publish the results shows you to be an honest broker, not a failure. If you don't put right publicly what went wrong, you will never restore your public image. The faster you put your image right, the quicker it will be forgotten.

Crisis management – a basic survival guide

Pre-crisis:

- Expect crises – every company has them.
- State the worst-possible scenario.
- State the next worst-possible scenario.
- In utmost confidence, talk to the very senior management in the company for two reasons:
  - if it's a real crisis then they should know about it;
  - if it isn't worth bringing to the attention of the senior management, there is a question regarding its seriousness.

N.B., one man's crisis is another man's salvation (e.g., closing a factory in the prosperous southeast to open up a plant in the northeast is not everyone's crisis).

At this stage, managers should look seriously at whether all possible steps are being taken to prevent the hypothetical crisis.

- Set up a crisis management team of senior people. If it is a vital problem it must be handled by a very senior director with the PR person advising on communications strategy. The PR person must not be put up as the spokesperson, however trivial the company may consider the matter. The most senior director of the company must act as the only spokesperson.
- Set up the physical machinery (e.g., faxes, telephones) to cope with communications. Have, for example, telephones ready, but don't label the area the 'Incident Room'. It could be equipment in routine use that could be made ready in an emergency.
- Set up an emergency reporting procedure for when an incident is seen to be likely. Don't allow staff to remain silent until it happens, but beware of panics and beware of crying 'wolf'.
- Finally, set up a system for payment of immediate needs, without prejudicing any future compensation claims by victims.

Planning the use of public relations

The six-point plan that follows was initially put forward as a framework by the late Frank Jefkins. It has now become widely accepted as a sound basis for PR planning, and could, in fact, be used for planning in all promotional fields. The RACE acronym underlies all PR planning (Fig. 5.3).

Point 1 – appreciation of the situation

This means that the following questions need to be asked:

- What is the current situation?
- What do people know or not know about it?
- Are there any misunderstandings?

Sources for answers to these questions can be:

The RACE acronym underlies all the principles of PR

Figure 5.3

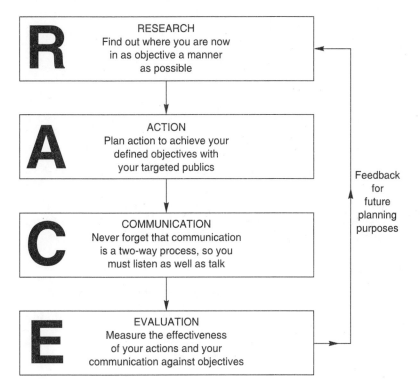

- observation;
- press cuttings/media monitoring;
- statistics:
  - national;
  - internal (sales, etc.);
  - industry (competition/exports);
  - financial/economic (share price);
- trends (inferred and stated);
- opinion polls (qualitative and quantitative).

Other factors affecting the situation include:

- industrial relations;
- weather;
- customer appreciation (complaints and praise);
- prices;
- economic/political situation;
- opinion leaders.

Are there any negative thoughts such as:

- Hostility?
- Prejudice?

- Apathy?
- Ignorance?

How can these be changed to positive thoughts such as?

- Sympathy?
- Acceptance?
- Interest?
- Knowledge?

A warning – all can't be done at once and the change needs to be continuous.

Point 2 – defining objectives

This is where you spell out the objectives of your programme. Is the aim to change attitudes from x to y? Are you wanting to increase knowledge within your public from x per cent awareness to y per cent awareness? What objectives would a PR programme aim to achieve? List them. Categorize and prioritize them.

Point 3 – defining publics

List and define which publics you want to reach:

- Internal: staff (production, promotion and sales, senior, middle and junior management).
- Associate:
  - suppliers;
  - distributors;
  - retail outlets;
  - shareholders.

- External:
  - customers;
  - potential shareholders;
  - potential employees.

- Local/community:
  - neighbours;
  - MPs;
  - local council (members and officials);
  - pressure groups (*ad hoc* protest groups, residents associations, national groups);
  - chambers of commerce/Rotary clubs/Lions clubs;
  - schools and colleges;
  - hospitals and health authorities.

Remember that you communicate with *people*, so it is essential to look into the above categories to identify the appropriate individuals). This can be done by:

- Trade publics:
  - job title/function;
  - company;

- industry;
- location.
- Consumers:
  - age and age group;
  - sex;
  - neighbourhood and location;
  - housewife/working wife/with or without children;
  - head of household/chief wage earner;
  - what they read, watch and listen to;
  - car owner/motorist;
  - possessor of durable goods;
  - user of retail outlets;
  - level of income.

The more of these factors that are known the easier it is to pinpoint the target, and yes, they are advertising/marketing techniques, and yes, they are valid in PR. Remember, very few organizations actually communicate with 'the general public'.

Point 4 – selecting the methods

This is the chronological order in which you should communicate with the media to make sure that information is distributed at the right time and place to have maximum impact. It is no good sending out a press release and hoping it sticks – media relations have to be planned.

Suggested order:

- Financial media (if raising investment, but not in place of contact via the financial management of the company/organization).
- Internal newsletters/house magazines (to reinforce routine management procedures, formal and informal communications do not replace them).
- Trade, technical and professional media (again, in addition to and not as a replacement for normal business discussions and negotiations).
- Special-interest magazines (such as *Ideal Home*, which have long lead times).
- Television (other than news, as programmes have a long lead time).
- General-interest monthly publications.
- Current-affairs weekly publications (such as *The Economist*, if appropriate).
- National Sunday newspapers.
- Local weekly publications (including Sunday newspapers).
- National daily publications.
- Radio (unless a programme or longer item is possible).

Constantly review the media you are contacting – the item may be appropriate in other sectors. Negotiate placement (which you can do if you have a plan). Do not always blanket mail. Think of particular editors, journalists, correspondents and freelance writers, and discuss their requirements.

Media relations techniques include the following, i.e., the ubiquitous press release is not appropriate for every occasion:

- news releases;
- press statements (written and oral);
- photo opportunities;
- product releases;
- case histories;
- briefings;
- interviews;
- media entertaining;
- press conferences;
- articles and features.

The essential substance can be obtained (not be made up) from the following:

- new products;
- new technical developments/technology;
- application of products and technology;
- corporate developments;
- issues and controversies;
- introduction of standards, regulations, laws, etc.

Other means of communication can also be used. There follows an overview of which method is useful for achieving what type of objective:

Printed material

Printed PR material might have the following purposes:

- to give sales information;
- to build corporate image;
- to be explanatory;
- to campaign for a cause.
- merely requesting (as in a questionnaire).

Forms of printed PR material include the following:

- leaflets;
- mail shots (from letters to multi-parts);
- catalogues;
- brochures;
- press advertising;
- news-sheets/newsletters;
- house magazines (internal/external).

Always select the form that best suits the purpose.

Participatory media

Participatory PR media (or methods that need human involvement for delivery) include the following:

- seminars;
- workshops;

- conferences;
- exhibitions;
- displays.

Again, select the form that best suits your needs, budget and timetable.

Audiovisual material

Audiovisual presentations might be in the following forms:

- flipcharts;
- overhead projectors;
- slides (carousels/pulsed tapes);
- films;
- videos;
- computer-generated material or websites.

Sponsorship

Sponsorship might be a method you select, but always ensure it has been well thought through:

- it must be relevant;
- participation should be taken on a sound basis;
- it can be expensive;
- it can be inexpensive;
- it can be ineffective;
- it can be effective.

If you let your heart, or your principal's heart, rule your head, make sure you have a healthy budget.

Point 5 – developing a budget

There are a number of ways of constructing a budget, but the main ones are:

- finger in the wind;
- top-down, i.e., see what you've got and work within it;
- the task method, i.e., decide what needs to be done and price it;
- historic plus, e.g., 10 per cent more than last year;
- percentage of sales/receipts.

The methods are not mutually exclusive, but it is best to be realistic, i.e., don't put forward a proposal with a huge budget. Remember, the four main elements of setting a PR budget are:

- labour – salaries/PR consultant's fees/PR practitioners and other staff that might be involved;
- office overheads – these are mainly fixed and can easily be calculated;
- materials – stationery, print, etc.;
- expenses – these must be controlled at all times.

Point 6 – evaluation

There are three key points to remember here:

1 It is important to measure the effectiveness against the objective (if the exercise fails to meet the objective, it is a failure).
2 It is important to take soundings before as well as after to establish changes.
3 Evaluation should be continuous (to review progress and preview future activity).

Evaluation/assessment methods can be either quantitative or qualitative:

Quantitative:

- column centimetres (measure them);
- ratings/readership (count them);
- enquiries received (count them);
- quality scored (score it);
- increased interest generally (measure it);
- increased sales/receipts (know past levels, and present levels, and measure the difference).

Qualitative:

- opinion polls (to gain insight into attitude changes);
- peer group/competitor attitudes (carry out in-depth research);
- media interest/sympathy. This may not result in immediate column centimetres, but can be judged on a one-to-one basis and bodes well for the future;
- effect of total positive and negative media coverage.

Summary of PR planning

The main stages in PR planning are:

- Situation analysis including the problem.
- Objective setting.
- Target-audience definition.
- Methods.
- Budget.
- Evaluation.

In theory, the budget should be decided when the programme is finalized.
In practice, the client (or employer) may say 'Here's the cash – that's it!'.
In a more detailed sense, here are some notes on planning:

- Set margins for the operation.
- Estimate the working hours and other costs.
- Select the priorities.
- Assess the feasibility of carrying out the declared objectives.

A six-point PR planning model would be:

1 Appreciation of the situation.
2 Definition of objectives.
3 Definition of publics.
4 Selection of media and techniques.
5 Planning of a budget.
6 Assessment of results.

You must always take into account:

- hostility;
- prejudice;
- apathy;
- ignorance.

What you are aiming to achieve is a transfer from this stance to the following:

Hostility → Sympathy
Prejudice → Acceptance
Apathy   → Interest
Ignorance → Knowledge

Remember, investigation is required to arrive at a helpful appreciation of the tasks involved and solutions needed. PR is about effecting change, not just creating favourable images.

Summary of Chapter 5

Within this chapter we have covered the following:

The background to, the reasons for, how to plan and how to implement a public relations communication programme.

1 Overview

This section describes what PR is and what it can do.

2 How does it get done?

This section looks at who does what internally and externally for PR.

3 The publics

This section takes a look at publics and what they want.

4 The methods for communicating

This is a comprehensive review of a large number of above and below the line communication methods and how they are used for public relations purposes.

5 Applications of PR

This section looks at how PR is applied in a range of real circumstances.

6 PR planning

This section addresses the specific issues about writing and implementing a PR plan that will work!

Self-test questions and opinion development

These are not exam questions, nor are they meant to represent the sort of question you might expect to face anywhere else. They are designed to help you check whether you have understood the content of this chapter. All you have to do is read the questions, give them some thought and maybe jot down some notes on what your response might be. Not all the questions will have factual answers – rather, they might encourage you to think about a topic or an issue and formulate an opinion based upon what is now, hopefully, a better understanding of the topic.

- What is PR?
- How would you say it differs from advertising?
- Why do you think PR is made fun of so much?
- What do you think the IPR could/can/does do to change that?
- Name four possible publics and their needs from an organization that wants to build mutual understanding with them.
- Name three possible PR objectives.
- How could you use TV for PR instead of, say, advertising or sponsorship?
- Answer the same question for radio.
- Name the possible crises that could be faced by the following:

  - a charity to help children;
  - a company known for buying its raw materials in the UK;
  - a cricketer and his sponsors;
  - a nuclear fuel plant;
  - a company that makes children's furry toys;
  - a church.

- Why do political lobbyists have to be so careful about their ethics?
- What are the six points in a six-point plan?
- Why do you need six? If you had to add a seventh, what would it be? Why?

Extending knowledge and understanding

You are encouraged to undertake the following activities to further your knowledge and understanding of the topics covered in this chapter in the following ways:

1 Visit the IPR website and work your way through it. What does this say about PR in the UK today? What interesting links are there? Do you think it could do a more professional or proactive job? Why do you think the IPR is needed? Spend some time working around the site, and try to visit other PR Association sites too, e.g., the PRCA in the UK, or for Ireland or the USA. By using a search engine and a bit of imagination you can find many. How do you think they compare?

2 Try checking out several PR agencies' own websites, remembering they are in business to help others manage their reputation and image – what do you think their sites say about them? A great site I found is http://www.soc.american.edu/friedheim/pr.html that has been set up by US college students to make links easy! But if this address doesn't work for you, don't worry, you can still surf and find lots of agencies – good luck – you might be amazed at what you discover.

3 Keep up to date with your PR trade press reading – whether it's on the web or on paper. What are the big issues *today*? What's their background?

4 What qualities do you think it would take to become a great PR practitioner? How many types of practice are there? Would you need to be a very different sort of person in each field? What do you think?

5 Try to find a PR plan for your own organization/one of your choice. What does it tell you? What does it tell you if you don't have one? Why not write one yourself?

6 Managing implementation

Learning objectives

By the end of this chapter you should:

▶ be aware of the importance of resource planning and management;
▶ understand the harmony required between internal and external resources;
▶ clearly understand the process involved in choosing a new marketing communications service provider;
▶ clearly understand the criteria used in selecting a new marketing communications service provider;
▶ have an insight into why it is vital to brief service providers thoroughly, from both the client and service provider perspective;
▶ understand the briefing process;
▶ know what should be in a good brief;
▶ be aware of the key issues involved in managing service providers;
▶ understand the importance of checking laws and controls that affect communications.

Making sure you have the right resources – internally

Overview

You will need two types of resource to be able to implement your marketing communications programme: internal resources and external resources. It is normal for the *internal* resource to be your first consideration when assessing your resource requirement situation.

The internal resource available to you might be adequate to carry out all the marketing communications functions you need. This might especially be the case if the functions are being managed by you and implemented by a team of specialists either in your office, in your country or even just within the organization across the world.

Thus, your starting point is working out what your communications programme is going to be, assessing the skills of the staff available and hoping that there is a match! But even if there is a match in skills, there also has to be a match in terms of workpower available for the size of task – in other words, have you got enough of the right people to do the job? This is often where a problem arises, especially if there is any element of seasonality in the business, thereby producing peaks and troughs of activity for the marcomms team.

If you have an opportunity to mould a team for the future, through recruitment, then here's a useful tip: work out what you will need in the team one month from when the new person would join and six months from when the new person would join – if there's a difference, recruit someone who can grow to be what you *will* want or who, indeed, has the skills you *will* need already. It is important to look ahead in terms of team development, knowing that you can buy-in short-term resources when you need them.

Specific issues

One of the most contentious issues being faced by many marcomms managers today is the question 'Who owns our website?' and the equally contentious issue of 'Who manages our website?'. The battle lines are usually drawn between the IT department, marketing and corporate affairs or PR departments. So who *should* own and run the corporate website?

Well, as a writer on marketing and marketing communications I am sure you would expect me to say 'the Marketing Department' without hesitation, but actually I have a different suggestion: why not get the marketing department to lead a team effort? Often there are other issues that need to be dealt with on the website, such as investor relations, customer communications or internal communications, and there might well be technological advances about which the marketers will have no knowledge but that could greatly alter the content, method or type of communication available through this valuable tool. Thus, a team effort, with user focus remaining the emphasis for all team members, might do the best job. But leadership skills will be put to the test, as will communication skills, so a good programme of continuous communication and discussion, with clear guidelines about responsibilities and no-go areas needs to be put in place from the first opportunity. I suggest that marketers take the lead in this area because they are the keepers of the 'identify, anticipate and satisfy customer requirements profitably' ethos.

Making sure you have the right resources – externally

How do marcomms managers choose the right external service providers?

There is no simple answer to this question. Indeed, as you read the trade press and see the way that advertising, public relations, direct marketing, sales promotions and all types of accounts move from agency to agency, you might begin to wonder whether any client ever does choose the right external service provider (hereafter referred to, in the interests of brevity, as 'agency', but without the implication that this refers to just advertising agencies – you might equally apply what is said to PR agencies, sales promotion agencies, design agencies, etc., etc., etc.!).

This general movement aside, both clients and agencies have an interest in an account remaining with the same agency for a reasonable period of time, as this allows the client–agency relationship to develop a depth that can lead to truly great advertising. However, the job of constantly reviewing the ability of an incumbent agency to deliver work that meets objectives, and the reviewing of the alternative agencies available, takes a great deal of valuable time on the part of the client or marketer, so it really is worth attempting to choose the best possible supplier in the first place.

Thus, as mentioned earlier, when considering your needs internally, you need to have decided, broadly speaking at least, what types of promotional effort you will require. Remember that even if you go to a full service agency, if it is an advertising agency you are likely to get an advertising solution to your marcomms problems; if you go to a below the line agency you will get a below the line solution; and so on. Possibly the business to business communications agency or a real, honest to goodness through the line agency (and they are few and far between) are most likely to offer you a true range of communication solutions.

Figure 6.1 shows the sorts of tools you might want to consider for certain objectives.

| **Figure 6.1** | *The role of different promotional tools in the promotional mix – advertising in context* |

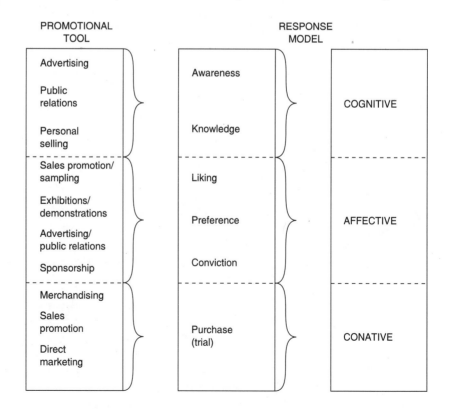

Once you have decided what type of supplier you are looking for or, indeed, what range of suppliers you might need, then you can begin the process of selection, appointment and management.

What follows is not an exhaustive 'how to' list, but rather a basic checklist for a client who is trying to choose an agency – of whatever type (the word 'agency' is not being used to refer exclusively to an advertising agency). There are two lists, one that deals with the process one might follow and one that looks at the criteria one might use when choosing.

The process of choosing an agency

- Decide what your needs will be: full service; specialist PR back-up etc.
- Decide the type of budget you will have: all with one supplier?
- Look at the output you like: which agency's name keeps cropping up?
- Which agencies do your competitors/admired rivals use: are they rumoured to be moving account?
- Which agencies produce work for those organizations, outside your own field, whose advertising has the spark you want for your own?
- Check with a trade publication for campaigns that use the type of communication tool you believe you will be using.
- If at this point you find you have seven or eight agencies to choose from, you could find out whether they have a show-reel of their work or a portfolio that they could send you, thus avoiding the need for them to send along a team to mount a full 'credentials' presentation.
- Build a list of about five agencies that appear to offer the range of services you need, handle the size of account where yours would fit well, and produce work you admire.
- Invite these agencies to give a 'credentials' presentation – this is the agency's chance to show you what it does for existing clients and gives you a chance to meet some of the agency personnel.
- Select two or three agencies that you are now happy with as your final selection.
- Brief these agencies so that they can mount a real 'pitch' for your account.
- During a pitch presentation, always look out for an agency that has met the criteria of your brief.
- Award the contract and tell the loser(s) of your decision.
- Agree any press announcements with the agency.

The criteria for choosing an agency

- Know what you want.
- Look for an agency that can offer the services you need.
- Be sure that the size of agency is right. If your account is small, try to get an agency where it will be mid-sized; small accounts can fall to the bottom of the priority list.
- Is the agency well located for you, your other offices, etc.? Although electronic communications mean that you do not need to be breathing down each other's necks, it makes sense to use an agency whose location makes it accessible to you, and good staff/suppliers accessible to it.

- Has the agency got the sort of track record with its past/existing clients that matches what you are looking for?
- What is the staff turnover at the agency like? High turnover of staff is not good.
- Is the chemistry between your team and their team good?

The Incorporated Society of British Advertisers can offer good advice when it comes to selecting an agency, and has produced a publication called *Choosing the Advertising Agency*, which can give further guidance, and which contains principles that can be applied to choosing any sort of marketing communications agency.

These days it is even possible to retain a consultant who will do all the initial searching and screening for you, but this can be costly. However, the marketer's own time costs money, so if time is tight and a consultant is being considered it is worth costing the true value of the time it will take the client to find a new agency, compared with the cost of having the initial stages contracted out.

Whatever process is worked through, it really is the client's responsibility to have a basic understanding of the services they will need and, similarly, a basic understanding of who does what at an agency, thus allowing any decision to be based on better knowledge. So let's take a look at today's full service advertising agency structure, so you can get to grips with who does what.

| **Figure 6.2** | *Full service agency structure today* |

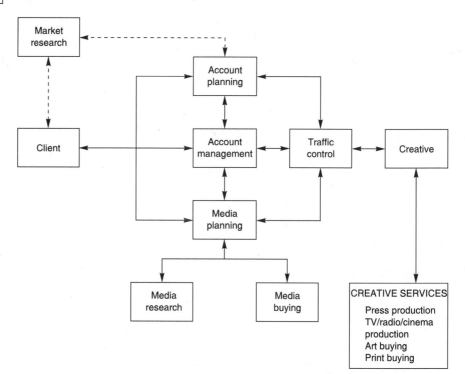

Advertising agencies: who does what?

The full service advertising agency has evolved over many years into what we see today. That is, because of the requirement of marketers to have access to a centre of excellence, full service agencies still exist and are growing in strength and corporate weight worldwide.

Account handling

Account handlers are the point of contact with the client, and the conduit through which all communication between the client and the agency flows. They are carriers of information from the client to the agency, translators of client language into agency language, internal co-ordinators of accounts within the agency, and the people responsible for presenting the agency's work back to the client. They need to be listeners, interpreters and co-ordinators. A team player, the account handler has a vital role in ensuring that the client gets what they want, because the agency has a true understanding of what is needed.

The different layers of account-handling responsibility will vary from agency to agency, with the titles bestowed upon the handler being dictated by both corporate culture and the needs of the client. For example, a marketing executive would quite happily deal with an account executive, whilst a marketing manager would probably prefer to deal with an account handler whose title also included the word 'manager'. Advertising agencies that have their cultural roots in the USA often carry the term 'Vice President' across the Atlantic and use it here in the UK.

Account planning

The account planner will often have a numerate background, or will at least be an expert interpreter of research and numerical data. This function comes very close to the client's own marketing planning, with many of the same market tracking surveys being on-line as within the client's own research department. The account planner will research, investigate and put forward proposals for action to the rest of the account team based upon market, audience, attitude, media and creative treatment research.

Media planning

Media planning is a vital function within an agency. The means of putting the message in front of the right person at the right time is key to the overall promotional and communication task. Within media departments there is usually a central research and planning function, with specialist planners and buyers being called upon as necessary. For example, whilst a generalist planner needs to take an overview of the campaign requirements, it makes sense to have specialist buyers who build firm relationships with either television or press media sales forces, for example, thus ensuring that the best buying deal is obtained for the client, with the planning requirements having been agreed at the outset.

A detailed knowledge of all above the line media must be complemented by free access to on-line media research data, allowing detailed planning to take place. Also, the account handler will ensure that the media planner has a full understanding of the range of other media being used by the client at the time of the campaign in question.

The creative effort

Within the creative department of a full service agency, there are those who are conceptually creative and there are those whose abilities are more practical.

The creative team

This term specifically refers to the art director and copywriter, who often work as a team for many years, if not for the whole of their careers. It is vitally important that there is a deep level of understanding within the team because they are the key players in the success, or otherwise, of a campaign. Often, teams that have worked together for years see their relationship as a sort of professional marriage, with each knowing the other so well that their thoughts often fly off in the same direction together at the same time.

Indeed, whilst one will be responsible for visual concepts and the other for the verbal message, it is the synergistic effect of the two elements together that makes a campaign work. The team that works well together will produce harmonious advertising almost automatically, and can attract clients to an agency because of its reputation for producing outstanding creative work.

Traffic managers

These people are responsible for ensuring that each stage of the creative process is fulfilled at exactly the right time to allow advertisements to be finally prepared and reach the media owner in the right format at the right time to appear as specified in the media schedule. Timetabling of an entire campaign is essential, and the traffic manager will liase not only with the creative and media departments but also with the account handler, ensuring the total internal co-ordination of the account.

Other services

Gone are the days when agencies could afford the overhead of their own television commercial production teams, or a stable of illustrators or photographers. The early 1990s saw the last of the in-agency film production units move off to become, at first, a profit centre within the agency and then a totally separate entity. Often, production departments devolved from agencies with a 'buy-out' of equipment from the agency by the original staff, who then set up as an independent production company. Many producers and directors still work on a totally freelance basis, being contracted in by independent production houses, who themselves work for agencies on a project-by-project basis.

Photographers, illustrators, composers and musicians tend to work as freelances, usually using an agent to represent their work to agencies.

Within an agency the art buyer, or in some cases the art director, is responsible for reviewing, say, photographers' portfolios on a regular basis, ensuring that the agency knows exactly how to get hold of the best food photographer, the best trick photographer or the best fashion photographer at very short notice. With specialist abilities being the order of the day, agencies need to call on those with the required skills on an infrequent basis – the freelance system works well in this environment.

Management issues

When all is said and done, an advertising agency works with a client company to plan, execute and monitor the effectiveness of an advertising campaign. Generally this means an advertising campaign that uses above the line media. However, most advertising agencies will have either specialist departments, devolved sister companies or links with other specialist providers of sales promotion, direct marketing and public relations functions at least, if not the full range of other miscellaneous below the line promotional services. As already mentioned, this is particularly the case in the business to business specialist advertising agency where the use of below the line tools is important and often uses more of the budget than above the line services.

Advertising agencies are in business to do business. If they are to survive and thrive they must provide the services their clients require. Thus, as clients' requirements change, the specific services offered and the way in which they are delivered will vary within the largest and the smallest agencies.

Buying 'à la carte'

As mentioned earlier, all the functions offered by a full service agency (account handling, account planning, media planning and buying, creative conceptual work and production facilities) can be bought direct by the client from independent companies or even freelance individuals. This is referred to as buying *à la carte*.

From the client's perspective the advantage of using a full service agency (of any type, because the full service versus *à la carte* buying of services applies equally to PR as to advertising) is that you have immediate access to a whole range of experts who are able to bring a fresh and un-jaundiced point of view to bear on your problems. However, it is a very expensive way of operating if you do not intend using all the services on offer – your fees are having to service the overhead, so you might as well use the facilities!

This has to be balanced with the huge amount of extra time that the client who chooses to buy each element of service individually must dedicate to the task. Sometimes it is easy to lose sight of the fact that the internal cost of staff who co-ordinate matters in-house is as real a cost to your company as the fees paid to an agency. The client should weigh up the objective pros and cons of using a full service agency as opposed to buying *à la carte*, as circumstances change and alter with time.

An understanding of basic approval procedures is also required. If you are the client you will want to know what is going on and whether it is meeting the brief you have agreed. How do you do this, without getting in the way? Quite simply you work with the agency before they begin to implement your programme to ensure they know when to seek your approval:

- it is usual for all creative concepts to need approval;
- finished artwork/animatics (for commercials) need approval;
- finished commercials need approval;
- media schedules need approval;
- literature proofs need approval;
- prototype gifts/samples/giveaways need approval;
- event plans need approval;
- exhibition-stand designs need approval;
- packaging and point-of-sale mock-ups need approval.

The best guideline is to approve the brief, approve the plan, approve the rough/mock/model/prototype and approve the finished item before it is shown/displayed/run/despatched.

It is the client's responsibility to make it quite clear that they require sight of any promotional item or method at each given stage. You might want to lay down rules that allow nothing to go beyond each stage without your signature on the artwork/contact report (a contact report acts like minutes taken at a meeting between client and agency).

Promotional output begins with the agency putting into action the promotional programme as agreed. However, another integral part of the whole promotional process that certainly has to be planned in from day one is the system of monitoring that will measure the effectiveness of what it is you are doing.

As the overall controller of a promotional programme it is your responsibility to ensure that each part of the promotional programme, each promotional tool, has in place its own monitoring system – a system that will monitor how effective that particular tool is being in achieving the objectives set for it. So, you need to measure the increase in sales levels in March if your on-pack promotion aimed to get proofs of purchasing being collected in March for redemption in April; you need to measure attitudes to your organization's environmental stance before you run your 'plant a tree' scheme, as well as after it, and so on. The method you need to use to measure effectiveness needs to be selected for and tailored to each promotional tool and each promotional objective.

Briefing

When it comes to briefing your full service agency there are essentially three types of brief that allow the information needed for a successful campaign to be passed around those who need it:

| **Figure 6.3** | *The overall briefing process* |

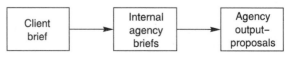

1 the client brief;
2 the media brief;
3 the creative brief.

The client brief

A poor brief from the client will waste the agency's time and can cost both the client and the agency money by leading, ultimately, to poor output with poor results. The damage can be long lasting and potentially disastrous for all concerned.

A brief is not a document that is merely handed over to an agency, it should be presented to the agency by the client in a briefing session that is designed to allow the agency to ensure that it has all the information it requires in order to meet the brief it has been given. Thus, it is worth stating that the briefing session demands preparation by both parties, so that the client is able to give the information required of them by the agency.

The agency representative, usually the account handler, will be looking to leave the briefing session with a document and appendices that give the agency all they need to know, as well as an impression from the client of the way they see the project working. That is not to say that agencies like clients to write the headlines and do the media selection even before the brief leaves their office! An account handler will try to stop the client doing these things, and should also resist the temptation to do them themselves, even if the client starts to press for a 'top of the head' response.

The brief is the start of the creative process.

Certainly, it should contain all the relevant information. At the end of the brief, the creative team should be clear to whom they're talking, why they're talking to them and what the advertising must say.

But it should also be a stimulus to creativity. A good brief will contain insights into the product category, the marketplace and the thoughts and feelings of the prospect. It will carry hints of likely directions; it will offer a promise that is easy to dramatize; and generate enthusiasm for the task.

A good brief is one that the creative team cannot wait to start work on; because they sense the opportunity to do great work.

If you master the art of good briefing, you will receive better creative work from your agency and earn the respect and loyalty of your creative colleagues. You will be the person whose jobs are consistently done well, on time and budget, because people enjoy working with you.

Ultimately, good briefing is one of the highest skills in agency management. This is not to belittle presentation skills or the ability to negotiate. But the quality of briefing has a direct effect on the quality of the creative work.

And the quality of your marketing communications determines your company's reputation and prospects. So let's look at this process from the 'inside'. We need to get an understanding from three different perspectives:

1 What the agency is looking for.
2 Using an agency briefing form.
3 Briefing an agency team.

What the agency is looking for – the account handler's viewpoint

So there you are, briefing the agency on a campaign. Sometimes they're terrific written briefs covering the whole marketing background. Sometimes they're not so terrific written briefs, as they cover the whole marketing background but completely miss the key points that the agency need to know.

There is one golden rule when writing a brief. Always imagine that you have to actually create the response. Imagine that at the end of the meeting, you have to go back to your agency, shut yourself in the office and produce a great campaign. You. Not the agency, not the creative team. And if you can't do it, well . . . That way you know what information to put in.

When taking a client brief, there are two things you, as the account handler, have to do:

1 collect the basic background information;
2 begin to develop the promise.

1 Background information

This sounds easy, but isn't always so. You often have to dig out the information. It may help to structure your notes around a checklist called POMMMM.

Product	What *exactly* are we selling?
Objective	Why are we advertising?
Market	Who are we talking to?
Media	How will we reach them?
Message	What must we say?
Measurement	How will we know it's worked?

If you've covered these fully, you've got the background. Give the agency everything you can lay your hands on!

- a copy of the brief;
- brochures/literature;
- let them take the product back with them;
- research? Who did it? Where is it?

Don't pretend you know all the answers if the agency wants to dig a little deeper.

- Who can tell them?
- Can they meet the technical people?
- Go out with a salesman?
- Visit a distributor?
- Is there really no research?
- Can they have sight of the marketing plan (is it confidential? can they sign a secrecy agreement?)?

All the time, think how you would feel if you had to sit down and write the ad.

- You would like the product to play with;
- you would like the literature to read;
- you would like some good, relevant background reading;
- you would like a good, clear thought-out brief.

2 Developing the promise

Digging out the background information is only part of the job of developing an agency brief.

A good briefer is schizophrenic. Your brain has to be divided into two compartments – both working flat out. One compartment is digging out basic facts, the other compartment is looking for clues that will help the agency.

When delivering a brief, you can literally divide your piece of paper in half, labelling the two halves: *facts* and *clues*.

In the *facts* half, you can note down any background information. In the *clues* half, scribble down the little points that come up that you feel may help to develop the promise and create the ad.

The trick here is to talk to the agency; anecdotes lead to great ads. Get excited. Ramble on a bit about the product, market, competition, big contracts, funny stories – anything.

And spot the *clues*.

'Well, we lose out on price. But if you take all the costs into account, we're cheaper'.

'In the end, they're all terrified of choosing the wrong one'.

'The bloody brokers take the easy way out. They just sell the product they understand'.

Sometimes a client throws out a clue that goes further than helping to develop the promise; they come up with an idea for the advertisement as well. For example, David Ogilvy was taking a brief from Rolls Royce, and was told that the car was so quiet, the noisiest thing about it was the damned clock! He went on to create a famous advertisement that used this fact to sell the car's uniquely quiet running!

It's not always easy to collect facts and pick up clues simultaneously. But always remember: you have to write the ad.

It does wonders for sharpening the brain.

Using an agency briefing form

An agency may or may not have a very detailed briefing form.

The briefing form should provide a way for you to order your thoughts, and present your arguments. It should be treated as an aid to analysis and communication, not as a kind of tedious examination form.

Often an agency will suggest that their client uses it as a 'blank' to complete prior to briefing. Here is an example of what such a document might contain as prompts/information for a client.

Product/service

1 What is your company selling?
2 What is the market buying?

There are two important questions here. The first, 'what is your company selling?', asks for a factual description of the product. For example, Bosch is selling a drill. The second asks for a judgement. In the case of Bosch, the market is buying a hole. To give another example, Redland is selling Rosemary clay tiles but the architect is buying a building material with warmth and character.

1 To help the creative team understand 'what we are selling', find relevant information: brochures, photographs, press releases, pages from the web site. If possible, bring the product itself into the meeting.
2 To help the team understand 'what the market is buying', look for relevant magazine articles and research.

Role of advertising

Why are we advertising?
There are many roles that advertising can fulfil. Some examples are :

- to reinforce existing behaviour;
- to overcome prejudice;
- to generate response;
- to get the brand on the candidate list;
- to boost company morale;
- to change perceptions;
- to improve distribution;
- to increase brand or company awareness.

You should be clear what the advertising is expected to achieve today, and in the long term.

What do we want people to do?
Send off the coupon? Circle the reader enquiry number? Call a Hotline? Fax their business card? Look up the web site? Ask for our brand at their distributor? Specify our brand by name? Not veto our brand when someone else suggests it?
You should be precise. How many coupons will count as success? What is the perception now, and what change is sought?

How will we know it has worked?
Wherever possible, you should ensure that a system of measurement is in place before the campaign breaks. Without this, you will not know if the campaign has worked. Accurate data is the only good foundation for subsequent campaigns.

Target audience

Demographics, attitudes, function.

1 This heading recognizes that business advertisements aren't read by job titles but by people.

For example : Security Manager, C2, aged 40 to 55 years old. Ex-policeman, passed over for promotion. Spends most of his shift reading, mainly spy novels and thrillers. Bored with his job. Feels that company security could be better, but people only want his opinion when things go wrong.

Suddenly, we're talking to an individual. If the agency has a clear picture of the lifestyle and attitudes of the prospect, they can address him in his own language.

2 Business to business markets are complex. The person who specifies the product will probably not be the person who buys it. There may well be other 'influencers', including the end user.
   For example, in the case of a fork lift truck:

Truck Driver	identifies the brand
Works Manager	selects the brand
Purchasing Manager	negotiates the price
Managing Director	signs the cheque (and vetoes if he hasn't heard of the brand)

Make sure that the agency understands who's involved and how they interact. (For example, should the advertising give the Truck Driver some arguments he can take to his Works Manager?)

Competitive frame

Who are the direct competitors – how are they positioned ?
   Don't just list competitive companies. This will mean nothing to the agency. Instead, paint a picture of the market. Who are the 'best' companies? (i.e., the ones you most admire). Who are the 'worst'? What makes them best and worst? Where does your own brand stand on this spectrum?

What is the prospect currently thinking/using?

1 All advertising is about changing perceptions. To do this, we must know the starting point. Does the prospect know that this type of product/ service exists? Is he satisfied or dissatisfied with what he's using at the moment? Does he have a negative view of our brand ('too pricey', 'too old-fashioned', 'too complicated', etc.). Challenging preconceptions can lead to great creative ideas.
2 Bring along samples of previous advertising, and competitor advertising. If we know what ads in this market usually look like, we can create an unusual one.
3 Make sure you consider all the competition, including indirect competi- tion. (For example, the 'competition' to automatic mailing equipment is a room full of company employees folding paper and licking envelopes.) Does the prospect have to compromise or improvise without our product or service? This can be a rich source of creative ideas.
4 Look in the trade magazines for 'burning issues', especially the editorial and the letters page. Is there a market trend we should know about? Or some impending legislation? Is there a preoccupation with cutting costs or raising quality? Maybe we can integrate this into our argument.

Single-minded proposition

This should be the single most compelling thing we can say about the brand. You should evaluate different propositions and aim for a killer.

A killer proposition is both *motivating* (it gives a powerful reason to purchase our product/service) and *differentiating* (it sets our product apart from others).

Imagine you are face to face with the prospect. What is the one thing you could say to him to make him want to know more?

Could he save his company time or money? Is there an urgent problem he can now solve? Or an opportunity he's missing? Is there some good news he hasn't heard yet? Or a danger he should know about?

The important thing is to concentrate on product benefits, not product features. As the saying goes: 'people do not buy $\frac{1}{4}$" drills because they want $\frac{1}{4}$" drills, but because they want $\frac{1}{4}$" holes'.

Why should they believe it?

We must be able to substantiate the promise, otherwise we will produce work that is glib and unconvincing. To quote David Ogilvy (for the last time) 'we tell the truth but we make the truth exciting'.

Other significant benefits/factors

Including practical considerations, mandatory inclusions.

Here you should list other important benefits that will help to form the body copy. You should also mention mandatory inclusions (standard disclaimers, Queens Award logos, exhibition stand flashes) that cause so much grief when they're mentioned *after* the ad has been created.

Tone and mood

What are the values of the brand ?

Every company has a unique personality. For example, Diversey Lever is bringing a new vision to cleaning and hygiene systems. Instead of merely pushing products, they offer total cleaning solutions, via a talented workforce.

The agency needs to understand your company's distinctive tone of voice. Is it relaxed and humorous? Challenging and aggressive? Caring and compassionate? Lyrical and romantic? And so on.

How to brief the agency team – as an account handler

Understanding the internal point of view from the agency's perspective is important to the manager of marcomms work – the more you understand the issues that will be faced by your suppliers the better a manager of that service provider you can be. So let's take a look at the viewpoint of the account handler within an advertising agency – what do they have to bear in mind to do the best job they can for you, the client, within their own organization? And how can you help them to do the best job they can on your behalf?

The account handler is the conduit between the client and the agency, and has to get the agency team to perform to the best of their ability – here are some notes that would be valuable to an account handler or, indeed, to anyone directly briefing creative and media teams!

By now the account handler should have collected all the *facts* and *clues*. Let's talk directly *to* the account handler in question . . . you've compiled a brief that's informative, imaginative and stimulating. Now, don't throw it all away!

Never, ever, apologize for a brief. Never say 'I'm sorry, we've got to do a quick ad for so and so'. The chances are you'll get poor creative work, and you'll deserve it.

Here are a few pointers:

1 Make the brief special. Fix a special meeting. Don't just turn up with an armful of papers and say 'if you've got a minute, can I brief you on this?'. If you squeeze briefs in as 'A.O.B.' and don't take the job seriously, neither will the agency. There's no rule that says you can't brief in the morning over a bacon sandwich or in the evening over a beer!

2 Show the agency that you're enthusiastic about the product. Bring the product/service and its application to life. Tell stories, paint pictures. Use your presentation skills to bring a bit of theatre to the brief. Remember, it's part of the creative process.

3 Have lots of relevant information: videos, magazine articles, competitive ads and literature, copies of the candidate media. Agencies can never have too much *relevant* information.

4 Brief problems not solutions. You should never ask the agency for a specific type of execution: a testimonial, an editorial style ad, a product demonstration. It sounds reasonable but it leads to mediocrity. It's better to concentrate on the problem that advertising must solve. If you can find 'originality' in the problem, you'll help the agency to find an original solution.

5 Insist the agency make a recommendation. The agency should give you what is, in their judgement, the best possible solution. They should believe one of their ideas to be better than the others (should they not?), and in that case why would they ever show you (or want you to see) their second-best. Of course, you may want to know why other solutions were rejected, but insist on one recommendation.

6 Show that you appreciate the creative product and the agency's role. Don't show the agency your secretary's idea for the ad.

7 Radiate confidence in your team. Confidence breeds enthusiasm and it takes enthusiastic people to produce great creative work.

8 Open up the briefing process. You may have technicians, product managers and sales people who are in love with the product. Their enthusiasm is contagious. Organize an agency visit to some satisfied customers. It's amazing what agencies can do when they really believe in a product. Conversely, it's hard to create great advertising when your heart isn't in it, or you can't understand why anybody would want the product.

| **Figure 6.4** | *The briefing process in more detail* |

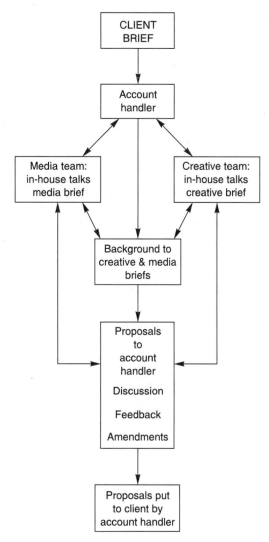

9 Give the agency team time to digest information, evaluate different solutions, and consider implementation. Terry Lovelock was given 10 weeks to write the Heineken slogan 'Refreshes the parts other beers cannot reach'. Give your team at least 10 working days. You wouldn't put a new product on the market overnight.

and finally . . .

10 Don't be stingy with praise. If you think an idea is elegant, ingenious or witty, say so. You won't appear uncool. Every agency has a portfolio of favourite ads that never ran. They get used to taking knocks, the way that professional footballers do. So it's nice to get some praise instead. Praise is very motivating.

The overall briefing process is summarised in Figure 6.4.

Briefing for non-advertising agency needs

Everything that is mentioned as being necessary for briefing an advertising agency applies equally well to briefing all other types of marcomms service providers – but with some specific amendments according to specific needs.

If you're dealing with a PR agency you might find that the person who is the account handler is also the person who will actually write the articles and news releases, talk with journalists and even organize conferences, etc., for you – so you are actually briefing the person who needs all the information, directly, rather than dealing with a 'go-between'. This means that it is easier to discuss the heart of the matter, but it doesn't mean that any less effort should go in to the brief preparation or the briefing process itself.

Management issues for service providers

You will find that the trade associations for each of the disciplines (the ISP for sales promotion, ISBA for advertising, etc.) will be able to offer guidance on the content of contracts that should be set in place when you appoint an agency of any sort. Both parties will benefit from a contract being in place, as this will form the basis of the expectations each party will have of the other as they work together.

Contractual agreements

Some organizations have standard Terms and Conditions for appointing suppliers, but often these are not adequate for the requirements of the marcomms manager. If they have to be used, then they should be used as a basis for the contract. Some other items that should be considered as additions (in a covering letter, which allows them to become a part of the contract) are given below.

Contact report procedure

It is normal for the service provider to supply reports of *all* contacts between the supplier and the client (including telephone calls, but excepting any written communication – rules vary about whether the receipt of an e-mail should elicit a contact report response and it is difficult to generalize: if an e-mail is sent then it could count as a written communication and therefore not require a contact report response, it becoming a part of the contractual relationship itself, but it would be best to take the advice of your own legal department on this issue).

These contact reports should be generated, often transmitted electronically these days, within 24 hours of the occurrence of the contact, and should state clearly and succinctly the content of the contact. It would be normal for the client to have a further 24 hours to query the content of any such report, but if they do not, then the report becomes a part of the contractual agreement.

An example of how this works in favour of *both* parties would be if a telephone conversation takes place between the client and supplier, and the client tells the supplier to go ahead and spend £20 000 on a particular item. The supplier sends a contact report saying that the client has approved

£30 000 worth of expenditure (maybe a simple typing error). The client has 24 hours to get back to the supplier and change the figure to the lower amount or else the supplier can go ahead and spend the higher figure. It just all makes sure that everybody knows what is going on at all times – after all, most marketing communications implementation takes place with tight deadlines and mistakes are easily made – this process is there to try to prevent mis-communication or mis-understanding from becoming a huge problem.

Account team personnel issues

If the client has appointed a supplier on the basis of a particular account team and their presentation of their efforts, the last thing they want to happen is for the people they thought they would be working with to disappear to work on other pitches or other accounts! That said, there are rules about not placing restrictive contracts on people and not allowing them to go about their business in a reasonable manner, so you have to be very careful about wordings here. Your main aim is to make sure that the supplier knows who you want to work on your account, by name and in what capacity, that if one or more of those people leave the agency or need to be reassigned, that you, the client, will be informed and will be able to have some say in selecting the replacement, or at least being able to have a 'trial period' for anyone new who is assigned to your account.

Marketing communications is often referred to as a 'people business', and it is true that the personal relationships involved are very important when it comes to building the most successful campaigns possible. This item addresses this issue.

Review periods and content

One of the best ways to manage the relationship is to keep reviewing progress: this should be done even when there is no output on the account. But, again to benefit both parties, the nature and timing of such reviews should be made clear: not only does the supplier need to know how much time and effort they will have to put into the review preparation and presentation procedure, but the client needs to make clear why they need to review what they want to review, when they want to review it.

Day-to-day management

If relationships are important in business it is because communication is important. And communicating within the client–agency relationship is vitally important because if either party does not understand the other then a great deal of money can be wasted on work that does not achieve the desired effect.

If a client has several agencies to deal with it is likely that the workload with each might ebb and flow, but that occasionally there will be a massive workload with many suppliers at once. This can mean that the client ends up repeating various tasks across suppliers. So why not brief suppliers together? No reason really, and many clients will do this. The other advantage that this has is that it allows all the suppliers to see how their work fits together.

Day-to-day working relationships are likely to ebb and flow with workload: and the agency has a responsibility to proactively try to develop the relationship too, so the responsibility lying with the client is mainly responsive and professional.

However often communication takes place, and whether it is professional or social, building understanding of needs, wants and desires will always lead to better work – the better the client is understood, the better the supplier can supply! So the golden rule is to keep communication clear and all should be well.

Regional and international factors

Throughout this text the main emphasis is on UK national marketing communications campaigns. Of course, not all campaigns are like this – some are local, some regional, some national, some international.

When you are setting promotional objectives you must, of course, define the geographical area within which those objectives are to be achieved. This will guide you in your selection of promotional tools.

When it comes to the international factor, it will again be fairly straightforward, when looking at your objectives, that you are supporting your products in, for example, the USA and the Far East, or you are not. Having established within your objectives where you need to support what product/brand, it is then the responsibility of the person managing the promotional programme to deal with that country/those countries on exactly the same basis as the UK, i.e., decide objectives, budgets, timescales, seek and appoint the appropriate agencies and establish planning and

---

How central control works to ensure that international promotional programmes have local relevance

Figure 6.5

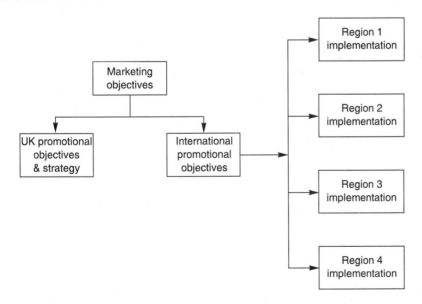

implementation guidelines for each programme. The way in which international promotional programmes are handled is no different to the way described in this text when talking about the UK. What will be different will be the specific nature of the balance of the promotional mix selected and how each tool can and should be used within the country in question (see Fig. 6.5).

Generally speaking, most large UK-based agencies of all types either have branches, sister companies or affiliated agencies in most countries worldwide. Even small agencies usually belong to international groupings of agencies nowadays. That means that there is no excuse for not using the indigenous population for all your promotional planning and execution. This is especially important when it comes to the creative treatment for your promotion. Beware of mere translation – it might seem like a logical solution to a pan-European campaign for example, but literal translation is a very dangerous tool. So much promotional communication depends on nuance and interpretation that it is worth considering getting creative work totally originated in each country for each country. If this is not possible, say, because of budgetary constraints, or not desirable because you do want a truly pan-European campaign, then carrying out pre-campaign research in each country will at least establish if the population there is receiving the messages you believe you are sending!

Controls affecting your communication output

Whether you are communicating just within the UK, or globally, what you can do and how you can say it will be constrained in one of two ways – either by law or by some sort of code of conduct.

Of course laws will differ from country to country, as will codes of conduct, or guidance, so it is a good idea to get advice in each country on what is allowable, as well as what is desirable. But since it will always be the client organization whose name will be connected to any problems that might arise, it isn't enough to tell your agencies that they have to abide by the rules – the client must check that the requirement to do so is in the contract, that they constantly ask the questions that get the right answers and that the agency is making them aware of when they might be 'sailing close to the wind'!

The UK has seen a spate of advertisements that have courted controversy with the specific aim of generating press coverage, thereby leveraging a relatively small advertising budget to create a lot of 'media noise'. For certain brands it could be argued that this has worked well, FCUK being a case in point, where controversy is very much a part of the brand proposition and sits well with the target market. The Benetton organization adopts a similar strategy, using its advertising to raise issues it feels should be discussed within society. Some say that this stance has created a unique presence for the brand, others raise the point that it can turn as many people off the brand as it turns on – maybe not too popular if you run a store trying to sell broad appeal youth clothing!

Laws and controls can change overnight, so a printed book is not the best place to reproduce such information. But at least a marcomms manager should know when to stop and ask the question, even if they don't know the answer, and they should also have some idea about where to look for that answer. With this in mind:

1 Check everything with your legal department, if you have one.
2 Know where to check the law and codes: generally each trade association for each communications discipline (e.g., ISP, IPR, PRCA, DMA) will be able to give advice and guidance on not only which laws apply but also what the self-regulatory codes of conduct say too!

An example of such back up would be the website offered by the Advertising Standards Authority at http://www.asa.org.uk.

Generally speaking, advertisements must be legal, decent, honest and truthful, as should all marketing communications tools. Specific laws and codes might change, but the rule of thumb must always be to be open and honest with those you seek to communicate with, or influence.

Summary of Chapter 6

Within this chapter we have covered the following:

The issues concerned with managing and implementing marcomms programmes, using internal and external resources.

1 The right resources – internally

This section shows how to assess what you have already against what you will need.

2 The right resources – externally

This section looks at how to assess what external resources you will need, how to find them, how to brief them, how to assess their pitches, how to appoint them and how to manage them. It contains comprehensive checklists and contact points as well as practically useful sections, such as 'What should be in a brief?'.

This section can be used when dealing with any type of marketing communications service provider, not just advertising agencies.

Self-test questions and opinion development

These are not exam questions, nor are they meant to represent the sort of question you might expect to face anywhere else. They are designed to help you check whether you have understood the content of this chapter. All you have to do is read the questions, give them some thought and maybe jot down some notes on what your response might be. Not all the questions will have factual answers – rather, they might encourage you to think about a topic or an issue and formulate an opinion based upon what is now, hopefully, a better understanding of the topic.

- How many people work in marcomms for your organization (or one of a friend/relative)? What do they do? How are they structured? Who do they report to? What does this tell you about the way that this organization views marcomms?
- How many agencies does your organization/one of your choice use?
- What do they all do?
- Do they do it well?
- How could they do it better?
- If you were to work in an agency – what job would you like and why?
- If you were to work on the client side, what job would you like and why?
- Why do you think agencies (of all types) are now positioning themselves as 'integrated marketing communications agencies'?
- If you were to set up an agency, what would it offer, to whom and why?
- Why do briefs matter?

Extending knowledge and understanding

You are encouraged to undertake the following activities to further your knowledge and understanding of the topics covered in this chapter in the following ways:

1 Visit some websites for the following types of agencies and find out what they offer and how – what does this tell you about them and how they see themselves:

- advertising agency;
- PR agency;
- sales promotion agency;
- direct marketing agency;
- media agency;
- website agency;
- integrated marcomms;
- business to business agency.

2 You are an account handler at an agency that has just lost a pitch for a piece of new business. You have a chance to ask the client who has turned you down five questions that will help you plan better for the future – what would your five questions be and why?

3 If you were to set up a small, business to business marketing communications agency, what business issues would you have to deal with? How would you operate? Where would you set up? Who would you hire? How would you market yourself (not *sell* yourself, but *market* yourself)?

Building the relationship over time

7

By the end of this chapter you should:

► be clear about the importance of retaining customers;
► understand the balance between attracting, retaining and increasing the business you get from customers;
► have a detailed understanding of the role of customer relationship management (CRM) in each of the stages of the 'ladder of loyalty';
► be clear about the issues affecting CRM for both long and short repeat purchase cycle products and services;
► understand the role of technology in CRM.

Learning objectives

Much of what has been said so far implies 'getting in touch with' a target audience or public. We have considered planning, what tools are available, even which tools are good at which jobs. What we now need to consider is how to *build* a relationship with a customer, getting them to ascend the ladder of loyalty and thereby gaining maximum lifetime value from them.

This might be a short chapter – but it's an important one!

Getting them in the first place

A great deal of marcomms effort and money is spent trying to get potential customers to try a product or service for the first time and, increasingly, we are seeing more time and money being spent on keeping the customers who have been gained, in making them not only advocates but also truly valuable aides to marketing to their peers!

Let's get this into perspective – the ladder of loyalty shows us how true lifetime value can be gleaned from customers.

The usual suspects

There have to be a very large number of 'suspects', in order to end up with a significant number of customers, clients and advocates. So the 'casting of

| **Figure 7.1** | *The ladder of loyalty* |

the net' for suspects will tend to be pretty wide, with suspects usually defined in general target groupings, such as:

> Males, B, C1, 55+, living in the North of England or Scotland, with traditional tastes, a down-to-earth approach to life and a preference to spend money carefully, seeking value for money in a beer, not seeking kudos.

Though this profile speaks of lifestyle as well as demographics, it is still very general in terms of targeting. It will be adequate for above the line media planning, it will even allow for regional upweighting and below the line communications planning. But all that this level of promotional effort will achieve is something of a hand-raising, or testing of the products effect, if you were, for argument's sake, launching a new beer.

Mass communication is generally used to get suspects to nominate themselves as 'prospects' – to put themselves into a grouping that says 'I am interested' rather than 'I might have been interested, but in fact I am not'.

Suspects are grouped in different ranges, from primary to secondary to tertiary – in other words, from hotter, to warmer, to cooler! With suspect groups being so broad-ranging and generalized it is unlikely that all members will have an equal propensity to be interested, thus we need the differentiation within this overall group.

The role of targeting

Because it can be expensive to contact suspects, there is a refining process that can be undertaken to narrow down the targeting: a good and sensible place to begin is by building an understanding of your existing customer base, finding out what these people, or, indeed, companies, have in common, and trying to find more people or companies, like them. This might sound like common sense but it is, in fact, what underlies a great deal of target market planning!

Once you know the type of person you are looking for, then you can decide on the best tool available to reach them. It might be that there are only another 60 organizations in the whole world with whom you are seeking to do business, in which case, the use of a very direct form of contact, such as a telephone call, letter, brochure, invitation to an event, etc., would be suitable. With business to business marketing and selling it is often the case that a sales force will be involved, and this very personal method of representing your organization's offering can be effective.

But in business to consumer marketing and selling, it is rarely possible for every suspect to receive a sales call from a sales person – however much the organization might like to do this!

The role of branding

That is when mass communication methods have to be assessed. Yes, it is true that there might be a mailing list for your primary suspects in existence somewhere – you might even be able to afford to use it! – but a direct mail item is rarely enough to turn a suspect into a prospect all on its own – indeed, many suspects will only respond positively to a brand name with which they are very familiar, even if they have never tried the product or service, nor know someone who has.

That is why so much time, effort and money is spent building brands that have a personality that will communicate the values and proposition of the brand to a mass audience very rapidly. Of course, this is an expensive exercise, with millions of pounds, dollars, yen and lire being spent every year trying to build associations between a brand name and logo and a specific positioning strategy.

The strength of this perceived relationship between a Suspect and a brand name has enormous value. Indeed, so great is the potential held within brand building that the international accountancy fraternity has now accepted a number of Brand Valuation Models into its accepted methods of valuing a company, or part of a company's assets, when it is selling to a buyer who wants a valuation based on more than manufacturing equipment owned and stock held!

The true value of a brand is, of course, its potential, and this is the problem – no matter how well a brand *has* performed in the past, how it will perform in the future is a matter that will be controlled by its future management.

The Levi brand has had an illustrious career globally – becoming at once the symbol for teenage rebellion and mass work clothing, but the late 1990s saw it in crisis as poor management led to the closure of several production plants. Poor management of a brand can bring it to its knees very rapidly – for example, whilst Levi was performing well in the denim market, what the managers forgot was that it was in the clothing market – and khaki, chinos and even leather all took their toll on the youth rebellion position it held, whilst cheaper alternatives produced in countries where production costs were dramatically lower than Levi's appeared in the work clothing market. With pressure from all sides, the brand could not sustain its previous broad appeal, and so has had to retrench and reassess its position globally.

However difficult it might be to position, build and manage a brand, it is still an important factor in bringing suspects towards a prospect position: it does this by allowing suspects to form opinions about whether the personality and offering of the brand will fit with their needs, wants and desires, by allowing them to at least begin to decide whether they want to put themselves forward as a prospect.

Prospecting for gold

A prospect is not a customer – a prospect is still a potential customer, someone who *might* become a customer, who has, maybe, something in common with many of your existing customers, but who has yet to buy from you.

Sometimes a prospect needs to be able to try the product or service you are offering free of risk (which usually means free of charge!). As such, you might have prospects who have no experience of your offering and prospects who have some experience of your offering – it is likely that those with experience (and the marketer would be responsible for ensuring that it was a good experience) would be seen as 'hotter' prospects than those with none.

It might seem odd to think of prospecting as part of customer relationship management, but it is. If you deal fairly and well with prospects you are increasing your chance of them becoming customers. You will also have set the tone of the relationship that your newly acquired customer will expect from you – so be careful to ensure that the promises you make to convert prospects to customers are promises that you can, and do, keep to your customers.

It might even be that your best prospects are *lapsed* customers. BT has an ongoing campaign aiming to convince those who have moved to their competitors to 'Come Back' – offering free reconnection as an incentive. Whilst this is indeed an excellent incentive to those who wanted to try the competitive offering, but who now might be swayed to return, those who never went away in the first place, those who have remained loyal customers, can feel somewhat aggrieved that they won't get free connection if they want an extra line, but that those who have not been supporting BT all this time now get a service for free for which they themselves have to pay! So you do have to be careful that you do not set up a system of seeming partiality.

So, there are various types of prospect:

- lapsed customers who have had bad experiences of your offering and are very unlikely to return, but might if you can convince them that you have changed;
- lapsed customers who had no bad experiences of your offerings, but who wanted to try an alternative – they might return if you remind them that they enjoyed dealing with you, and if you give them an added incentive to return, as well as trying to tie them into some sort of loyalty scheme (maybe building points, so they don't go off for a better quick deal to one of your competitors);
- those who never have been a customer, but who have had some sort of free (or risk-reduced) trial of your offering, which was (hopefully) a satisfactory experience, and who now need to be converted from 'trier to user';
- those who have never been a customer, have knowledge of your offering and feel positive about it, so might be prepared to try it at a low risk or risk-free level;
- those who have never been a customer, have no knowledge of your offering so need to be made aware of it, hopefully in a positive way;

● those who have never been a customer, know of your offering through third parties who have had bad experiences – so will need a lot of convincing to try it even for free!

Obviously, each category of prospect poses a different challenge for the marketer, and for the marcomms manager, with different objectives and tools being set and used. Offers and incentives should be tailored to best meet the needs of the target group, and the method of communication should be chosen to get the right message through to the right number of the right people at the right time. This is a very important factor in terms of marcomms planning: get too many people asking for a free test drive at the same time and you end up with a large number of disappointed people who had raised their hands to move from suspect to prospect – and that's not good!

Aiming to score a conversion

Once you have found and categorized your prospects, you can decide what it is that is most likely to convert them to customers. Is it the promise of a three-year warranty, or free petrol for 3000 miles, or a weekend for two in Paris or a money-off voucher for their next holiday? Is it 10 per cent off their next purchase, or this one? Is it that chance to save for money off something of their choice?

What is it, other than your offering alone, that will get them to buy, buy now, and then buy again? Is it a lower price, or easy payments? As you can see, sales promotions can be seen at the fore in this area! But promotional offers alone cannot do the job of converting a prospect to a customer – there has to be a reason for the customer to want to be a customer, other than the specific offer itself, or else they will move to one of your competitors as soon as your competitors offer a better promotion.

If you sell large items, such as cars, holidays or, say, manufacturing equipment, you might have to deal with a very long repeat purchase cycle, so getting a customer turns into keeping a customer very rapidly, when it is impossible to sell them lots of little repeat purchases over time, as someone marketing fmcg's could, for example.

Long repeat purchase cycle CRM

Thus, CRM for long repeat purchase cycle products and services differs significantly from that which works best for short repeat purchase: long repeat purchase cycles would be anything longer than, say, a month.

The forms of tool used in long repeat purchase cycle vary from simple letters, direct to the customer (often delivered by permission e-mail these days) to very special offers on related goods and services that come about from being an honoured member of an owners'/users'/customers' club.

The aim with this type of programme is to treat the customer as though they are a prospect for the next purchase, but to keep emphasizing all the advantages of being an existing customer – making them understand what they would lose if they were to choose another supplier next time they buy.

The Internet offers lots of opportunities to keep in touch with valued customers, but only if that is the way they choose to be kept in touch with, for car companies it is often the tactile, involving medium of a glossy motoring magazine that they choose as their customer relationship vehicle. Basically you need to choose the type of communication method that works for the target audience, in this case your customers, and then make sure that the content is relevant and interesting and the appeal is high. Otherwise, why would they miss it if it stops – or, worse still, they might be glad when it does because the communication is too frequent or too irrelevant!

It is tempting to think that frequent communication with customers is the best way to keep them 'warm', but, in fact, the best way to keep a customer satisfied is to deliver what your product or service promised in the first place (so, no matter how good your customer retention programme, you will lose customers if your offering fails to deliver!) and keep in touch with them at a frequency that is right for them with information, entertainment and rewards for their custom in the right balance.

Getting the right balance is something that not even the most experienced marketer can guess at – it is vital to carry out research, and to go right back to basics and *ask the customers!*

Indeed, one of the most vital elements of any successful CRM programme is the ways in which the customer has the opportunity to talk back to the marketer – and to know that they have been heard! In other words, it is not enough to allow for feedback and comment loops – the whole communication programme has to be designed to work in both directions. By allowing you to talk to your customers, by allowing them to talk to you, and by telling them you have heard them and by showing them that what they say matters to you by telling them when their comments have been acted upon, *then* you will begin to build the most successful CRM programme you can.

Lakeland Plastics is a mail order, and store based, retailer of kitchen and homeware equipment and supplies. It's sales catalogue is engagingly written, contains good, clear photography of the products for sale, and also contains quotes from satisfied customers, sometimes telling of the unusual ways in which they use certain pieces of equipment – often giving prospects an additional incentive to purchase a certain item! They also carry requests from customers to help them find replacements for old items they might have had from their grandmother's kitchen – so Lakeland often introduce a modern version of the item to their range. When items arrive at the customer's home each parcel contains a hand-signed note from the packer who put the package together, and the company's returns process is very simple.

Little touches often mean the most to customers: the telephone call a month after you buy a used car to check that all is well; the birthday card from your insurance company; money-off vouchers for dry cleaning a week after the wedding date; information on how to help toddlers learn best when baby is a year old! They all say 'we care' to customers. Some use technology to keep track of complex data that makes sending birthday cards to thousands of people on the right day each year seem simple, whilst some small organizations just keep a simple card file index! The *way* you do it isn't what the customer is interested in – it's that you bother!

fmcg CRM

And what about the fmcg customer – the person whose name and address you might not have because you don't deliver to their door – they simply pick up your product from the supermarket shelf?

Well, increasingly it is possible to use the shopping profiles generated by supermarket's retailer cards to gain a better understanding not only of your customers' profile, but also to know what else they buy when they pick up your products – thus allowing you to learn much more about how cross-brand promotions might work for you, or when to contact customers to best remind them how much they enjoy *your* brand just before they go shopping – every week, or month!

So, not only is it now possible to *get* the name and address of someone who might be a regular purchaser of your brand of tea, biscuits or toilet tissue, but also to get that information about those who are *not* your customers, so you can approach them with an offer that might capture them for yourself!

That said, you can also use club membership schemes to build databases, run promotions that require at least one proof of purchase so that you capture addresses that way or you can buy lists of shoppers on a broader scale for associated products (shampoo for conditioner; moisturiser for hand cream, etc.). Thus, you can build a relationship with your own customers either through your own brand's relationship with them and the opportunities you have with your own product or service for getting them to give you information about themselves that allows you to contact them with more, relevant data at a later stage, or via other customer database lists.

Servicing the client – right every time!

If the customer is always right, then the client is the person, or company, who is right time after time after time! The key difference between a customer and a client being that the repeat purchase relationship is established with a client. That might mean that they have bought three cars from your company, though from different dealers, over the last eleven years, or that they have been using your brand of washing powder for most of their adult life!

Whatever the specifics, these are loyal customers, their business has been valuable to you for some time, and you want it to continue to be that way. You need to nurture these clients, seek their opinion and input into your product and service development processes, ask them *why* they are loyal, learn from this and try to benefit from what you learn by applying the lessons to other, 'not yet a client' groups of customers.

They are likely to feel they have a close and binding relationship with your brand, your offering. They are the purchasers you are least likely to lose to a competitor, but it is dangerous to become complacent about their love for you! Many clients can feel as though they are being taken for granted, whilst attention is lavished on prospects and new customers – it is very important to build a special part of your CRM to deal with these, your VIPs!

People who have shopped at a store for 50 years are appalled when change is proposed. Those who have been loyal to a supermarket for a few months will feel they should be rewarded for this display of fortitude – given that there is so much competition for their attention!

Estimates vary about how much more it costs to get a new customer than to keep an existing one – and of course this will depend on how much it costs to get one in the first place – but one thing is certain, it *does* cost more! So making the most of what you have is important.

You might simply want to repeat-sell, you might want to up-sell, you might want to take the client onto the next level: that of advocate. Whatever the objective, you must treat the client in a different manner than the customer or they will gradually lose the incentive to stay.

Speaking up on behalf of advocates

When a customer believes in you enough to keep on buying from you, when they feel valued as a special client, they will want to pass on that warm glow to others – and you can help them to speak up on your behalf by encouraging them to do so, either directly or indirectly.

Direct methods include 'member get member' schemes, where the original client will get some sort of reward for introducing a new customer (maybe money off their next bill or a gift voucher, etc.), whilst indirect methods would be advertising campaigns or direct mail that encourage the original client to want to speak out about their long relationship with your organization because it will show them to be clever/prudent/discerning, etc.

Advocacy can be a simple referral by example, 'My Mum always used Fairy Snow so I will too', or complex, 'I am an Independent Financial Advisor and I recommend this policy'. The marketer must decide just how important advocacy is to their proposition. To some it is so important that they even *buy* advocacy, in the shape of professional endorsement. Whenever a golfer endorses a golf club, or a footballer a pair of football boots, all suspects, prospects and even customers and clients are aware that money has changed hands and that the golfer or footballer in question is clearly being paid for their visible support of that brand. But, even so, there is a built-in belief that the golfer/footballer would never use a product that would diminish their ability within their sport, so the product *must* be good after all! That's why billions of pounds are spent globally every year on professional endorsements for products, and that is unlikely to stop!

But the real client, the real loyal customer makes a truly wonderful advocate, and many marketers have spotted this and utilized its potential. In Canada a company called Subway found a young man named Jared who lived on their low-fat sandwiches for months, and increased his exercise, losing a huge amount of weight and saying that the Subway product had changed his life! Jared has inspired thousands of others to do the same sort of thing, and he now stars in the company's TV advertising as an example to others to take advantage of Subway's low-fat offering. An advocate who is shouting very loudly!

Other advocates come in the form of those who endorse products but without payment changing hands. In the UK it is claimed that Delia Smith can make or break a company, or even a whole system of food production, if she says yes or no to a product on her cookery programmes. She is almost single-handedly responsible for the huge variety of olive oils we now find in our supermarkets, she popularized the sundried tomato and cranberries exploded into UK supermarkets when she included them in several recipes. It has even been claimed that just one of her television programmes that showed how to boil and poach eggs meant that three times more eggs were bought in UK supermarkets during the week that that programme was shown than would normally be the case! Yes, advocacy even for the humble egg can work wonders!

Some products or services almost miss out the client part of the ladder and leap straight from customer to advocate: getting your carpets professionally cleaned is not something we do every day – maybe we only do it once every five or six years, and we might have moved out of the area in any case – but that carpet cleaner will need the advocacy of satisfied customers if s/he is to build a reputation based on recommendation – and recommendation is very important in all types of areas: hairdressers, cleaning services, garages, decorators, plumbers, dentists, doctors, etc., etc. – they all rely on personal recommendations to get a great deal of business. So advocacy works on many levels, from the word of mouth in the local supermarket to multi-national endorsement campaigns – but they all have one thing in common – it is all about people who know the company's offering speaking out on its behalf. In other words, they are going beyond being mere users, they are becoming a part of the promotional effort itself.

Summary of Chapter 7

Within this chapter we have covered the following:

How marketing communications works to build a relationship with customers over time.

1 Getting them in the first place

This section looks at why it is worth keeping customers and introduces the 'ladder of loyalty'.

2 The role of targeting and branding

These sections look at how why it is important to get the right customers, and how to attract them.

3 Prospecting for gold

Here we look at how to get suspects to identify themselves as prospects, and what to do with them when they do.

4 Aiming for a conversion

This is where turning prospects into customers is considered.

5 Servicing the client

Here we consider how to keep customers coming back time and again.

6 Speaking up for advocates

By making sure that those who use you speak up for you, you can open up a whole new form of communication!

Self-test questions and opinion development

These are not exam questions, nor are they meant to represent the sort of question you might expect to face anywhere else. They are designed to help you check whether you have understood the content of this chapter. All you have to do is read the questions, give them some thought and maybe jot down some notes on what your response might be. Not all the questions will have factual answers – rather, they might encourage you to think about a topic or an issue and formulate an opinion based upon what is now, hopefully, a better understanding of the topic.

- What is the 'ladder of loyalty'? What does it mean?
- How can you decide who your Suspects might be?
- List three types of marcomms activity you could undertake to get suspects to nominate themselves as prospects for:

  - a brand of biscuits;
  - a brand of beer;
  - a new family hatchback car;
  - a new office stationery company;
  - a printing company that specializes in self-adhesive label printing;
  - a new emergency generator that would be suitable for building sites.

- For a company selling cars, how many levels of 'hotness' do you think there might be for sub-dividing prospects?
- What sort of customer services should the following types of companies offer, and why:

  - a make-up manufacturer;
  - a disposable nappies manufacturer;
  - an accountant;
  - a dry cleaning company;
  - a health centre;
  - a college.

- List the things that could *stop* you being a customer of any brand/retailer/company you use at the moment. How do they prevent these things happening?
- How could you encourage people like you, who are loyal to the above brand/retailer/company to speak out on behalf of the brand/retailer/company?

Extending knowledge and understanding

You are encouraged to undertake the following activities to further your knowledge and understanding of the topics covered in this chapter in the following ways:

1 Have you got a bank? How long have you been with them? How hard would it be to move away? How easy would it be for you to switch bank? How could other banks tempt you and help you to move? Take some time to investigate the different targeting, services and customer relationship building programmes used by banks today – ask friends and relatives about their banking experiences to add to your own, and use the Internet to compare offerings, as well as the tone and style of what the bank sees as its image.

2 Have you got a car? If not, work with someone who has – you need someone who has bought a car (new or previously owned) from a dealer. Break down the whole suspect onwards relationship you/your friend have had with the brand, the dealer, the model and the specific vehicle. How did you/your friend move from suspect to prospect to buyer to user. Are you already an advocate? A client? Why? How does the manufacturer communicate with you as a customer? How does the dealer communicate with you as a customer?

3 I recently had all my carpets professionally cleaned by a small local firm – just one man and his son, with his wife taking the telephone bookings. Not only did I get great, fast, efficient service, but I just received (two weeks later) a Thank You card from the family, signed by all, to acknowledge my custom, and saying they hope I mention them to friends. Low cost, not complicated – but it works. Find as many examples of great customer relationship management as you can that *do not* involve complex, high-cost data mining etc.

4 How much of the direct mail you receive is part of a CRM programme, and how much of it is trying to get you (a suspect) to become a prospect? Start sorting all your direct mail into 'purpose' piles, and see what you find!

Communication planning and implementation in the real world – case studies that will challenge your ability to really 'do it'!

Three original case studies follow. Some facts and figures have either been omitted or amended slightly to ensure confidentiality. Otherwise they are what they seem to be – built around real companies and brands operating in the real world, today. Each sets the scene then challenges you with questions. Even if you are studying alone you can take your time to work through the questions and think about how you would tackle them.

The case studies are truly contemporary, don't rely on big budgets and have unique challenges for today and tomorrow – enjoy!

Utterly Butterly – building an utterly British brand in a busy marketplace

Summary

This buttery spread was launched into a busy market, had to work its way through a descriptive minefield and find a place in the heart of the British public, as well as on the chiller shelves of supermarkets. By adopting an utterly British, utterly quirky personality, and by communicating this through an impressive, above and below the line communications campaign where integration was vital if the campaign's quirkiness was to be capitalized upon, the brand is now well established and able to fully exploit its position in the market.

The case

The Utterly Butterly story – background to spreading the word!

Market context (April 1995)

The total spreads market in the UK was experiencing a 3 per cent volume decline and there had really been very little innovation in the marketplace since 'I Can't Believe It's Not Butter' (ICBINB) launched in 1991. By 1995, ICBINB sales were growing by 20 per cent per annum and the market was seeing the introduction of some Own Label copies from the major multiples. Generally speaking, the market was dominated by brands that had been around for 15 years or more: Flora, St Ivel Gold, Clover, Vitalite.

St Ivel context

St Ivel had one established brand, 'Gold', which was declining by 10 per cent per annum and their recently launched brand 'Mono' was struggling. Despite this, the company vision was to grow its share of the spreads category and become a strong challenger to Unilever in the UK.

Consumer context

Health-positioned brands were seen as less appealing because of a more balanced approach to health, though the gap between butter and spreads was still large in terms of taste perception and delivery. 'Anchor Spreadable' and 'Clover' bridged the gap but were too expensive for many mass-market families, whilst the successful launch of ICBINB had demonstrated the appeal of a more buttery spread at a modest premium but still fell short of many consumers' taste expectations. In terms of taste, butter was still king!

Trade context

Basically, the retailers were very receptive to added-value innovation, given the poor margins being earned on butter.

Deciding on which side your bread is buttered – what position to adopt?

It was clear that ICBINB had paved the way for a new sector that delivered a more butter-like taste, with the convenience of traditional margarines at an accessible price. The brand had also achieved this in an impactful manner that differentiated it in personality terms from the more traditional brands in the market. Research suggested however that the product still fell short of consumer expectations on taste. In this respect its name 'I Can't Believe It's *Not* Butter' worked against it.

St Ivel mapped the market and decided that a positioning that borrowed the best elements of traditional butter brands and added modern personality would help develop the sector that ICBINB had established but with a more positive proposition. It was felt that the St Ivel brand heritage would help provide the traditional elements but on its own would not differentiate a new offering nor provide modernity.

Thus, the research and development of not only the product itself but also the naming, packaging and marketing communications programme that would hopefully launch and establish this new brand were embarked upon.

L is for Legalities – name it don't shame it!

Legally, St Ivel was not allowed to use the word 'butter' in the name of a new product. ICBINB had successfully argued that describing the product as not butter was acceptable. However, St Ivel wanted a more positive statement of taste than, 'We're not butter'!

In a brainstorming session someone said 'What we want is a name that is utterly buttery'. But buttery is an extension of butter and so illegal. The addition of an 'l' however formed a brand new word 'butterly' and the brand name was born. Apart from making it legal the 'l' also added an element of quirkiness that has become one of the key personality traits of the brand.

Shaping up to the task – we're not square!

Pack design had a key role to play in differentiating the brand. The oval shaped tub was developed to set the new product apart from their 'square' competitors. Simple graphics were also used to focus attention on the name and communicate the uncomplicated nature of the product. Finally a foil seal was used instead of wax paper to associate the brand with more premium foil-wrapped butter and differentiate the new offering from competitors.

The communications effort

Here are the points that were made by Marketing Director Tony Lucas during an interview:

Background: The advertising idea 'Have you gone Utterly Butterly' was used as the anchor point for all our communication. The St Ivel organization and our customers were encouraged to succumb to this challenge, which brought together the name, proposition and personality in a single, highly memorable statement.

Going Utterly Butterly meant declaring your undying devotion for the product but also in doing so revealing the more eccentric side of your personality. This activity was reflected in the advertising and the quirky, eccentric brand personality soon became established. The unexpected benefit was that this was seen to be a 'very English' thing to do, which helped to set us apart from the more 'brash, American' personality of ICBINB.

The tools: TV was the principal means of communication in order to achieve cut-through in a competitive market. Critically, during the first year, we achieved a higher share of voice than our nearest competitors and built brand awareness quickly.

The TV campaign comprised 40-second and 10-second commercials to build both involvement and salience. The creative idea of showing English familiar stereotypes going Utterly Butterly was very popular and achieved extremely high awareness. The creative also proved popular with St Ivel personnel because of the fact that a St Ivel factory and product development personnel featured within the storyline. This proved useful when sales dramatically exceeded forecast for the first 6 months following launch! It's all well and good having a runaway success, but someone has to make sure that production and distribution can meet the requirements of the retailers!

Ongoing brand building: share data and advertising tracking combined with post-launch focus groups and spontaneous consumer feedback (by the 1000s!) into our consumer care team confirmed that we had a very popular personality-driven brand! We have continued this monitoring right throughout the campaign, as we heartily believe in knowing what our marketing communications investment is generating for us in terms of brand awareness, understanding, emotional attachment and, of course, sales!

Thus, it was clear that the marketing tasks post launch were:

1 to drive brand penetration and usage;
2 to maintain the 'brand premium' in the light of own label copies; and
3 to build on the success of the launch with extensions in the catering channel (using large catering tubs and individual portion packs) and convenience channel (using 250 g packs).

Equally, the ongoing communication task was fourfold:

1 to keep the personality fresh and involving;
2 to establish a strong product story, a genuine source of competitive advantage, to maximize usage;
3 to continue to build brand awareness within a context of ever-increasing competition; and
4 to support the range extensions and brand premium.

During the period since launch these objectives have been successfully delivered by the following methods:

● continuous media presence (principally TV);
● continuing to refresh our TV executions bringing new twists to the core theme;
● featuring 'product' involvement within the story line;
● evolving the strap line into 'It's the taste that drives you Utterly Butterly';
● developing a strong BTL (Below The Line) campaign to communicate the brand personality at point of purchase: e.g., 'Utterly Butterly' first birthday celebration linked TV and packaging;
● devising ways of getting consumers, customers and St Ivel staff involved with the brand: e.g., The Utterly Butterly Wing Walking Team on the Uttlerly Butterly Biplane (of which we have also had die-cast models made that we can use as incentives, prizes and giveaways); e.g., making the world's largest crumpet;
● most importantly by maintaining an eccentric attitude to building the brand and using every opportunity to surprise and entertain our consumers: e.g., National search for a Wing Walker.

Throughout the whole of the life of the Brand we have also emphasized the role of internal communication – this was especially important since we did actually feature real members of staff in our advertising campaigns, as well as shooting on real manufacturing locations. Our staff are our team, and a real asset – so we have worked hard to keep them on board and involved as much as possible.

I'm not really at liberty to say how much we have spent on our marcomms, but it's obviously been big budget stuff, using as much TV and other above the line work as we have. Press, posters, radio – they've all played their part, as have a host of what we feel are really inventive, and quirky, below the line methods. The point that I do feel I should emphasize is that, whilst we have used a large budget, we have by no means had the biggest budget in the sector! We have aimed to gain maximum effectiveness and efficiency of spend, rather than spend as much as we can, and I believe that consistency over time has really paid dividends.

What we have aimed for, and achieved, is to establish and build a brand that has a future in a busy and potentially lethal marketplace.

With such a strong and affectionate base to work from, we have no end of wonderful ideas about how to sustain the brand's quirky British positioning!

Conclusions

Utterly Butterly quickly established a distinctive personality that reflected the quirkiness of English humour, our love for eccentrics and our longing for the taste of real butter. This was backed up by an innovative pack design and an excellent product. In other words, it was both different and better.

By campaigning these core themes single-mindedly and at every opportunity Utterly Butterly has held on to this position and become one of the strongest brands in its category. In a crowded market spontaneous brand awareness is way ahead of most competitors at 36 per cent, and is still growing.

Weight of purchase is higher than any other product in the category and at 21 per cent and climbing, penetration is in line with market leaders. Utterly Butterly is currently the fastest growing brand in the category!

You can see what Utterly Butterly is up to today by visiting them at http://utterly-butterly.co.uk.

Your challenge

Where do you think Utterly Butterly should go over the next two years? What direction? Should it build on where it is, or go in a new direction? And when you have decided, come up with the formal marketing communications programme (again for the next two years) that would deliver these objectives.

Technidrill – big B2B value for small B2B expenditure

Summary

This case highlights the way in which a relatively small, niche industrial company has to use its limited resources wisely in order to be able to do an effective job of communicating with a truly global marketplace. Based in France, but supplying precision engineered drilling equipment to companies around the world, often in trouble spots or areas where it is not easy to do business, Technidrill is showing that it can grow in a complex, ever-changing and pretty harsh business environment.

See how simple can be best, and how the personal touch works in any language!

The case

The background

The Cote d'Azur, The Riviera, the South of France – all these phrases conjure up images of bronzed bodies lying on beaches lapped by an incredibly blue sea and of film stars and pop celebrities partying into the small hours or racing about on motor boats with secret lovers!

But, whether you might think it or not, the ancient town of Nice, with the Negresco Hotel overlooking its stunning Baie des Anges and its world famous Promenade des Anglais, can boast a thriving manufacturing base as well as being well located to service the needs of France, Italy, Switzerland and the Benelux countries as a distribution location. Not as glamorous a picture, but the reality of it, nonetheless!

So, in 1989, when three engineers with a wealth of engineering expertise and long careers working for various companies, decided to set up their own company in their hometown of Nice, it wasn't actually such a crazy idea. Certainly the pace of life is not as frenetic as in the north of the country, but the South of France has its own way of doing things that means they normally get done! However, they realized immediately that the only way for three engineers to operate a company successfully was for each of them to take an area of expertise and work to develop it.

Jonas Ellerstrand, a Swede who had lived in Nice for many years, became the President of the company, and took most of the responsibility for marketing and sales planning. The initial idea was to become agents and manufacturers of consumable materials for the drilling industry, a plan to which Technidrill has largely adhered.

Indeed, in 2000 they were still in a position where more than 90 per cent of their turnover came from consumables, but they also now market and sell on behalf of an Italian drilling machine manufacturer, Ellettari of Piacenza.

'Technidrill', as the company was named, is doing well – it is building alliances and is also growing its number of affiliated distributors worldwide – this being the strategy adopted in order to increase potential sales globally of the products manufactured in Nice.

By virtue of the fact that they supply very technical products to a small marketplace, distributed around the world, Technidrill's marketing, marketing communications and sales operations have always had to be 'lean' to say the least, and yet still have to get the complex messages about range, reliability and quality to a lot of people who might be operating in some very inaccessible geographic locations.

The organization and the offering

The products manufactured and sold by Technidrill are, as the name might imply, a range of drilling equipment for mining exploration, geotechnical drilling, civil engineering, special foundation, water well drilling, directional drilling (river cross drilling) and sometimes their products are also used for 'slim-hole' oil and gas drilling.

Thus, potential customers are relatively small in number, might well be found in some geographical concentrations (dependent upon geographical features such as mineral deposits, etc.) or might be anywhere in the world where an engineering project requires drilling equipment.

Technidrill has a factory in Carros, an industrial area near the airport in Nice, where they specialize in the manufacture of tubular products and particularly friction-welded products, i.e., composite drill rods and pipes. Two people, Jonas Ellerstrand and Pierre Bovet, are based at Carros and are responsible for export sales. There are two other people who sell for Technidrill – one based at Carros and one in Paris – who actually work through Technidrill's wholly owned subsidiary DGA in Viry.

France, and sometimes neighbouring countries such as Switzerland and the Benelux, are very much seen as comprising the domestic market with, truly, The Rest Of The World representing the remaining market.

On home turf

In the domestic market, the aim really is to be flexible with what can be offered to customers, but over the years the emphasis has come to show most demand for manufactured tubular products, diamond and TC (tungsten carbide) tools, tricones, DTH (down-the-hole hammers and tools), core barrels with accessories.

Other than the products that they manufacture themselves, Technidrill distributes some and buys and sells others, mainly from American, British, Spanish, Canadian and Polish manufacturers.

The target here is the end users of drilling equipment, i.e., large, medium and small-sized drilling contractors.

In December 1998, Technidrill acquired a distribution company (that still retains its pre-Technidrill name of DGA-GS) that is now taking over as the domestic sales centre, situated in Viry Haute-Savoie, about 20 minutes by road west of Geneva.

This office complex also contains a warehousing facility and a Sales Manager controls three sales people. Another key reason for this acquisition, other than geographic location and reputation, was to gain access to the former owner of this company, today as a consultant, but probably in the future as a partner in the parent company Technidrill/DGA-GS.

Playing away

In theory the whole world is a potential export market: but realistically western Europe, north Africa, North, Central and South America (USA, Canada, Mexico and Chile), Australia, Japan and Southeast Asia (Hong Kong being the biggest market here), West Africa (through Ghana), South Africa and timidly East Africa (through Tanzania) are the areas that Technidrill focuses on.

The director of sales, Pierre Bovet, Swiss by birth but, again, a long-time resident of Nice, covers Switzerland, Germany, Austria, Spain, Portugal and North Africa. Jonas Ellerstrand covers the rest!

Pierre mainly sells to the drilling companies directly, as he is closer to his markets and he has a more technical background than Jonas. He also presents the full product range to all contacts he makes in his geographic areas.

Jonas develops the distribution market in the countries mentioned above, almost only selling the manufactured products, as the distributors in the world have access to similar products as those distributed by Technidrill, so don't require their involvement.

In 2000 the export sales were approximately 14 million French Francs.

An alternative way of looking at Technidrill's offering would be to categorize its markets by product type, but this only really applies to the domestic market, as most export sales are of the manufactured, tubular products.

Playing as part of a team

Layne Christensen, Technidrill's partners, today have a non-controlling investment in Technidrill. Layne Christensen are both involved in contracting (drilling) and the manufacture and distribution of the other products offered by Technidrill. However, their dilemma is to try to avoid being perceived by their customers as competitors of drilling equipment, which is not always very easy. Hence, they are now concentrating on the contracting part of the business, making 'alliances' with different manufacturers in the world.

In the USA particularly they have a marketing and sales company, DESI (Drilling Equipment Supplies Inc.), with offices in four locations covering the whole country, and they also have a presence in Australia.

Technidrill's aims

Domestic market

To be the national leader both in the manufactured and distributed products in the drilling and coring field, both through marketing and intense sales work.

When they realized they couldn't achieve that goal through their own sales people, they decided to make an external acquisition in 1998.

Their goal now, is to increase the domestic sales by 10 per cent per annum, which has been achieved for each year since the acquisition.

Export market

Here Technidrill is mainly concentrating on manufactured products, but they are introducing more of the distributed ones in the countries that border on what they see as their domestic marketplace.

Their main goal is to position Technidrill internationally as a well known and respected supplier in their application field.

Their goal here is to increase export sales by 15 per cent per annum.

The communications effort

Technidrill finds that the 80:20 rule applies in most of their business (80 per cent of their business coming from 20 per cent of their customers), and they are well aware that they are much smaller than their multinational conglomerate competitors. Thus, they have adopted a strategy of ensuring lots of personal communication, mainly face-to-face or by telephone or e-mail, with a great deal of global travelling to allow for frequent customer visits to clients, customers and prospects alike.

They use no above the line communication techniques at all at present, though 2001 sees them appointing a communications agency to help them reassess this decision.

When I interviewed him, these were some of the observations made by Jonas Ellerstrand about the communications techniques they use the most:

Telephone calls: never underestimate the power of telephone contact – a real relationship can be built between client and marketer over the telephone. It works particularly well when it is between two people who have met and spent time together, and a few trade shows and dinners can be a valuable grounding for telephonic communication where we are able to glean lots of information and feedback on past purchases, immediate needs, likely future needs and any plans for the long term that the client might have. Talking to a person, not a company, is the best way I know to find out what your customers *will* need in the future – that way we try to stay ahead of the competitors and make sure we can satisfy our customers' needs tomorrow as well as today. By keeping in touch on a planned, pro-active basis, as well as by responding fast to calls from the client, it is possible to 'shut out' competitors, by constantly proving you are the caring provider.

Personal business letters: again, another Cinderella in the world of marketing communications, but the role of a business letter, where the writer has taken the time to write it in the language of the recipient, carries a lot of weight. Sometimes a business letter, actually printed on paper and mailed is *not* the right answer – this is especially that case where the mailing system is unreliable, so e-mail can be used in its place. But it is important to treat e-mail as though it is a *serious* communication, not just something you dash off as you rush out of the office. It can damage a good relationship if the recipient thinks you don't care enough to spend the time it takes to form proper sentences and use grammar properly. Of course, we use letters and e-mail to keep in touch in a more formal way than telephone calls, so the letter should be more formal, even if it is mailed electronically.

Meetings and personal entertainment: both Pierre and I spend a huge amount of time 'on the road' visiting our allies, partners, customers, clients and prospects. Often, in our business, it is this personal touch that sets us apart from our competitors in that we, the heads of the company, are actually there with customers and able to make promises and negotiate *as* the company not *on behalf of* the company, which is what the salesmen who work for our competitors have to do. By taking the time to visit our partners and customers we are showing a real commitment to our joint success – and that's how we work, by making sure that our suppliers, partners and customers all know we are all part of one team, all aiming to make sure that customer satisfaction is Number One on our list of priorities.

Entertainment doesn't have to be lavish, but it does have to fit the cultural and personal expectations of each person with whom we are meeting – that might mean lots of breakfasts in North America, or lots of very late, long dinners in North Africa; it might mean working well where alcohol consumption is high on the agenda, or being in a dry restaurant and sipping tea. It usually means a combination of late nights, early mornings, long journeys, hanging around at airports and the confusion of constantly changing time zones. When travel is involved, planning must be top of your list of priorities – it's too easy to miss that call from Australia when you are flying to Seattle, so good communications tools and making sure you keep on top of all the call backs, all the e-mails and all the restaurant bookings is important.

Trade shows and exhibitions: because of our size it just isn't realistic to take stands at every show at which we would like to have a presence. We make sure we are represented on the stands of our partners and allies, we are often asked to support our customers when they appear at certain shows, but what we mainly aim to do is to keep quite a low (and low-cost) profile at most shows, but use them as a chance to meet and entertain key people – either prospects or customers.

A printed brochure: we find that we use a lot of printed brochures, because a lot of people still like to have something in their hands that they can see and feel, and which you can leave with them after you have met. Of course we are able to send brochures to our partners to use at trade shows, and we can mail them to anyone who makes enquiries of us, but the main use is to prove that we can give you something *now* – not just direct you to a website. We also have technical data sheets printed separately, so we can keep the information in the brochure more general, focusing on high quality photography and general specifications, rather than having to reprint every time we change specific specifications or introduce new options under existing lines. These sheets also give us the chance to make our offering under-standable in many different languages. The agency will probably get us to update our brochure, but I don't think we have yet reached the point where we can stop printing a brochure forever. Maybe in a few years, but not now.

Our website: we've kept it simple, we have built in a small amount of interactivity and we know that our customers like it! We can update information overnight, we can keep generalities the same, but we don't have the resources to build a flashy website, nor do we believe that our customers would want it. They can contact us through the website, but most existing customers have direct e-mail contact with their nominated personal contact within the company – sometimes they will be e-mailing several people directly about different aspects of their order, maybe sending delivery details to despatch, checking criteria with production and telling sales about invoicing information. The website acts as another gateway for existing customers, and reassures them that we are technologically adept! It can act as a noticeboard for us too – so we can e-mail customers to tell them that there's something new to see on the site, for example! We know that competitors, suspects, competitors of our suppliers and the whole industry can access our site, as well as get to other linked sites via our own, so we don't put anything confidential out there at all. Our address is http://www.Technidrill.com.

The use of guarantees and certifications: obviously we have guarantees based on either international specifications or our own stated specifications, but sometimes even though we are not at fault, we give 'commercial' free-of-charge products or reimbursements. This builds trust and shows we really do believe that the customer is always right. One supplementary indication of our dedication to quality is that Technidrill has been certified with ISO 9002 since 1998, which is something we use in our communications with customers all over the world. At the moment we find this is something that is becoming increasingly important, particularly in Europe, Australia and Asia; however the Americans are not very impressed yet, but they will get there!

How much does it all cost? well, with respect, I am not prepared to tell you exactly how much we spend on marketing communications, but we do spend more than 5.6 million FFr on the commercial department; this includes salaries and charges. The Nice office spends about 800 000 FFr on travelling, meeting, entertaining, etc., for the overseas markets, and the French sales department spends approx. 600 000 FFr for the same.

How effective are we? We do, of course measure the effectiveness of what we are spending through the sales results, but this is not our only measure of success. Indeed, much of what we do has such a long sales cycle that we are investing in communications today that might not bring in an actual sale for two years, so measuring sales is almost only a measure of historical success, without any indication of current or future success. The contacts and rate of inquiries are also measured, e.g., the number of proposals made to customers, the number of new customers, monitoring the word of mouth communication about

Technidrill and its products, reactivity, personal contacts, hits and contacts made through the website, etc. Whilst these are not all indicators of effectiveness of one tool alone, they do show the holistic effect of all our actions – including how satisfied our customers are with our products and services.

Conclusions

Technidrill proves that small budgets, the personal touch and some of the simplest communications tools can all be used to produce great effects! You don't need complex databases and datamining software if you have few enough clients and enough energy, application and foresight to know them all – you only have to ask the man on the other end of the telephone and he'll tell you what they want – if you're lucky he'll also tell you why you keep getting his business and why, if you don't, why you didn't!

In many business to business markets it's the same story – you have relatively few clients, even on the global stage, you can actually physically meet with most of them if you choose and you can use simple, one-to-one communication methods on an ongoing, proactive and reactive basis to build real working relationships with suppliers, partners and customers, even when you aren't one of the Big Boys!

Your challenge

Assume that Technidrill has decided to bring in an outside marketing communications consultancy and agency to help it further develop its marketing communications planning and implementation.

1 How should Technidrill go about finding such an agency? What criteria should it use when seeking them out?
2 What should it brief them to do for a pitch? Write the brief.
3 When you have written the brief, change sides and write the proposal too. How does the proposal meet the brief?
4 What challenges has the brief highlighted that are specific to Technidrill, and how have you met them?

The realtor's reality – from your doorstep to the world

Summary

When it comes to selling houses, the Internet really has taken away a lot of the guesswork, with photographs and virtual tours becoming the norm. Now you can view potential new homes from around the world just by visiting a website! But to sell a house in North America you have to do a lot more than have a snazzy webpage – and Debbie Sheppard should know. Over more that two decades she's sold hundreds of houses in Vancouver, Canada, and by looking at how she works with a wide range of above and below the line methods, mass communication and personal, face to face tools for communication we can see how communication can work from the doorstep and right around the world! Realtors, Real Estate Agents, or Estate Agents – depending on where you are based in the world – will face much the same issues as described in this case, and the key factors in this case can be applied across most Western countries.

The case

Sell, sell, sell!

'We've decided we want to sell our house', is how it begins. Debbie Sheppard has heard it hundreds of times. And selling a house isn't just about selling a house, of course, there's always a reason – a life-changing reason such as 'We need more space for the baby', or 'We're getting divorced', or 'We're starting over', or 'The kids have gone to college'. Whatever the reason, there always is one, so when Debbie gets involved with someone who is wanting to sell their house, she is getting involved with someone who has decided that their whole life must change in some way. And she has become a driver in that change.

Now, moving home is said to be one of life's most stressful situations, but that stress doesn't start and end on moving day, it starts long before the day you call the realtor and doesn't finish until everything is unpacked again, all the remodelling is finished and you finally feel 'at home' in your new home – and that can take some time!

But before you even get into your new home you are faced with selling the one you have. With most home purchases being a part of some sort of 'chain', where each potential purchaser has their own property to dispose of, getting rid of the house you have, at the price you need to be paid, is often vitally important to being able to move to the house you want. And the realtor is the one who can sell it for you – at the price you want and preferably within a week! So, no stress for the realtor there then!

Seriously, the realtor is seen as a source of experience and local knowledge, as someone who can negotiate on the sellers' (vendor's) behalf and as the person who will somehow find that person, or family, who are fated to be the next inhabitants of your home.

And that's where the problems start – it's *your* home, so it looks and is used in the way *you* want. The next inhabitants are unlikely to want to live in *your* house, they are likely to want to live in the house you happen to live in right now, but in a different way than you live in it. So, the realtor is also often the person who has to tell some hard home truths to the vendor about how to, literally, put their house in order to make it as desirable as possible, and that can be as tricky as telling someone that they have bad breath! Communication skills are called into play from the first moment for the realtor!

Putting your best foot forward

Debbie has helped to get unkempt houses into shape, has offered heritage homes that need lots of tender loving care and has helped growing families to spot the potential in dividing up living areas or opening them out into bigger spaces!

The issue here is that each specific product offered for sale is different (different location, specifications, size, features, etc.) and will appeal to a different target group (couples, empty-nesters, young families, animal lovers, etc.). So whilst a standard process can be followed, the specifics need to be amended every time! She is selling a vision of a future, not just the house as it looks today.

The communications expertise needed by realtors is twofold: the ability to highlight the features that will sell the property, and the ability to get this message to the right target audience for the property.

Most people expect Estate Agents and realtors to lie about the property they are offering, to 'talk it up'. Debbie has always worked hard to set herself apart from such 'double talk' and all her descriptions aim to focus the attention of the reader on the real positives, whilst not seeking to ignore the inevitable negatives!

It starts at the front door, and works in both directions! Communicate now!

Getting the product into the best shape possible means that Debbie works with vendors to bring their property up to the required standard as fast as possible. At the same time she will be commissioning photography, virtual tour filming, print runs, press advertisement space and writing copy.

This is what Debbie has to say about the communications tools she uses:

The most obvious thing that says that a house is for sale is the sign on the property, in a position where most people will see it. If the property is set away from a main road, then a directional sign is also an essential tool. Clear copy and big print so everyone can see who to contact are essential too, as is a well presented garden or lawn area!

I can put up the best designed, most professional, biggest sign in the world but, if it's in front of a run-down front door, with peeling paintwork and unpolished brass, surrounded by a flowerbed full of weeds but no flowers, it won't help to get the asking price, so I have to work *with* my vendors to make sure that their entrances and the exterior of their home are as inviting as possible. Often a couple of tubs of flowers at the front doorstep can have a great positive impact.

If someone is about to nominate themselves as a prospect you don't want to turn them off by making them think immediately that they'll have to spend time and money just getting the outside of the house or the garden in order – besides, a lack of care for the exterior might encourage a potential buyer to think that there's been poor maintenance all around, and thus make them more suspicious of the property's pedigree.

Once I know a property is for sale I will do a few things immediately:

- I will bring the property to the attention of my colleagues at the office (I belong to a realty group called Homelife Classic Realty, a Canada-wide company that adds a huge reach to my communications) they then visit the property with me and get an idea of what's for sale – this helps them represent the property to their clients;

- I get the property onto the Homelife Classic Realty website as soon as possible (see end of case study for address);
- I make sure that the Multiple Listings Service is made aware of the property so that it can be placed on their website (see end of case study for address) and can be put into their weekly publication that lists properties for sale in the area, gaining coverage of additional realtors in the area and realtors who might be seeking out properties for their clients within this area;
- I try to ensure that a group of realtors representing the Multiple Listings Service (i.e., they are associated with many different realty companies) visit the property;
- I access my own client database – this isn't as grand as it sounds, because I take the time and trouble to know what all my clients are looking for, so I usually know who to telephone right away, often bringing them to the property on the day of the listing, and can mail selected people from my lists of previous clients just in case this new property might be of interest to them;
- I will decide which of the local newspapers has the best profile for this type of property and use my standing space order for the newly listed property – local newspapers are not just a great way of telling those who live in the community about what's available, but often those looking to move into an area will use these local newspapers as a valuable source of reference (some newspapers have accompanying websites onto which they will load these advertisements);
- having either commissioned photography, taken it myself, or having downloaded it from a pre-existing bank of photography (sometimes the people who buy a house come back to the same realtor to sell it for them – at least, that's what we try to make happen), I get the in-home commentary sheets drawn up – these are very full descriptions of the home, usually two to three pages long, and include a colour photograph, a map of the site and full contact details for myself. They are left in quantity inside the house for other realtors who bring their clients, for the homeowner to give to the 'drive-bys' that they might encounter and for anyone who might visit the house (friends, relatives, etc.) to take and pass on;
- I will contact the cameraman who shoots Homelife Classic Realty's 360 degree virtual tours that I will then upload onto my own website (see end of case study for address) as well as making sure that the links are in place from the MLS website, the Homelife Classic Realty's website and any others that I feel might be useful for this particular property;
- I will get a flyer (single publicity sheet with photograph) put together for all the Real Estate companies in the area;
- I will respond immediately to any queries that come in on the property, I will call anyone I think might be interested in it, and I will make sure that all my colleagues, and even competitors, know how to get in touch regarding the possible sale of the property.

Real Estate is truly international these days – I recently had a couple visit from the UK who found me on the Internet, had done their research via the Internet and were able to arrive in Vancouver with a relatively short list of viewings for me to arrange. That couldn't have happened, easily, without the Internet, but all those homes were being offered for sale locally too, so this really is an 'around the corner, around the world' business.

What pays off?

Realtors get a percentage of the price of a house as their fee: the average would be about 7 per cent on the first Can$100 000 and about 2.5 per cent on the balance. The amount is split between the listing company and the selling company. Thus, the lower the selling price, the less the margin they have out of which they cover their costs, although the percentage weighting is designed to encourage the realtor to spend the right amount of money to make the sale, knowing they won't lose out too much if the vendor drops their final price! So the amount of money they spend on trying to sell a house has to be the right amount spent in the right way to get a sale at the asking price, but not so much that they can't cover their costs if the vendor agrees to drop the price, and not so little that there isn't enough interest in the property to make a sale at all! It is a fine path to tread, and that's why marcomms costs need to be viewed as coming from an overall pot, with the realtor needing to be prepared to take the risk associated with offering a property for sale, maybe for months!

A constant monitoring of the type and quality of leads gained from each communication method is what is called for here – and that's just what Debbie does, as well as comparing information like this with that gathered by her colleagues: this allows everyone in all real estate offices, or the real estate industry, to benefit.

And it's not just leads, but the number of sales made, the proximity to the asking price and the length of time the house has been on the market that make a huge difference to the overall profitability of life as a realtor, so these aspects must all be monitored too. Debbie has spent nearly two decades working on the right way to do it – but she acknowledges that every home poses a new challenge!

Conclusions

The Internet is now truly integrated into the marketing communications process for property sales worldwide, with some very sophisticated programs and some wonderful images being available globally. But this case study shows that you still have to think about how the whole communications programme will work in harmony, rather than just put a photo on a website and hope someone looking for a house sees it!

Some websites you might want to visit:

http://www.debbiesheppard.com
http://www.homelifebc.com
http://www.realtylink.org

Your challenge

You are a marketing communications agency that has been brought in by Debbie's realty company to give a talk to all the realtors like her about how they can make their marcomms effort work even better by developing an eCRM system that works more efficiently from the centre. The feeling is that the realtors will believe that the company is trying to 'steal' their individual customers/clients. Write the speech explaining how good eCRM and non-eCRM can work with integrated marketing communications to build business for Debbie and all her colleagues.

Index

THE
BUSINESS CASES
WEB SITE

BUSINESS CASES

◢ Quality case study materials from quality
authors

◢ Instant access to cases & tutor support
material

◢ 'Quick view' summaries & author profiles

◢ Download PDFs and 'copy' for use on
specified courses

◢ No registration fee

◢ Pay on - line or open an account

Check out this excellent site today
www.businesscases.org